ETHNIC MINORITIES AND THE MEDIA

ISSUES in CULTURAL and MEDIA STUDIES

Series editor: Stuart Allan

Published titles

News Culture
Stuart Allan

Television, Globalization and Cultural Identities
Chris Barker

Ethnic Minorities and the Media
Edited by Simon Cottle

Modernity and Postmodern Culture
Jim McGuigan

Sport, Culture and the Media
David Rowe

ETHNIC MINORITIES AND THE MEDIA
Changing Cultural Boundaries

EDITED BY
Simon Cottle

OPEN UNIVERSITY PRESS
Buckingham · Philadelphia

Open University Press
Celtic Court
22 Ballmoor
Buckingham
MK18 1XW

email: enquiries@openup.co.uk
world wide web: www.openup.co.uk

and
325 Chestnut Street
Philadelphia, PA 19106, USA

First Published 2000

A catalogue record of this book is available from the British Library

ISBN 0 335 20270 5 (pbk)   0 335 20271 3 (hbk)

Library of Congress Cataloging-in-Publication Data
Ethnic minorities and the media: changing cultural boundaries/edited by Simon
Cottle.
       p.   cm. — (Issues in cultural and media studies)
    Includes bibliographical references and index.
    ISBN 0-335-20270-5 (PB) — ISBN 0-335-20271-3 (HB)
    1. Mass media and minorities.   I. Cottle, Simon, 1956 – II. Series.
P94.5.M55 E867 2000
302.23′086′93–dc21   99-056966

Typeset by Type Study, Scarborough
Printed in Great Britain by Biddles Limited, Guildford and Kings Lynn

CONTENTS

NOTES ON CONTRIBUTORS

Simon Cottle is Professor of Media Communication in the Sociology Department at Bath Spa University College. His books include *TV News, Urban Conflict and the Inner City* (Leicester University Press 1993) and *Television and Ethnic Minorities: Producers' Perspectives* (Avebury 1997); he is co-author with Anders Hansen, Ralph Negrine and Chris Newbold of *Mass Communication Research Methods* (Macmillan 1998).

John Fiske is Professor of Communication Arts at the University of Wisconsin-Madison. He has written numerous books including *Television Culture* (Routledge 1987), *Power Plays, Power Works* (Verso 1993) and *Media Matters: Race and Gender in U.S. Politics* (University of Minnesota Press 1996).

John Gabriel is Professor of Sociology and Head of Department at London Guildhall University. His books include *Race, Culture, Markets* (Routledge 1994) and *Whitewash: Racialized Politics and the Media* (Routledge 1998).

Marie Gillespie is Lecturer in Sociology and Anthropology at the University of Wales, Swansea. She is author of *Television, Ethnicity and Cultural Change* (Routledge 1995).

Herman Gray is a Professor of Sociology at the University of California, Santa Cruz. His most recent book is *Watching Race: Television and the Struggle for 'Blackness'* (University of Minnesota Press 1995) and he is currently working on a book about black cultural politics in the US.

Ramaswami Harindranath is Senior Lecturer in Cultural Studies at the University of the West of England, Bristol. He co-edited with R. Dickinson and

O. Linne *Approaches to Audiences* (Edward Arnold 1998) and he is currently working on a book about culture in a global perspective to be published by Open University Press.

Charles Husband is Professor of Social Analysis and Director of the Ethnicity and Social Policy Research Unit at the University of Bradford. He has published widely in the field of ethnicity, racism and the media and edited *A Richer Vision: The Development of Ethnic Minority Media in Western Democracies* (John Libbey 1994).

Karen Ross is Director, Centre for Communication Studies, Coventry School of Art and Design, Coventry University. She has researched and published widely on the broad subjects of 'race', disability and gender in mass media and her books include *Black and White Media: Black Images in Popular Film and Television* (Polity 1996).

Annabelle Sreberny is Professor at the Centre for Mass Communication Research at the University of Leicester and was Director (1992–9). Her most recent books include *Women's Communication and Politics* (Hampton Press 1999) and *Media in Global Context* (Edward Arnold 1997); her current research explores diasporic consciousness and gender dynamics in the global context.

Teun A. van Dijk is Professor of Discourse Studies at the University of Amsterdam. He has written books on text grammar, the psychology of text processing, and news and racism including *News as Discourse* (Lawrence Erlbaum 1988), *Racism and the Press* (Routledge 1991), *Elite Discourse and Racism* (Sage 1993) and *Ideology* (Sage 1998).

Clint C. Wilson II is Professor of Journalism at Howard University in Washington, DC. His most recent books are *Race, Multiculturalism, and the Media*, written with Felix Gutierrez (Sage 1995) and *A History of the Black Press*, completion of work by the late Armistead Pride (Howard University Press 1997).

SERIES EDITOR'S FOREWORD

Simon Cottle's edited collection *Ethnic Minorities and the Media: Changing Cultural Boundaries* constitutes an incisive intervention into a number of controversial debates about media representations of 'race' and ethnicity in societies such as those in Europe and North America. Each of the eleven contributors engages with a key aspect of these debates from a new vantage point, showing how the cultural boundaries of identity formation may be discerned precisely as they are imposed, transformed and contested across the mediasphere. As the editor makes apparent from the outset, the media engender an array of crucial sites whereby the cultural dynamics of racial and ethnic discrimination (frequently characterized as an 'us' versus 'them' opposition) are being actively invoked in hegemonic terms. At the same time, however, he points out that these same spaces also can be used to affirm social and cultural diversity and, as such, help to create the conditions for the articulation of resistance to these forms of discrimination. It is this shared concern to examine afresh the fluidly contingent forces of cultural power being played out in media discourses, institutions and audiences which lies at the heart of this timely and sophisticated collection.

The Issues in Cultural and Media Studies series aims to facilitate a diverse range of critical investigations into pressing questions considered to be central to current thinking and research. In light of the remarkable speed at which the conceptual agendas of cultural and media studies are changing, the authors are committed to contributing to what is an ongoing process of re-evaluation and critique. Each of the books is intended to provide a lively, innovative and comprehensive introduction to a specific topical issue from a unique perspective. The reader is offered a thorough grounding in the most salient debates indicative of the book's subject, as well as important insights into how new modes of enquiry may be established for future explorations. Taken as a whole, then, the series is designed to cover the core components of cultural and media studies courses in an imaginatively distinctive and engaging manner.

Stuart Allan

ACKNOWLEDGEMENTS

An edited volume necessarily incurs many debts of thanks, and this one is no exception. I would like to thank Martin Barker, Charles Husband and Teun van Dijk for offering their interest, support and kind words at the outset of this project. I thank, too, all the authors in this volume for providing their very different chapters. These collectively represent, I think, some of the very best, critically engaged, scholarship in this most humanly pressing of fields. My sincere thanks, then, to all contributors who produced their chapters on – or even before – time, and I here publicly forgive the laggards among them who, for reasons not always within their control, began to unhinge my sanity along the way. Such is the lot of the editor!

Once again, I would also like to say a personal thank you to Professor J.D. Halloran for all the support and encouragement that he has kindly offered to me over recent years. His formative influence upon the field of mass communication research and research into issues of media and racism would here be difficult to overestimate. I would also like to thank all the producers both past and present of *Black Pyramid*, an independent film and video collective based at St Pauls, Bristol, for agreeing to share with me their insights into the problems of making minority television programmes while struggling to make a difference. Thanks, then, to Lorna Henry, Ian Sergeant, Femi Kolade, Shawn Sobers and Rob Mitchell.

This book, in no small measure, bears the imprint of the series editor, Stuart Allan, whose editorial talents have effortlessly moved back and forth between the minutiae of syntax to the book's abstract conceptualization. Stuart has also proved to be a dab hand at wielding an axe when necessary, though mercifully his gentle swing and precision cuts have proved (relatively) pain free. I thank Stuart for helping to make this a better book than it might otherwise have been, and for his consistent support, editorial acumen and unfailing good humour – all essential qualities in the very best of editors. Thanks too, to my colleagues at Bath Spa University College, particularly Rob Mears for his gracious support across the years and Andy Brown for his theoretical knowledge of all things 'race'.

Finally, as always, heartfelt love to my family, Lucy, Ella, Theo and Sam, and to my mother Rita Cottle, for putting up with the often dissociated presence in their midst.

Introduction
MEDIA RESEARCH AND ETHNIC MINORITIES: MAPPING THE FIELD
Simon Cottle

Mapping the field

Today in countries such as those in Europe and North America, the relationship between the media and ethnic minorities is typically characterized by continuity, conflict and change. This book aims to explore the complexity of this interaction by bringing together a range of the latest findings produced by some of the leading international researchers in this field – a field, as we shall hear, which is also essentially contested.

In academic discourse, as in wider society, contending definitions of 'race', 'racism' and 'ethnicity' – to name but a few of the key terms with which we must grapple – currently struggle for theoretical and political recognition. These terms and their corresponding theoretical frameworks, sometimes called the **problematics of 'race'**,[1] variously provide us with the means of thinking about and/or thinking through some of the most fundamental categories, distinctions and discriminatory processes that humanity has yet produced for itself and within which, or in relation to which, many of us conduct our lives and construct a sense of who we are, where we belong and where we want to be. Specifically, three general 'problematics' currently contend and debate the field of 'race' and ethnicity in terms of **'race relations'**, **'racism/racialization'** and, most recently, **'new ethnicities'**. We shall encounter each in the discussion that follows. Approached through these frameworks ideas of 'race' and ethnicity can be evaluated positively or negatively, seen as imposed from outside or mobilized from within, and accounted for with reference to deep-seated social inequalities or the pursuit of cultural differences. Fundamentally, though, questions of 'ethnicity' and 'race' are about the drawing and redrawing of boundaries.

Boundaries define the borders of nations and territories as well as the imaginations of minds and communities. By definition, and often by design, they serve to mark out the limits of a given field, territory or social space. Depending on where one is positioned or is able to stand – whether inside or outside, at the centre or on the margins, or perhaps crossing and recrossing borders – they serve simultaneously to include some of us, exclude others and to condition social relations and the formation of identities. Over time, boundaries can become deeply embedded in the structures and institutions of societies, in their practices and even in their 'common sense'. Once institutionally sedimented and taken for granted, these boundaries all too often harden into exclusionary barriers legitimized by cultural beliefs, ideologies and representations. In such ways, the marginalized and the excluded can become ontologically disenfranchised from humanity, misrecognized as 'Other', exploited and oppressed and, *in extremis*, vulnerable to systematic, lethal violence.

The media occupy a key site and perform a crucial role in the public representation of unequal social relations and the play of cultural power. It is in and through representations, for example, that members of the media audience are variously invited to construct a sense of who 'we' are in relation to who 'we' are not, whether as 'us' and 'them', 'insider' and 'outsider', 'colonizer' and 'colonized', 'citizen' and 'foreigner', 'normal' and 'deviant', 'friend' and 'foe', 'the west' and 'the rest'. By such means, the social interests mobilized across society are marked out from each other, differentiated and often rendered vulnerable to discrimination. At the same time, however, the media can also serve to affirm social and cultural diversity and, moreover, provide crucial spaces in and through which imposed identities or the interests of others can be resisted, challenged and changed. Today the media landscape is fast changing.

Global and local developments in media markets, corporations and technologies are transforming the media environment, leading to new possibilities as well as to new forms of containment with respect to the production, circulation and consumption of media representations of ethnic minorities. Forces of political deregulation, global competition and the convergence of (digitalized) technologies – principally telecommunications, computers, broadcasting and satellite and cable delivery systems – have all reconfigured the global operations, institutional structures and strategic goals and market capabilities of major media players (Herman and McChesney 1997; Mohammadi 1997; Thussu 1998). These same forces have also contributed to the proliferation of media systems and output, growing audience fragmentation and the strategic importance of niche marketing within and across the borders of nation-states – forces that look set to continue into the foreseeable future.

Set against this wider tide of strategic corporate change, however, are the daily encounters and growing (tactical) uses made of new – and old – interactive technologies of communication by ethnic minority groups and diasporic communities. Today these communication technologies include international telecommunications, audio and video cassettes, mobile phones, mobile music systems, the Internet and email, digital cameras, photocopiers and fax machines, camcorders, and home-based computerized music recording and production systems. These time-space collapsing technologies present new communication opportunities for embattled and/or dispersed ethnic minorities, not least by helping to sustain subcultures and networks and keeping alive memories and myths of homelands as well as collective hopes for the future (Sreberny-Mohammadi and Mohammadi 1994; Gillespie 1995). These technologies facilitate instantaneous flows of information and ideas as well as the ritual exchange of symbols and images, thereby serving to construct and affirm 'imagined' – and now increasingly – 'virtual' communities.

Between the international media conglomerates and the daily mediated communications of ethnic minorities, there stands an array of 'intermediate' minority media organizations – the minority press, local cable TV stations, local radio, independent commercial television production companies, community-based film collectives. These organizations steer a difficult course between universalist appeals, market imperatives and systems of patronage on the one side, and particularistic aims, community based expectations and felt obligations on the other. Taken together they contribute an important, albeit under-researched, dimension to the communication environment of ethnic minorities and their struggles for 'authentic' and/or pluralistic representations (Cottle 1997; Dayan 1998; Browne 1999).

Integral to these struggles are demands that relate specifically to the cultural-politics of representation based on calls for enhanced media access and recognition, whether in mainstream and/or via minority media and outlets. Here limited gains, as well as continuing constraints and setbacks, characterize the contemporary ethnic minority media scene. The mainstream media, though differentiated by medium, outlet, genre and subject interests, all too often produce shocking examples of xenophobic reporting and racist portrayal, while often publicly committing to the ideals and practices of an inclusive multi-ethnic, multicultural society. Institutional inertia, as well as countervailing tendencies, are at work in the operations and the output of today's mainstream media, as are ideas of **multiculturalism** and the representations of **white backlash culture**. Contradiction and complexity, continuity and change characterize the media today.

Ethnic Minorities and the Media examines how representations of 'race' and minority ethnicity are reproduced, elaborated and challenged within today's media. Particular attention is devoted to the forces that currently shape and constrain their inflection across the media sphere, and how ethnic minorities themselves respond to, use and deploy media within their every-day lives, cultures and identities. The subtitle of this book, *Changing Cultural Boundaries,* deliberately seeks to draw attention to the ways in which processes of change are currently impacting on the production and reception of ethnic minority media representations, as well as the necessity for many of the media's representational practices to be challenged and changed. No one can seriously deny the importance, not to say urgency, of this field of investigation. How could they given the enormity of the human conse-quences – both historical and contemporary – that ideas of 'race' and eth-nicity have played, and continue to play, in structures of domination and inequality and in the political mobilization of cultural differences and iden-tities.

Towards new departures

Historically, ideas of 'race' developed as a means to differentiate social groups as biologically discrete subspecies marked out by physical or pheno-typical appearance, innate intelligence and other 'natural' dispositions. These ideas are generally traced back to the Enlightenment and scientific attempts to measure, calibrate, typologize and rank people in a hierarchy of superiority and inferiority. Within the context of western imperialism and colonialism, such efforts served to naturalize, in the most literal sense of the term, oppressive social relations. In so doing they sought to legitimize sys-tems of power and domination – systems that also found expression in the production and circulation of popular cultural imagery and artistic forms (Said 1978; McLintock 1995; Pieterse 1995). Today, scholars debate ideas about 'race' in relation to the historical encounters between different peoples (Jahoda 1999); their 'disciplinary' force in legitimizing imperialism and colonialism (Said 1978); their basis in the philosophical tenets and cul-ture of Enlightenment thinking (Goldberg 1993); or how they arose through the contradiction between Enlightenment ideas of equality and the inequal-ities of capitalist modernity (Malik 1996a). In other words, ideas of 'race' are debated not in relation to the discredited reductionism of biology but in relation to the changing social and discursive formations of history.

When approached in this way – historically, socially, discursively – we find that ideas of 'race' in fact assume different forms and are intimately entwined with systems of cultural representation – processes that continue to this day. Following the Holocaust, the ultimate racist exclusion, the use of explicit racist language and images within western multi-ethnic societies is likely to confront public opprobrium. In such circumstances it is understandable that essentialist ideas of racial difference may now become re-coded into more 'acceptable' ideas of primordial ethnicity or deep-seated cultural differences. Here culture itself becomes largely naturalized as the carrier of collective ancestry, traditions and group/national belonging and destiny: 'the concept of race arises through the naturalization of social differences. Regarding cultural diversity in natural terms can only ensure that culture acquires an immutable character, and hence becomes a homologue for race' (Malik 1996a: 150). The **'new racism'** of public language and discourse, for example, does precisely this when addressing potential immigrants, migrant workers, refugees and asylum seekers (as well as ethnic minorities 'within' the territorial confines of the nation) as cultural 'outsiders' who do not belong to a traditional (mythical) 'way of life' (Barker 1981; Solomos 1986, 1989; Murray 1986; van Dijk 1991; Gilroy 1992).

Confronted by such **racism(s)** – those that dare not mention their name – we need to deploy sensitive analytical tools if we are to recover exactly how racialized and racist meanings are embedded within, and reproduced through, the discourses, language, narratives and images of media representations. We also need to recognize the historically variant forms that racism(s) can assume, and how these are produced within and through different state, institutional and everyday practices. And we must also seek to understand how the ideas and practices of 'race' inform, and are informed by, other forms of social exclusion and oppression – whether those of class, gender, sexuality, ethnicity, age, nation or state. 'There is considerable historical variation', as Goldberg writes, 'both in the conception of races and in the kinds of social expression we characterise as racist' (Goldberg 1990: 295). Essentialist ideas of (demonized) national character and (tribalized) ethnic differences are often mobilized by state and media in times of war and conflict, further illustrating how racist discourses are not necessarily confined to minorities or need necessarily depend on the physical markers of skin colour (Allan 1999; Allen and Seaton 1999; Beattie *et al.* 1999b). Racism, then, remains an imperializing and opportunistic discourse capable of accommodating all. These issues are disturbing and should challenge us all to take very seriously indeed the media's representations of 'race' and ethnic minorities. They do not exhaust, however, the complexities of the interactions between ethnic minorities and the media.

The contributors to this collection seek to engage, for the most part, with the changing relationship and interactions between **ethnic minorities** and the media in the **United Kingdom** and in the **United States**. This is deliberate. As the opening statement to this introduction suggests, the relationship between media and ethnic minorities is characterized by complexity, and one way of opening this up to considered discussion is to focus on particular contexts – especially when seeking to identify and theorize new developments and how these depart from previously established research findings. Both the UK and the US have established research traditions in media research, and both have generated considerable research in the field of ethnic minorities and the media – which is not to suggest, of course, that important work has not been produced elsewhere. Strong parallels (as well as differences) exist between these two countries with respect to the multi-ethnic nature of their societies and in the encounters of ethnic minorities with the media – reflecting histories of enforced and voluntary minority settlement, systems and structures of inequality and political struggles for change (Small 1994; Parekh 1997; Stone and Lasus 1998).

A detailed comparative study of the changing cultural politics of ethnic minority media representation in both the UK and the US has yet to be written. The research studies presented here demonstrate that strong parallels do indeed exist and that findings, theoretical discussion and methodological frameworks generated in one national context often have relevance in another, whether in respect to changing representations, changing contexts of production, or changing cultures of identity, and how each separately, and in combination, register and contribute to changing cultural boundaries. Many of the chapter contributions also have relevance of course for those studying the minority media fields in other multi-ethnic, inegalitarian and increasingly media-dependent societies. Whether focused on the globalizing practices of transnational media corporations, diasporic and transnational communities and/or fundamental questions of minority ethnic media access and representation these concerns, by definition, transcend narrowly conceived national borders and may well 'travel' and speak to other minority experiences and contexts. It is hoped that readers of this collection, wherever they are based, will be stimulated to ponder, discuss and even better still to study and research for themselves the extent to which the ideas and findings advanced by the different authors on these pages in fact apply to their own situations and changing cultural boundaries.

Each of the chapters that follow is written by a leading researcher in the field, draws upon their latest research and thinking, and can be read as a self-contained and authoritative statement demonstrating new research departures. When read together, however, this collection also encourages you to situate each of these insightful discussions in relation to each other, in relation to the wider processes of change (and continuity), and also in relation to past research frameworks and findings. To this end each of the chapters that make up the rest of this book shall be introduced so as to highlight their distinctive contribution to the wider research field.

Changing representations

Today researchers make use of powerful theoretical frameworks and sophisticated tools of analysis. Varieties of neo-Marxism, multiracial feminisms and post-colonial studies, for example, all currently inform and contend with both established and emergent approaches to the study of the media including political economy, sociology of organizations and professions, cultural studies, discourse analysis and new audience studies. The theoretical encounters within and between these respective approaches often produce lively, sometimes acrimonious, debates centring on fundamental questions of knowledge, epistemology, methodology and the role of politics in academic study. Like all fields of academic endeavour with direct political relevance, such contestation is hardly surprising, nor should it necessarily be lamented. The clash of frameworks and methodologies can prove useful in staking out a field of shared concern and can also help to push the boundaries into new and productive areas.

Frameworks and debates help guide the questions asked by researchers and the approaches that they adopt, and they also help to 'test out' the robustness of research procedures, the validity of research findings, and the political relevance of the work undertaken. That said, when confronted by the array of approaches currently debating the essentially contested field of 'race' and ethnicity, it is perhaps all too easy to lose sight of the common ground, as well as some of the more fundamental differences structuring the debates and disagreements. Here we can refer once again to the wider problematics of 'race' and how each has informed research agendas and priorities and helped to conceptualize different objects of inquiry. Their influence can be detected throughout much of the research field now subject to review.

Over recent decades, a considerable body of research conducted in both the UK and the US has examined the media's representations of ethnic minorities. The collective findings of this research effort generally make for depressing reading. Under-representation and stereotypical characterization within entertainment genres and negative problem-oriented portrayal within factuality and news forms, and a tendency to ignore structural inequalities and lived racism experienced by ethnic minorities in both, are recurring research findings.

In Britain in the late 1950s through to the 1970s, for example, studies observed how immigrants were reported in relation to the so-called 'race riots' of 1958 (Miles 1984), public health scares (Butterworth 1967), problems of 'numbers' and tensions of 'race relations' and how this effectively concealed problems of British racism (Hartmann and Husband 1974; Hartmann *et al.* 1974; Critcher *et al.* 1977; Troyna 1981). In the 1970s and across the 1980s, studies of news, and other factuality genres, identified the ways in which a 'moral panic' orchestrated around 'mugging' (Hall *et al.* 1978), the portrayal of street violence (Holland 1981) and inner city disorders served to criminalize Britain's black population and ignored continuing social inequalities and growing anger at policing practices and harassment (Sumner 1982; Tumber 1982; Joshua *et al.* 1983; Murdock 1984; Burgess 1985; Downing 1985; Hansen and Murdock 1985; Solomos 1986, 1989; Cottle 1993a). In the 1980s and 1990s, studies have charted virulent press attacks on anti-racism campaigns, the vilification of black representatives and the support given to statements of 'new racism' by prominent politicians, as well as xenophobic reportage of refugees and migrants – actively disparaging attempts to further multicultural and anti-racist agendas (Murray 1986; Gordon and Rosenberg 1989; van Dijk 1991; McLaughlin 1999; Philo and Beattie 1999). Across the years, numerous studies have also observed the media's use of stock stereotypes of black people as 'trouble-maker', 'entertainer' and 'dependant' (Hartmann and Husband 1974; Barry 1988; Twitchin 1988; Hall 1990a).

In the US in 1968 the National Advisory Commission on Civil Disorders published its report into the causes of the major 'disturbances' that erupted across many US cities (Kerner 1968). In an oft-repeated passage it stated:

> The Commission's major concern with the news media is not in riot reporting as such, but in a failure to report adequately on race relations and ghetto problems . . . In defining, explaining and reporting this broader, more complex and ultimately far more fundamental subject the communication's media, ironically, have failed to communicate.
>
> (Kerner 1968: 382)

More recently, bell hooks maintains,

> there has been little change in the area of representation. Opening a magazine or book, turning on the television set, watching a film, or

looking at photographs in public spaces, we are most likely to see
images of black people that reinforce and reinscribe white supremacy.
(hooks 1992: 1; see also Martindale 1985; MacDonald 1992; Corea
1995; Ramaprasad 1996)

These and many other studies, then, provide us with evidence of the general patterns, impoverished representations and sometimes starkly racist
portrayal found in both the UK and US mainstream media. As *general* findings, however, these may suggest a relatively static and uniform picture of
ideological or representational closure and, in consequence, cover over historical processes of change. Studies are now beginning to recover, for example, how the changing ideas and political agendas of 'assimilation',
'multiculturalism' and 'anti-racism' have informed the development of TV
representations across the years (Daniels and Gerson 1989; Pines 1992;
Daniels 1994; Ross 1996; Bourne 1998) as well as those of the press
(Wilson and Gutierrez 1995) and cinema (Shohat and Stam 1994). The
influence of 'liberal' TV producers (Seymour-Ure 1974; Braham 1982) as
well as 'responsible' newspaper journalists and newspapers (Paletz and
Dunn 1969) have also been observed to have contributed to, respectively,
the downplaying of white racist fears and the selective curbing of sensa-
tional press treatments of civil disorder. These studies point to further
representational complexities and differences in and across the media. And
we must also note the limited but real advances in ethnic minority media
presence in recent years, whether in respect of TV genres of light entertainment, comedy and advertising in the UK (Givanni 1995; Hall 1995; Beattie *et al.* 1999a), or successful 'soaps' based on black characters in the US
(Downing 1988; Jhally and Lewis 1992; Gray 1995), as well as in the commercial crossover (and commodification) of the 'black culture industry'
more generally (Cashmore 1997). These, too, are important features of
ethnic minority representation.

Today, studies increasingly deploy an array of textual methods of analysis
when examining the myths, narratives, discourses and language embedded
within media representations of 'race'. The work of Mercer (1994) and Hall
(1997), for example, demonstrates how recent images of black bodies often
deliberately 'embody' ambivalent meanings that play on ideas of cultural
difference, stereotypes and intertextuality prompting readings that go
'against the grain'. Other studies also generally detect at least some discursive contestation and/or challenge to dominant viewpoints across mainstream genres and within minority media outlets whether, for example, in
'raced' representations of urban disorders in the US (Gooding-Williams
1993; Fiske 1994a, 1994b; Jacobs 1996; Hunt 1997) or the portrayal of

inner city 'riots' in the UK (J. Lewis 1982; Burgess 1985; Hansen and Murdock 1985; Cottle 1993a).

To be clear, none of the above suggests that dominant views of 'race' no longer inform media representations or serve to 'racialize' media events – they most certainly do – but rather that this outcome is precisely that, an outcome which has to be secured and managed if definitions, interpretations and prescriptions are to be effectively imposed on such 'events'. In other words, media representations of 'race' are a product of social and discursive processes mediated through established cultural forms; they are not a foregone conclusion and they most certainly are not beyond challenge or change.

Sensitized to the textual forms and discursive nature of media representations, recent studies have tended to reflect the growing influence of cultural studies and the wider linguistic (and cultural) turn in contemporary social theory. Here empiricist ideas of representation and 'ideology' have become increasingly challenged by approaches exploring the ways in which 'reality' is constituted (and/or known) within language, discourse and representations. Approached in such discursive terms, representations do not so much 'distort' reality as productively provide the means by which 'reality' is actively constructed and/or known (whether via 'social realist' or 'social constructionist' epistemologies). While this culturalist turn has helped to sensitize many to the discursive forms in which 'reality' is literally made to mean or 'signify', a strict adherence to structuralist (and post-structuralist) preoccupations with language, texts, signifying systems or 'regimes of truth' must always, according to its critics, collapse into forms of textual determinism, cultural relativism and political idealism (Ferguson and Golding 1997). For these commentators, the culturalist analysis of 'texts' should be integrated into a deeper appreciation of the 'contexts' of production and reception and becomes fatally undermined if permanently severed from the sociological (empirical) analysis of social relations, unequal life chances and the wider play of power.

Drawing a theoretical line in the sand an influential variant of cultural studies theorizes popular culture as the terrain on which, and through which, hegemonic struggles for consent are ideologically conditioned and discursively played out and thus seeks to keep both the interactions (and 'articulations') of the 'cultural' and the 'social' in view (Hall 1980b, 1999). British cultural studies in the 1970s and 1980s through its reworking of European structuralisms (Saussure, Lévi-Strauss, Barthes) and variants of Marxism (Voloshinov, Thompson, Williams, Gramsci, Althusser) has proved to be extraordinarily influential (Hall 1980a, 1980b), and its ideas have informed analyses of media representations of 'race' (Hall 1978; Hall *et al.* 1978; Gilroy 1987; Hall 1990a, 1992c). *Policing the Crisis* (Hall *et al.* 1978), for example, had sought to analyse how black youth had become criminalized and symbolized as a new 'folk devil' by the media in the 'mugging' scare of the early 1970s. This 'moral panic', it was argued, helped pave the (ideological) way for a new form of state 'authoritarian populism' (neo-conservative politics) that itself was a response to processes of national economic decline and growing political dissensus. This analysis relating representations of 'race' to wider state interests and processes of ideological reproduction has proved seminal though its explanation of the exact mechanisms linking media institutions, professional practices and cultural representations to political forces of change may now appear under- (or over-) theorized and in need of empirical support.

Recent studies in the US (discussed further below) have made similar connections between 'media events' and deep cultural anxieties around issues of 'race' (Fiske 1993, 1994a, 1994b; Reeves and Campbell 1994; Hunt 1997, 1999). These studies generally observe how 'raced' media events serve conservative political projects but may also sustain counter-hegemonic discourses. Studies such as these, then, remind us how media representations can both register and contribute to the shifting political-cultural climate of 'race' – a conflictual and contested terrain that by definition is constantly on the move. Today this terrain increasingly accommodates ideas of 'multiculturalism'. In my study of a UK regional television news programme, for example, I observed how ethnic minorities are now often portrayed in deliberate 'multiculturalist' ways through a (superficial) focus on cultural festivals, individual success stories and the cultural exotica of ethnic minority cultures (Cottle 1993a, 1993b, 1994). These representations are examined with reference to the established conventions of this particular news genre with its populist pursuit of positive stories and 'celebratory' features around lifestyle and consumption, as well as a growing multicultural sensibility inside the newsroom. Despite the best intentions of the producers, such 'multiculturalist' representations, I argued, may actually serve to reinforce culturally sedimented views of ethnic minorities as 'Other' and simultaneously appear to give the lie to ideas of structural disadvantage and continuing inequality.

Interestingly, recent US studies have arrived at similar findings and discerned a new and subtle form of 'modern racism'. This is interpreted as the unintentional outcome of news producers who seek to move beyond 'old fashioned racism' by portraying African Americans in more positive ways but who thereby create an impression of black social advance and thus undermine black claims on white resources and sympathies (Entman 1990; Campbell 1995; Lule 1997). Similar criticisms have also been levelled by Jhally and

Lewis (1992) at the so-called 'enlightened racism' of successful 'black' TV programmes such as *The Cosby Show*, 'which tells us nothing about the structures behind success or failure' and 'leaves white viewers to assume that black people who do not measure up to their television counterparts have only themselves to blame' (Jhally and Lewis 1992: 138) (for an alternative interpretation see Downing 1988). Herman Gray has also questioned the 'advances' represented by such portrayals, maintaining that: 'In the world of television, [America's] open and multiracial society operates within a carefully defined social, cultural and economic assumption that keeps alive the assimilationist assumptions of racial interaction' (Gray 1986: 232).

These and other studies, then, increasingly point to the dynamic nature and subtleties of media discourse and representation, features that cannot always be captured through simplistic and static applications of the concept of 'stereotype' (Mercer 1988, 1989, 1994; Daniels 1990; Cottle 1992). Given the common-sense status of this concept in public and media criticism, it is perhaps worth pointing out some of its limitations when unthinkingly applied to media representations of 'race' and ethnicity. Criticisms of the concept of 'stereotype' include, for example, its apparent conflation of universal processes of cognition with those more socially motivated or ideological processes of perception; its competing realist and idealist political premises – should representations portray the 'negative' realities of 'raced' lives and thereby seemingly endorse wider cultural typifications or portray a more 'positive' imaginary but then be accused of distorting reality?; its assumption that meanings are 'contained' within its terms and are not dependent on (differentiated) audience interpretations; its pulverization of textual complexity and meanings, the latter of which are assumed to be confined to, embodied within, and 'read off', depicted characters – though these in any case all too often are methodologically 'flattened' in quantitative counts of occupational roles; and its displacement of how, for example, narrative, irony and audience expectations of genre may all contribute to the communication of meaning. In more practical terms, the concept of stereotype may also prove increasingly out of step with the changing cultural politics of representation. Recent ideas concerning new ethnicities and the cultural politics of difference, with their fluid understanding of contested subject-positions (Hall 1988, 1992a, 1999; West 1993) prompt a more diversified stance towards the politics of representation – one that increasingly questions essentialist stereotypes whether 'negative' or 'positive'.

A ritual view to representations of 'race' also promises to move beyond the relatively static ideas of stereotypes (Carey 1989; Ettema 1990; Hunt 1999). 'A ritual view of communication is not directed towards the extension of messages in space but the maintenance of society in time', says Carey, and it involves, 'not the act of imparting information but the representation of shared belief' (Carey 1989: 43). Ettema (1990), in a study of 'press rites and race relations', develops this approach and demonstrates how the mass media not only reinforce social consensus by routinely affirming shared beliefs but also 'mediate situations in which individuals or institutions actively engage each other – often to further their own ends – in a stylized public event – a "public enactment"' (Ettema 1990: 310). This approach is important because, again, it reveals how some representational opportunities or openings can sometimes be won within an unfolding narrative enacted (and contested) through time. These openings, then, are not entirely predetermined by the forms of news texts or contained by the strategic advantages of dominant social interests.

Hunt (1999) further illuminates the power of this ritual approach in his detailed analysis of the 'media event' of the O.J. Simpson case. This study observes how different political projects sought to mobilize their interests in and through four principal narratives that surrounded the black celebrity's televised trial and his subsequent acquittal for the murder of his wife and her friend. Narratives of the 'Celebrity-Defendant', 'Black "Other"', 'Domestic-Violence' and 'Just-Us' variously served, according to Hunt, as hegemonic discourses in support of the status quo or as counter-hegemonic discourses aimed at disrupting the status quo and its current treatment of women and black Americans. The study thus 'acknowledges the potent effect of integrative, hegemonic forces like ritual without discounting the possible infiltration of counter-hegemonic ideas' (Hunt 1999: 46).

Fiske (1994a) has also deployed ideas of 'media events' to capture the seemingly 'hyperreal' media exposure granted to major stories like the O.J. Simpson case. This media event became such a phenomenon, according to Fiske, because it served to express the deep conflictual cultural undercurrents of 'race' within American society as well as the increasingly 'mediated' nature of our 'postmodern times'. Fiske attends to the succession of 'media events' involving black men in recent years, for example, O.J. Simpson, Rodney King, Clarence Thomas, Willie Horton, Mike Tyson and Marion Barry, and argues:

> These men do not figure as unique individuals, but only as the products of the white imagination; they figure as embodiments of the white fascination with and terror of the Black male and his embodiment of a racial-sexual threat to white law and order.
>
> (Fiske 1994a: xv)

These representations of 'race', then, serve to racialize, criminalize and sexualize black men and, by processes of symbolization, the wider black community.

Notwithstanding the 'postmodern' nature of our societies these findings in fact resonate with those from earlier times. A chilling example helps make the case. In 1938 Ames reported on her study of (pre-modern) American society in the 1930s and how, 'Newspapers and Southern society accept [racist] lynching as justifiable homicide in defence of society', particularly with respect to 'the protection of white women', and how 'This attitude of society in the south – this sympathetic understanding of a barbarous act while regretting the fact – influences editorial opinion' (Ames 1938; see also Omi 1989). Notwithstanding the developments and complexities of media representations it seems that significant sections of today's media continue to reproduce racist myths and white fears.

In their different ways each of the three chapters that comprise Part I on 'Changing representations' interrogate the continuing influence of white racism within today's media. This is so, notwithstanding the development of new technologies of communication, growing multicultural awareness within sizeable sections of the media audience, and the increasingly unacceptable public use of explicit racist language. Each chapter provides us with new departures in the analysis of contemporary media representations and together these alert us to the necessity of engaging with, and critically challenging, the discursive and representational forms of contemporary media racisms.

In Chapter 2, 'New(s) racism: a discourse analytical approach', Teun van Dijk outlines his discourse analytical approach and the insights that this delivers when applied to an example of 'new(s) racism'. Van Dijk's work has been at the forefront of recent international developments in discourse analysis as well as in the applied examination of communicated racism in both text and talk (van Dijk 1987, 1988a, 1991). His discussion provides us with invaluable tools for the analysis of mediated 'new(s) racism' often embedded within the structures and presuppositions of language. The example used in this chapter is a news report taken from the popular British newspaper the *Sun*, a tabloid that has often been criticized for its racist portrayals in the past. In the light of continuing press reporting of refugees, 'economic migrants' and asylum seekers in Britain in xenophobic, ethnocentric and racist terms, van Dijk's approach is all too relevant to our times and will hopefully equip others to examine, expose and challenge the subtleties of new(s) racism wherever it is found.

Fiske, as we observed above, has recently interrogated some of the US's most spectacular, hyperreal 'media events' involving black Americans and how these have served to visualize white fears and imagination in powered displays of cultural representation (Fiske 1993, 1994a, 1994b). In Chapter 3, 'White watch', John Fiske develops his earlier analyses with particular reference to practices of racialized surveillance since, in his view, 'the relations between the seer and the seen, between the knower and the known, are ultimately ones of power'. Videotapes and televised pictures have featured prominently in recent media events, whether the live televised broadcast of O.J. Simpson fleeing the attentions of the police and his subsequent court trials, the videotape of Marion Barry, the former Black mayor of Washington, DC, allegedly accepting drugs from an ex-girlfriend, or the videotape of the Los Angeles Police Department beating Rodney King that subsequently led to televised scenes of the Los Angeles 'riots' or (discursively contested) 'radical shopping' (Fiske 1994a). Developing theoretical ideas from Foucault, Fiske argues that the growth of contemporary forms of social surveillance are involved in the construction of a 'regime of truth' which serves to abnormalize and racialize black people and maintain the social order of whiteness. Fiske's chapter thus challenges us to rethink the apparent neutrality of technologies of surveillance and examine how these produce and communicate racialized knowledge which differentially penetrate into white and black lives.

In Chapter 4, 'Dreaming of a white . . .' John Gabriel also interrogates ideas of 'Whiteness' and the roles played by both established and new media in its construction and circulation. His discussion therefore develops previous themes of the discursive complexity and articulation involved in racialized representations, especially in relation to those of ethnicity, gender and sexuality as well as the varying roles played by different forms of media – cinema, television, radio, the press, the Internet, CD-ROMs – in affirming and popularizing forms of white consciousness and racist backlash culture. Gabriel situates these developments in relation to the shifting politics of 'race', global processes of change and the intertwined histories of the US and Britain. Whiteness should not be regarded as a monolithic discourse, he maintains, nor are whites a homogeneous ethnic group; rather, whiteness is a 'pathological discourse which has been constructed to create the fiction of a unitary and homogeneous culture and people'. Today many whites feel anxious and under threat and this produces, according to Gabriel, a white backlash culture expressed in and across today's different media.

Changing contexts of production

In comparison to studies of media representations of 'race', racism and ethnicity, studies of media production in this context are relatively few and far between – a finding that reflects an imbalance in the wider field of media communication studies more generally, the practical difficulties of securing research access to media production domains, and the influence of theoretical frameworks disposed to privilege the 'moment' of the text. Currently this imbalance threatens to underestimate, and under-theorize, the important forces that both condition and constrain, as well as facilitate and enable, ethnic minority media involvement in the production of representations. Studies of media representations often lack a theory of 'mediation' and, in consequence, collapse the forces of production into culturally defined 'frameworks of knowledge' that are thought to be at work in the production (or, to borrow Stuart Hall's terms, the 'encoding') of media output (Hall 1980c). As such, they tend to overlook Hall's recognition of 'the relations of production', the 'technical infrastructure' and the 'institutional structures' that also condition and shape the practices and output of media workers. There is much more to 'media production', of course, than the professional incorporation of surrounding cultural discourses. Neither can 'production' usefully be confined, as theorized in structuralist accounts, to the 'production' of meanings within 'texts' and systems of signification, or processes of identity formation 'produced' exclusively within/through contending narratives and discourses. That said, 'production' is not hermetically sealed behind institutional walls nor confined to organizational decision making and professional routines, and nor is it simply the (unmediated) expression of market forces. 'Production' involves all of these forces in dynamic combination and much else besides.

Research into media production has particular relevance for our understanding and theorization of racialized and racist media representations as well as for the under-representation of ethnic minorities as media professionals and cultural producers. Miles (1989) has usefully differentiated between the processes and mechanisms involved in the reproduction of social exclusion, disadvantage and racist discrimination – processes that by definition cannot all usefully be analysed and understood as 'racism'. Historical processes and structural factors can lead to exclusions and disadvantages that are not, in consequence, consciously intended or ideologically premised on racist ideas. When we consider the operations, institutions and practices of the media we should therefore not be surprised to find that a complex of factors and processes may also be at work here too, resulting in ethnic-minority under-representation. Of course this is not to deny that racist thinking and **institutionalized racism** may also be involved. But if we want to better understand the forces that contribute to the under-representation of ethnic minorities within the media workforce as well as their misrepresentation in terms of media portrayal, we have to grapple with all the complexities at work.

Viewed through a wide-angled lens, media production is shaped by prevailing state policies and socio-political responses to ethnic minorities, as comparative studies of different multicultural nations demonstrate. Political ideas of assimilation, integration, pluralism, multiculturalism and/or anti-racism can all variously inform the regulatory frameworks and cultural climates in which mainstream and minority production can either flourish or flounder (Riggins 1992; Dowmunt 1993; Husband 1994a; Frachon and Vargaftig 1995; Jakubowicz 1995). State regulatory frameworks and media policies are themselves subject to international forces including, as mentioned above, globalizing market trends, increased commercialism and technological developments, as well as other impinging geopolitical realities. Media industries and organizations are competing in uncertain times and volatile markets, and they strategically seek to position themselves in relation to regulatory authorities, competitors and consumers. Changing media structures and processes therefore shape the production contexts and frame the operations, budgets and strategic goals of media institutions, and these are condensed within senior decision making and must be professionally (pragmatically) negotiated by media professionals and producers in their daily practices.

Only a few studies have empirically examined how these and other forces impact on the production environment and producers of ethnic minority representations (defined here as 'about', 'for' or 'produced by'). Such studies include, for example, those of producers and the production of TV documentaries (Elliott 1972; Anwar and Shang 1982; Roscoe 1999); local radio programmes (Husband and Chouhan 1985) and black liberation radio (Fiske 1993: 227–33; Albert-Honore 1996); commercial TV magazine programmes and regional news (Cottle 1993a, 1993b); public service (BBC) multicultural programming (Cottle 1997, 1998); independent commercial and community-based TV and film (Salam 1995; Cottle 1997); minority cable TV (Tait and Barber 1996; Ismond 1997a, 1997b); the British Punjabi press (Tatla and Singh 1989) and the Black minority press more generally (Benjamin 1995); independent video and film collectives in Britain (Pines 1988; Hussein 1994) and in Britain and the US compared (Snead 1994). Key factors and constraints identifed at work here include, *inter alia*, limited finances, resources and training opportunities, systems of patronage and corporate gatekeepers, institutional conservatism and organizational hierarchy, producers' attitudes and cultural capital, source dependencies and source inhibitions, professional norms of balance and objectivity, professional status claims, cultural obligations and the 'burden of representation', audience expectations, temporal production cycles, and the conventions and aesthetics of media forms. Some of these forces 'at work' will be unpacked and discussed further below, as well as in some of the chapters that follow.

Together, however, these studies suggest that both individualist and instrumental explanations of media production do not fully encapsulate the complexities involved. There is more going on than simply the enactment of individual ideas and preferred cultural outlooks, or the manipulation of the media by senior corporate figures and/or surrounding political interests. Indeed, early studies of 'race' and the media by James Halloran and others had pointed to the complexities involved in explaining the media's 'failure to communicate' when indentifying the involvement of, *inter alia*, the 'event orientation' of news, the operation of deep-seated news values ('negativity', 'drama', 'conflict', 'personalization', 'violence'), the commercial logic of the media industries, as well as the 'inferential frameworks' or cultural/professional outlooks and expectations of the media workers concerned (Halloran 1974, 1977; see also Kushnick 1970; Knopf 1973; Hartmann and Husband 1974).

Accordingly, we must also attend to the various structures, contexts and dynamics that inform and shape media representations – regulatory, institutional, commercial, organizational, technological, professional, *and* cultural/ideological. To date, by far the most developed area of production research concerns journalism and news organization and the levels of production and professionalism. A brief review of some of these key findings thus helps to illustrate some of the complexities 'at work', complexities that are often missed and under-theorized in analyses of the cultural discourses 'at play' within media texts.

Journalist and proprietor prejudice

Anecdotal evidence provided by working journalists and observers suggests that many journalists and news proprietors do indeed harbour racist views and sentiments (Hollingsworth 1990: 132). Proprietorial involvement in setting news policy, hiring and firing senior editors, and even dictating headlines are also well documented (Pilger 1986, 1998). Much might seem to depend, therefore, on the personal views of proprietors, senior editors and ordinary journalists. However, on closer examination, research suggests that other more influential structures and processes are at work.

Ethnic composition and journalist training

The ethnic composition of journalists, their recruitment, professional training, on-the-job socialization, and problems of retention are clearly of relevance here. If journalists are found to come predominantly from white middle-class homes, select educational institutions and/or share similar middle-ground political values, undoubtedly this will influence the sensibilities and knowledge base informing journalist output. Recent data and discussion of Britain's ethnic minority journalists confirm that a gross imbalance between white and ethnic minority journalists continues to structure training and employment patterns and opportunities within the news media industry (Ainley 1998). Of the estimated 4012 national newspaper journalists only 20 (0.5 per cent) according to Ainley, are Black or Asian, while a mere 15 (0.2 per cent) out of 8000 work for the provincial press. In the broadcasting industry matters are slightly improved with an estimated 100 (2.7 per cent) Black or Asian editorial staff among 3700 – here, the equal opportunities policies, ethnic minority monitoring and training schemes of the BBC are thought to have helped, though Ainley (1998) reminds us that half of all Black staff work on black-only radio and television programmes. (For US data and discussion see Downing 1994; Wilson, this volume.)

Such figures are an indictment of the news media and demand concerted action to bring about real improvement. Ethnographic studies of news organizations and professionalism nonetheless also indicate that processes of journalist socialization (and retention) may be as important as journalist recruitment. Colleague esteem, successful newsroom acceptance and promotion and career moves depend upon conformity to a news policy and news organization goals, not their disruption (Breed 1955; Mazingo 1988; Cottle 1993a; Wilson, this volume). Researchers have also often commented on the ostensible lack of conflict within newsrooms and the unspoken acceptance of both shared news values and a widespread professional ideology of 'objectivity' – an ideology that may well have the effect of distancing ethnic minority journalists from acting as advocates for those minority groups and interests they might otherwise seek to serve (Cottle 1998; Allan 1999).

Competition and marketplace pressures

News organizations, for the most part, are in business to make profits and all compete for readers and audiences. Political economy research raises a third explanation based on the wider system of commercial constraints and pressures bearing down on the 'cultural industries' and their news output (Murdock 1982; Golding and Murdock 1996). Surviving in a competitive marketplace means seeking the maximum audience/readers and the maximum receipts from advertisers. In this context, news is produced just like any other commodity for the largest possible group of consumers. Within a predominantly white society and culture, economic forces can centre 'middle ground' white opinion and interests since this is where the largest market and profits are found, and thereby marginalize minority interests, voices and opinions. Also, high market entry costs and potentially smaller audiences, and hence advertiser reluctance to pay for advertising in such outlets, all inhibit the successful formation and growth of minority ethnic news media – though some have managed against the odds to secure a niche market (Tatla and Singh 1989; Riggins 1992; Benjamin 1995). In the mainstream, market pressures also contribute to press sensationalism, populist forms and formats, and can lead to the orchestration of 'race' controversy in pursuit of readers, ratings and revenue.

Bureaucratic organization and new technologies

Bureaucratic and organizational pressures within the newsroom, as well as impersonal economic forces outside, are also at work. Confronted with the daily pressures of news deadlines and the uncertainty of tomorrow's news events, news teams seek, as far as possible, to 'tame the news environment' and 'routinize the unexpected'. One way of doing this is to rely on key institutional sources of news, such as the police or government sources, for example, who serve as the nation's primary definers of reality (Hall *et al.* 1978). The result is that little energy or resources are devoted, as a matter of routine, to the search for non-institutional voices and viewpoints. When coupled with a professional journalistic claim to impartiality and objectivity which, ironically, is achieved in practice via the accessing of authoritative (that is, authority) voices, so the bureaucratic nature of news production is geared to privilege the voices and viewpoints of (white) social power holders, and not those excluded from powerful institutions.

That said, recent sociological studies of news source interventions, as well as ritual studies of news representation and production referenced earlier (Hunt 1999), now suggest that questions of news access may not be so clear cut and are contingent on the contestation of competing sources. The changing cultural-political field of 'race' and the unfolding narratives of particular news stories can also contribute to a wider caste of news actors, voices and viewpoints than may be anticipated, as certain stories break through news thresholds and become mobilized by different political interests and projects and stimulate 'pack journalism' (Cottle 2000a). In the context of the UK, the unprecedented media exposure that has built across the years following the racist murder of the young British student Stephen Lawrence in 1993 is a case in point. Across the years 1993 to 1998 *The Guardian* newspaper, for example, produced no fewer than 347 news reports on this one murder and its aftermath. Generally media attention has focused on the actions, pronouncements *and* failings of the police, the courts, a public inquiry as well as senior government ministers suggesting that a powerful combination of social and cultural forces are at work in the creation of this high profile 'media event' (Cottle 2000b).

Researchers also need to attend to new digital technologies of news production and delivery which, in combination with increased commercial pressures and political deregulation, have recently begun to reconfigure newsrooms and journalist practices. Journalists are increasingly under pressure to work 'flexibly' as multi-skilled workers producing news for multimedia news outlets. A recent study of just such a multimedia 'news centre' demonstrates how the introduction of new technologies and multi-skilled practices have contributed in practice to undermining community source involvement. This was so notwithstanding the possibilities of electronic news production systems, the Internet, email, video telephones, video cameras and so on to enhance search facilities, community access and widen forms of minority ethnic news participation (Cottle 1999). Quite simply the multi-skilled journalists fashioning news for TV, radio and on-line had neither the time nor the professional imagination to enhance ethnic minority community involvement through the use of these new technologies.

Deep-seated news values

News values, 'one of the most opaque structures of meaning in modern society' (Hall 1981: 234), have long been noted to help select, order and prioritize the production of news representations (Galtung and Ruge 1981). In the context of ethnic minority reporting, then, it is perhaps unsurprising that news often forefronts images of ethnic minorities in terms of conflict, drama, controversy, violence and deviance (Halloran 1974, 1977; Hartmann and Husband 1974; Troyna 1981; Cottle 1991). The question here, though, is not whether these news values are exclusive to ethnic minority reporting because clearly they inform other news stories as well, but rather to what extent they figure in a disproportionate number of stories about ethnic minorities framed in such ways. We should question to what extent 'news values' can really be assumed to be universal given the professionally produced variations found in and across different news forms. The recent development of, and controversy surrounding, the so-called 'public journalism' in the US, for example, with its advocacy of democratic participation helps to illustrate how 'news values' need not be seen as written in stone (Glasser and Craft 1998).

News forms and news genres

News organizations typically work to an identifiable editorial position and in-house style. Journalists also reproduce these distinctive news forms according to a number of genre and sub-genre conventions. These too exert a shaping impact upon the selection and framing of news stories about ethnic minorities, as the discussion of local news representations of 'race' above, has already suggested. We can also observe how processes of 'tabloidization' or, in more derogatory terms, 'dumbing down', led by commercial imperatives and professional perceptions of their audience are today changing television schedules, programme formats and newspaper appeals. These processes indirectly and directly impact on subject selection and silences within and across the news (and other forms of 'factuality' programming) and often inform the sensationalist and/or superficial spin that accompanies their presentation – processes already documented to have deleteriously influenced the TV representation of ethnic minorities and issues (Cottle 1993a; Ross 1996).

The above has done no more than briefly indicate some of the interrelated structures and processes of news manufacture that condition and shape – both directly and indirectly – the production of news representations of ethnic minorities. Not everything, it seems, can necessarily be accounted for with reference to the hegemonic play of cultural power and discursive contestation embodied within media representations – behind the scenes there is often more going on than meets the eye. Today, as we have already heard, the media landscape is fast changing and the three chapters that comprise the second part, 'Changing contexts of production', examine this changing scene in relation to the production of television programmes and press representations of ethnic minorities. The three chapters address different levels of interrelated change. These comprise the changing patterns of newsroom recruitment of ethnic minority journalists and the impact of traditional processes of journalist socialization; the informing context of commercial and corporate change and the response of professional programme makers to these new media constraints and pressures; and the changing global and technological landscape of the media industry more widely and its impact on the production and circulation of representations of 'blackness'.

In Chapter 5, 'The paradox of African American journalists', Clint Wilson addresses the contemporary position of African American journalists in US newsrooms. The chapter first historically contextualizes the current situation of African American journalists in relation to earlier calls for change, and provides up to date data on the employment of black journalists and editors in today's newsrooms. Wilson argues that the situation, though slightly improved in recent years, nonetheless remains woefully inadequate and seeks to explain why it is that news representations continue to ignore black perspectives, notwithstanding the employment of some black journalists. Wilson focuses on how processes of institutional socialization and sanctions within newsrooms continue to work against necessary change in news media content. In effect, he argues, the pressures for change and the forces of news media institutional socialization have created a paradox for black journalists.

In Chapter 6, 'A rock and a hard place: making ethnic minority television', Simon Cottle also attends to the production environment and professional practices of ethnic minority media workers. Here, however, the focus shifts to the production of 'multicultural programmes', that is, programmes produced by, for and about Britain's ethnic minorities, by the public service broadcaster the BBC, as well as by independent commercial companies and community-based producers. Producers and the production of multicultural television have often been overlooked in theoretical discussions. Drawing on his recent empirical research, Cottle illuminates, with the help of the producer's accounts and experiences, how a number of commercial, corporate and cultural constraints are pragmatically accommodated by today's producers. These constraints and accommodations are shown to thwart programme intentions and cast doubt on corporate statements of commitment towards multicultural programme production.

In Chapter 7, 'Black representation in the post network, post civil rights world of global media', Herman Gray explores the structural transformations in the global media industry and ponders what this means for black television programming and black media representations. He raises questions about the 'meanings of blackness' when played in the distant reaches of the vast corporate marketplace made possible by satellite, cable, the Internet and other forms of global delivery, as well as the possibility that the persistence of racialized programming patterns and viewing preference may suggest the presence of a 'post civil rights discourse'. Gray concludes, however, that though media representations do obviously signify at multiple levels and in different times and places, they continue to bear the traces of their conditions of production and the historicity of their time and place.

Changing cultures of identity

Studies of ethnic minority audiences, remarkably, remain a rarity. Given the recent enthusiasm for ideas of 'active' audiences in recent media approaches (Dickinson *et al.* 1998), this silence, with a few exceptions only, is perhaps all the more surprising. In another sense, however, it simply continues the institutional logic and academic inertia which, until recently, has conspired to ignore what ethnic minorities themselves might think, want, or say about media representations, the media's involvement within their everyday lives, or their media hopes for the future. This situation is now under pressure to change. In these 'new (media) times' of technological proliferation, accelerating global reach, fragmenting markets and increased competition, minority audiences can become targeted as potentially lucrative markets and their consumer tastes and media requirements may, in consequence, be deemed worthy of market research. A growing 'multiculturalist' sensibility combined with a corporate PR (public relations) culture has also, no doubt, encouraged major media players to publicly commit themselves to multicultural aims and occasionally sponsor research aimed at finding out what they should already know – and many ethnic minorities, of course, have always known.

More theoretically, academic interest in processes of audience reception involving 'interpretative communities', 'polysemic texts', differentiated 'decoding', situated contexts of domestic appropriation, and media use within local settings and cultural milieux, has also recently combined with research interests previously signalled within the 'new ethnicities' problematic. Together these conceptual approaches are now prompting new and significant work in this area (J. Lewis 1991; Jhally and Lewis 1992; Gillespie 1995; Barker 1997, 1998). Linking both these new approaches to audiences and the new ethnicities problematic are shared concerns with cultural processes of sense-making and how these inform the construction of identities and communities – whether 'interpretative' and/or 'imagined'. This culturalist approach to audiences thus promises to deliver deep insights into processes of communicated meaning and sense-making. As such it is a far cry from earlier sociological attempts to map and record processes of media communication and diffusion as in, for example, a study of the Detroit riot of 1967 which involved interviews with 500 arrested 'Negro' men (Singer 1970), or the behaviourist simplicities that suggest a 'causal' media effect prompting 'copycat' rioting (Scarman 1986: 173–5).

Market surveys, prompted by the commercial logics that underpin their design, are generally poorly equipped to delve into the complexities of minority and diasporic interpretative processes and/or situated media appropriation and use. Recent academic surveys have revealed, however, important patterns of majority and minority media use, programme preferences and attitudes towards majority and minority ethnic provision (Halloran *et al.* 1995; Mullan 1996). When aggregate results are followed up with interviews, as in both of these studies, qualitative findings emerge that often reveal collective minority dissatisfaction and frustration with the media's seeming inability to provide representations that portray their communities and cultures, their difficulties and diversity, in ways that are thought to be valid or fair – findings also exposed and discussed by Karen Ross (this volume). Viewer response mail has also provided researchers with retrospective insights into how white and Black viewers have differentially responded to and made sense of early 'symptomatic' TV texts, that is, programmes that register the racial tensions of their time (Bodroghkozy 1995). Interviews with ethnic minority audiences of contemporary media 'texts' have also revealed differential readings (Bobo 1995).

These latter studies invariably move beyond a concern with differentiated 'attitudes' towards media output and pursue a deeper appreciation of interpretative processes with the help of a model of audience 'decoding' (Hall 1980c). This model anticipates differential audience responses, given the 'polysemous' nature of media texts which are thought capable of sustaining 'dominant-hegemonic', 'negotiated' and 'oppositional' codes of audience reading. This model informed David Morley's early empirical study of audience responses to the UK television news programme *Nationwide* though, revealingly, he noted how a group of black students 'make hardly any connection with the discourse of *Nationwide*. The concerns of *Nationwide* are not the concerns of their world. They do not so much produce an oppositional reading as refuse to read it at all' (Morley 1980: 134).

In-depth qualitative studies of 'raced' responses to selected 'media events', whether the Los Angeles 'riots' of 1992 or the trials of the black celebrity O.J. Simpson, are also revealing. Hunt (1997) observes, for example, how 'black-raced' informants exhibited a consciousness qualitatively different from that exhibited by 'Latino-raced' and 'white-raced' informants when 'reading' the same mainstream television news portrayal of the Los Angeles 'riots'. According to Hunt, 'They were generally hostile toward KTTV assumptions that localized the significance of the events, that blurred the event's connection to issues of systematic racial and economic injustice in the US' (Hunt 1997: 163). He concludes that 'we are presented with a case where textual interpellations and audience resistance are intimately connected to raced ways of seeing' (ibid; see also Fiske 1993, 1994a, 1994b; Hunt 1999).

The complexities of audience reception and sense-making are not exhausted, however, with reference to these 'raced' ways of seeing. The interactions and various uses made of different media technologies and their insertion into everyday cultural practices and cultural milieux involves more than this – important though the structuring logics and outlooks of 'raced' media involvement undoubtedly are in shaping media responses and interpretations. Questions of identity and media interpretation are unlikely, when viewed from the new ethnicities problematic, to simply render down into what can often appear to be essentialized audience positions and predicted differences of 'raced' decoding. The complexities and contestation of multiple 'subject positions' or 'positionalities' discursively mobilized within and through 'new ethnicities', **hybrid-cultures** and contested cultural spaces would rather suggest a more fluid and complex set of cultural responses within processes of media reception and identity formation (Barker 1997, 1998). Here concerns of mediated 'race' and racism appear to have become decentred within emergent work conducted within the new ethnicities problematic. Current use of the terms 'transcultural', **diaspora** and **diasporic consciousness**, terms increasingly substituted for those of 'ethnic minority' and 'ethnic minority culture', further signal this theoretical shift towards culturally fluid, spatially transnational, and multi-layered discursive (and affective) 'reading' positions and how these are sustained within the cultural boundaries of diasporic experience (Dayan 1998; Hall 1999).

The chapters in Part III, 'Changing cultures of identity', help to illustrate the importance that is currently attached to this area of empirical research and theorization and provides four very different discussions. In Chapter 8, 'In whose image? TV criticism and Black minority viewers', Karen Ross outlines and discusses findings from an innovative study of black audiences commissioned by the BBC. The study involved 353 members of different black minority communities and made use of different methods – focus groups, interviews, viewing diaries, questionnaires. Ross considers the ways in which black minority audiences interact with television images and explores the perceptions which different black minorities hold towards televisual output. Salient audience themes raised, and discussed, include audience ideas of 'stereotyping' and the marginality of black minority characters, the dominance of 'racism' themes in programmes featuring black characters, cross-cultural relationships, and the impact of negative images on both white and black audiences. The chapter also explores some of the methodological concerns which arise when research with black minority communities is undertaken by white researchers and problematizes the notion that *only* black researchers can *do* black research. Ross concludes that 'What black minority viewers want is not something huge and extravagant but something small and relatively easy to provide: the opportunity to see themselves, in all their diversity, portrayed credibly on that most powerful of media – television'.

In Chapter 9, 'Ethnicity, national culture(s) and the interpretation of television', Ramaswami Harindranath calls into question the tendency within recent audience reception studies to work with a static view of ethnicity and a crude and reductionist understanding of cultural differences. Too often, he contends, influential audience studies like Liebes and Katz's *The Export of Meaning* (1993) run the risk of reproducing racial stereotypes when television's interpretations are thought to be determined by the ethnic community to which the respondent belongs. Drawing on his recent cross-national research and deploying theoretical ideas drawn from H-G. Gadamer, Harindranath acknowledges the centrality of the notion of collective identity in processes of audience interpretation but proposes a more complex link between understanding and collectivity. His discussion identifies the presence of a 'third' culture, a hybrid between his two selected national cultures. Not only is this pertinent to debates concerning 'cultural imperialism', but also it suggests a vital avenue for audience research concerned with cross-cultural consumption of mediated knowledge and the complexities involved.

In Chapter 10, 'Transnational communications and diaspora communities', Marie Gillespie explores how transnational media play a role in sustaining South Asian diaspora formations and consciousness by focusing on the everyday cultural and discursive practices among British Asian youth living in Southall, London. Gillespie argues for the relevance of an anthropological approach and illustrates her case with findings from a study of the reception of two TV versions of the Mahabharata, a foundational text of Indian society and culture, widely viewed in India and in the diaspora. She shows how Hindu women in London and Delhi selectively appropriate and contest key narratives for their own purposes, and in so doing subvert patriarchal and nationalist discourses in the construction of their own worldviews and identities. The key finding reported here is that young British Asians make shared use of transnational TV programmes and video films and that TV talk about them, far from being trivial and inconsequential, constitutes an 'embryonic public sphere' involving forms of self-narration and a forum in which different identities are experimented with and performed.

In Chapter 11, 'Media and diasporic consciousness: an exploration among Iranians in London', Annabelle Sreberny discusses findings from recent research into one of Britain's near-invisible Muslim and 'unmarked' ethnic communities. She reflects on the developing ideas and theorization of 'diaspora' and notes how work which focuses on racism, xenophobia and the dynamics of exclusion in western societies often overlooks the importance of cultural memories and attachments to other spaces and places that ethnic communities often hold dear. Sreberny explores this dimension of diasporic experience and consciousness, and examines how the contemporary media forms of diasporic communities can 'bind' such transnational communities together and serve to maintain minority ethnic cultural identities, and cultural attachments. What we need, she argues, are empirically grounded studies of how diaspora is experienced, lived in the everyday, and what kind of roles different media play within the complex set of psychological, sociological and cultural locations that comprise diasporic realities.

On the right to communicate

The chapters in this book all contribute new departures in the media-ethnic minority field, and each presents new research findings with respect to 'changing representations', 'changing contexts of production' and 'changing cultures of identity'. Implicit to the structure of this book, as well as this brief sketch of the research field, is the argument that each of these areas of research and theorization are indispensable for an understanding of the interrelated complexities informing the interactions between media and ethnic minorities and changing cultural boundaries. These different research emphases and approaches are productive of different insights as well as theoretical tensions – some of which have surfaced and remain unresolved in this introductory 'mapping'. Hopefully, however, the different levels of analysis and insights produced by each can be acknowledged as necessary for improved understanding. Political economy remains an indispensable tool in the analysis of the changing configuration of media industries and new production technologies. Cultural studies and forms of discourse analysis are no less necessary in the interrogation of media texts, representations and meanings. Sociological approaches to media organizations and professional practices, for their part, continue to produce improved understanding of the processes and practices by which media workers routinely grapple with institutional constraints and cultural obligations. And ethnographic and other qualitative approaches to the studies of audiences are now producing real advances in our appreciation of audience media involvement in processes of identity formation and identity maintenance.

Implicit to all the chapters that follow, despite their inevitable differences, is a shared concern with how the media currently represent, respond to, and perform in relation to ethnic minorities living with multi-ethnic, multicultural societies. Often informing these critical discussions, then, is a normative evaluation of how the media ought to represent, respond or perform in relation to ethnic minorities, and it is this commitment which often animates detailed research and provides the critical cutting-edge of engaged scholarship. The term 'multicultural' is perhaps pivotal here and contains within it fundamental questions (and immanent disputes) about the relationship between cultural identity and diversity, citizenship rights and responsibilities, and the exercise and organization of state power and civil society. It also begs questions about the normative role of the media in relation to all of these issues. When 'multicultural' is converted into an 'ism' – 'multiculturalism' – as it so often is today, this tends to flatten thinking about cultural heterogeneity and glosses over the differentials of power and historical privilege embedded in the institutions, practices and thinking of 'multicultural' societies. In other words, 'multiculturalism' often presents as a 'pat and pedestrian doctrine' and parades as 'the dogma of presumptive correctness' (Goldberg 1994: 1; see also Shohat and Stam 1994; Hall 1999). Difficult issues that go to the political heart of what it means to live in a 'multicultural' society are thereby side-stepped.

In a final afterword chapter, 'Media and the public sphere in multi-ethnic societies', Charles Husband thinks through and renders explicit his normative ideas about the role of the media in multicultural societies and how the media should help to construct a multi-ethnic 'public sphere'. Rooted in ideas of contemporary political philosophy, Husband challenges the inadequacies of much multicultural policy and Eurocentric human rights discourse. He argues for a policy of differentiated citizenship rights that acknowledges the distinctive histories and current experiences of differing ethnic groups and proceeds to develop a case for a further human right, a communication right – 'the right to be understood'. This right, he contends, must be enacted in and through a multi-ethnic media public sphere. Husband's chapter is perhaps a little more demanding than the other chapters in this volume; it challenges us all to think through exactly what we should expect, and demand, of the media in multi-ethnic societies and why. It provides a fitting conclusion to this collection.

Note

1 Ideas of 'race', racism and ethnicity have been, and continue to be, subject to heated debate and this informs the politics of language choice and use. This book is no exception. Thus, each of the contributors to this volume use and often define their preferred terms in the context of their own chapter discussions and these follow their informing political viewpoints. Some, for example, seek to signal the positive meanings of 'Black' and/or its political mobilization through capitalization, while others use lower case 'black' to describe enduring conditions of disadvantage, discrimination and racism experienced by different minority groups and people of colour. Others prefer to refer to specific minority groups such as 'African-Americans' in the US or 'African-Caribbeans' in the UK and acknowledge the important experiential and other bases of difference both within and

between minority ethnic groups. These and other language choices, then, signal the politics of difference and often give expression to three underlying **problematics of 'race', racism and ethnicity**. Terms set in bold throughout the remainder of this book refer the reader to the discussion of key terms and concepts (see pages 215–20).

Part I
CHANGING REPRESENTATIONS

NEW(S) RACISM: A DISCOURSE ANALYTICAL APPROACH
Teun A. van Dijk

Introduction

In this chapter we critically study the way news in the press may contribute to what is sometimes called the 'new racism'. Since news reports are a type of text, our approach will be 'discourse analytical'. This means that we do not treat news as transparent 'messages' whose 'contents' may be analysed in a superficial, quantitative way. Rather, we examine the complex structures and strategies of news reports and their relations to the social context. In our case, the social context consists of the activities of journalists in newsmaking, as well as the interpretations of readers, in the increasingly multicultural societies of western Europe and North America. More specifically we want to know what role the media in general, and news in particular, play in the reproduction of 'racial' and ethnic inequality in these societies, and aim to do so through a systematic analysis of news discourse structures.

The new racism

In many respects, contemporary forms of racism are different from the 'old' racism of slavery, segregation, apartheid, lynchings, and systematic discrimination, of white superiority feelings, and of explicit derogation in public discourse and everyday conversation. The *New Racism* (Barker 1981) wants to be democratic and respectable, and hence first off denies that it is racism. Real Racism, in this framework of thought, exists only among the Extreme Right. In the New Racism, minorities are not biologically inferior, but different. They have a different culture, although in many respects there are 'deficiencies', such as single-parent families, drug abuse, lacking achievement values, and dependence on welfare and affirmative action – 'pathologies' that need to be corrected of course (for a character-istic example, see D'Souza 1995; and for a critical analysis of this book, see van Dijk 1998).

Both in the US and Europe, several variants of this kind of racism have been studied, for instance as 'symbolic racism' that is opposed to policies of affirmative action, such as busing (McConahay 1982; Dovidio and Gaertner 1986). From the point of view of a black scholar, Essed (1991) similarly analyses the many micro-inequities in the life of black women in terms of what she calls 'everyday racism'. Such and other forms of racism are typi-cally indirect and subtle (Pettigrew and Meertens 1995). These are not limited to ordinary people, or the street, but are also practised by the elites, as we shall show in more detail for the media below (van Dijk 1993).

The role of discourse

Especially because of their often subtle and symbolic nature, many forms of the 'new' racism are 'discursive': they are expressed, enacted and con-firmed by text and talk, such as everyday conversations, board meetings, job interviews, policies, laws, parliamentary debates, political propa-ganda, textbooks, scholarly articles, movies, TV programmes and news reports in the press, among hundreds of other genres. They appear 'mere' talk, and far removed from the open violence and forceful segregation of the 'old' racism. Yet, they may be just as effective to marginalize and exclude minorities. They may hurt even more, especially when they seem to be so 'normal', so 'natural', and so 'commonsensical' to those who engage in such discourse and interaction. They are a form of ethnic hege-mony, premised on seemingly legitimate ideologies and attitudes, and often tacitly accepted by most members of the dominant majority group. This unique control of the majority over the prevalent forms of public discourse, policies and social conduct makes minority resistance (or white dissidence) against such racism even more difficult and precarious. It needs no further argument that the consequences of these forms of discursive racism in the lives of members of minority groups are hardly discursive: they may not be let into the country, the city or the neighbourhood, or will not get a house or a job.

Discourse analytical approaches

Traditional approaches to the role of the media in the reproduction of racism were largely content analytical: quantitative studies of stereotypical words or images representing minorities (see, for example, Hartmann and Husband 1974; Deepe Keever *et al.* 1997; for review see Cottle 1992).

Discourse analytical approaches, systematically describe the various structures and strategies of text or talk, and relate these to the social, political or political context. For instance, they may focus on overall topics, or more local meanings (such as coherence or implications) in a 'semantic' analysis. But also the 'syntactic' form of sentences, or the overall 'organization' of a news report may be examined in detail. The same is true for variations of 'style', 'rhetorical devices' such as metaphors or euphemisms, 'speech acts' such as promises and threats, and in spoken discourse also the many forms of 'interaction' (for an introduction to the various levels and approaches of discourse analysis, see van Dijk 1997b). These structures of text and talk are systematically related to elements of the social 'context', such as the spatio-temporal setting, participants and their various social and communicative roles, as well as their goals, knowledge and opinions. During the 1990s work on racism increasingly made use of such discourse analytical notions (Smitherman-Donaldson and van Dijk 1987; Wodak *et al.* 1990; van Dijk 1991; Jager and Link 1993; McGarry 1994; Banon Hernandez 1996; van Dijk 1997a).

The discursive reproduction of racism

How is discourse involved in the reproduction of (or resistance against) racism? To answer that question, we must know what racism is. Summarizing a complex theory, we shall simply assume here that racism is a social system of 'ethnic' or 'racial' inequality, just like sexism, or inequality based on class. That system has two main components, namely a social and a cognitive one. The social component of racism consists of everyday discriminatory practices, on the micro-level of analysis, and organizations, institutions, legal arrangements and other societal structures at the macro-level. Since discourses are social practices, racist discourse belong first of all to this social dimension of racism.

On the other hand, social practices also have a cognitive dimension, namely the beliefs people have, such as knowledge, attitudes, ideologies, norms and values. In the system of racism, thus, racist stereotypes, prejudices and ideologies explain why and how people engage in discriminatory practices in the first place, for instance because they think that the Others are inferior (less intelligent, less competent, less modern, and so on), have fewer rights, or that 'We' have priority for a house or a job. These beliefs or 'social representations' many members of the dominant (white) ingroup have about immigrants and minorities are largely derived from discourse.

That is, discourse as a social practice of racism is at the same time the main source for people's racist beliefs. Discourse may thus be studied as the crucial interface between the social and cognitive dimensions of racism. Indeed, we 'learn' racism (or anti-racism) largely through text or talk. Because they control the access to, and control over most public discourse, the political, educational, scholarly and media elites have a specific role and responsibility in these forms of discursive racism (van Dijk 1993, 1996). By their control over the crucially important power resource of public discourse, the various elites at the same time are dominant within their own ingroup (of which they are able to influence the prevalent ethnic opinions), as well as over minority groups, whose everyday lives they are able to control by their discourse, policies and decisions in positions of power.

The role of the media

There is no need to argue here the overall power of the media in modern 'information' societies. Together with other powerful elite groups and institutions, such as politicians, corporate managers, professionals and professors, they have – sometimes indirectly – most influence on the lives of most people in society. Whereas the power of corporate managers may have less impact on public discourse and opinion, and more on the economy, the market, production and (un)employment, the power of the media is primarily 'discursive' and 'symbolic'. Media discourse is the main source of people's knowledge, attitudes and ideologies, both of other elites and of ordinary citizens. Of course, the media do this in joint production with the other elites, primarily politicians, professionals and academics. Yet, given the freedom of the press, the media elites are ultimately responsible for the prevailing discourses of the media they control.

This is specifically also true for the role of the media in ethnic affairs, for the following reasons:

* Most white readers have few daily experiences with minorities.
* Most white readers have few alternative sources for information about minorities.

- Negative attitudes about minorities are in the interest of most white readers.
- More than most other topics, ethnic issues provide positive but polarized identification for most white readers, in terms of Us and Them.
- The media emphasize such group polarization by focusing on various Problems and Threats for Us, thus actively involving most white readers.
- Minority groups do not have enough power to publicly oppose biased reporting.
- The dominant (media) discourse on ethnic issues is virtually consensual.
- In particular there is little debate on the 'new' racism.
- 'Anti-racist' dissidents have little access to the media.

In sum, when power over the most influential form of public discourse, that is, media discourse, is combined with a lack of alternative sources, when there is a near consensus, and opponents and dissident groups are weak, then the media are able to abuse such power and establish the discursive and cognitive hegemony that is necessary for the reproduction of the 'new' racism. Let us now examine in some more detail how exactly such power is exercised in news and newsmaking.

Newsmaking

The role of the press in the system of racism is not limited to news reports or editorials, but already begins with the daily routines of newsmaking (Tuchman 1978; van Dijk 1988a). Minorities have less access to the media also because they do not control the many 'source discourses' on which daily newsmaking is based: press conferences, press releases, briefings, information brochures, documentation, interviews, and so on. Their opinions are less asked or found less credible or newsworthy, also because most journalists (and virtually all editors) are white.

News structures

Especially also on ethnic issues, for which alternative sources of information are scarce, news on TV or in the press often provides the first 'facts', but at the same time the first 'definitions of the situation' and the first opinions – usually those of the authorities or other white elites. We shall therefore systematically analyse the structures and strategies of news discourse, and see how they enact or contribute to everyday elite racism (for an introduction to these structures of discourse and news, see van Dijk 1988a, 1988b, 1997b).

Topics

Interestingly, whereas there are a large number of types of topic in the press, news about immigrants and ethnic minorities is often restricted to the following kinds of events:

- New (illegal) immigrants are arriving.
- Political response to, policies about (new) immigration.
- Reception problems (housing, etc.).
- Social problems (employment, welfare, etc.).
- Response of the population (resentment, etc.).
- Cultural characterization: how are they different?
- Complications and negative characterization: how are they deviant?
- Focus on threats: violence, crime, drugs, prostitution.
- Political response: policies to stop immigration, expulsion, and so on.
- Integration conflicts.

In each of these cases, even potentially 'neutral' topics, such as immigration, housing, employment or cultural immigration, soon tend to have a negative dimension: immigration may be topicalized as a threat, and most ethnic relations represented in terms of problems and deviance if not as a threat as well, most typically so in news about crime, drugs and violence minorities are associated with. On the other hand, many topics that are also part of ethnic affairs occur much less in the news, such as migrants leaving the country, the contributions of immigrant workers to the economy, everyday life of minority communities, and especially also discrimination and racism against minorities. Since topics express the most important information of a text, and in news are further signalled by prominent headlines and leads, they are also best understood and memorized by the readers. In other words, negative topics have negative consequences on the 'minds' of the recipients.

In general what we find is a preference for those topics that emphasize Their bad actions and Our good ones. However, Their good actions and Our bad ones are not normally emphasized by topicalization (and will therefore also appear less in headlines or on the front page, if reported at all). This general strategy of positive self-presentation and negative other-presentation is prevalent in most dominant discourse about immigrants and minorities, not only at the level of topics, but also at the other levels to be analysed below.

Quotes

Given the way that news reports are constructed on the basis of many source discourses, we may expect that such source discourses and their authors also get explicitly cited, and their authors described more or less explicitly. Depending who has access to and control over journalists also will be able to influence whether or not they are actually quoted. What one would expect, and what one indeed finds, is that in general, even in ethnic news, minorities are quoted less, and less prominently than (white) elites. If sources are quoted, we may also expect that those are selected that confirm the general attitudes about the group in question. Minority representatives will seldom be allowed to speak alone: a white person is necessary to confirm and convey his or her opinion, possibly against that of the minority spokesperson.

Local meanings

Besides the overall meanings or topics of news reports, we also need to examine the 'local' meanings of words and sentences. Most traditional text and content analysis focused on the words being used in news about minorities. Derogatory words in racist discourse are well known, and need not be spelled out here. The new racism, as described above, however, avoids explicitly racist labels, and uses negative words to describe the properties or actions of immigrants or minorities (for instance, 'illegal'). Special 'code-words' (such as 'welfare mothers') may be used, and the readers are able to interpret these words in terms of minorities and the problems attributed to them. And it needs no further argument that attitudes about groups and opinions about specific events may influence the 'lexical choice' of such words as 'riot' on the one hand, or 'urban unrest', 'disturbance' or 'uprising' on the other hand, as is also the case for the classical example of 'terrorist' vs. 'rebel' vs. 'freedom fighter'. Thus, most mentions of 'terrorists' (especially also in the US press) will stereotypically refer to Arabs. Violent men who are our friends or allies will seldom get that label. For the same reason, 'drug barons' are always Latin men in South America, never the white men who are in the drugs business within the US itself. In other words, when there are options of lexicalization, choosing one word rather than another often has contextual reasons, such as the opinions of the speaker about a person, a group or their actions.

Modern linguistics and discourse analysis, however, goes beyond the study of isolated words, and also studies the meaning of sentences or sequences of sentences and their role in the text as a whole. Thus, sentence meanings also show what specific roles participants have, for instance as responsible agents, targets or victims of action. What we find in such an analysis is in line of the general strategy mentioned above: Minorities are often represented in a passive role (things are being decided or done, for or against them), unless they are agents of negative actions, such as illegal entry, crime, violence or drug abuse. In the latter case their responsible agency will be emphasized.

Much of the information in discourse, and hence also in news reports, is implicit, and supplied by the recipients on the basis of their knowledge of the context and of the world. Also in news and editorials about ethnic affairs, thus, many meanings are merely implied or presupposed and not explicitly stated. Because of social norms, and for reasons of impression management, for instance, many negative things about minorities may not be stated explicitly, and thus are conveyed 'between the lines'. For instance in a sentence like 'The rising crime in the inner city worried the politicians', it is presupposed, and not explicitly stated, that there is rising crime in the inner city, as if this were a known 'fact'.

What distinguishes an arbitrary sequence of sentences from a (fragment) of discourse, is what we call 'coherence'. One of the conditions of coherence is that subsequent sentences refer to situations, actions or events that are (for instance causally) related. But, as suggested above, beliefs about such facts may be biased, and hence also may affect coherence. For instance, if Dutch employers claim that high unemployment among minorities is caused especially by lacking qualifications (and not by discrimination), then their version of the relations between the facts makes their discourse coherent-for-them, but possibly not for others. Thus, also in ethnic affairs reporting, the coherence of news is relative to the way journalists represent ethnic events (in their so-called 'mental models' of these events).

Another feature of coherence is not based on the 'facts of a model', but rather on 'functional relations' between the meanings of sentences themselves. One meaning for instance may be a generalization, a specification or an example of another. News in general is written top-down, usually following relationships of specification: beginning with the general summary of an event in headline and lead, the rest of the news will specify details. However, we have seen that in ethnic affairs coverage, if such details are bad for Our image, specifications may fail. This is the case more generally in discourse meaning: the levels of description and amount of detail on each level will depend not only on contextual relevance, but also on whether or not this will contribute to (de)emphasizing our good properties and their bad one. For the same reason, another functional relation that is bound to occur is that of contrast – for instance emphasizing Their lack of initiative and emphasizing Our help.

Such a semantic construction of oppositions in underlying attitudes about the ingroup and the outgroup typically appears, as we have seen above for other discourse about minorities, in what are called 'disclaimers'. These are specific semantic moves that realize in one sentence the strategy of Positive Self-Presentation and Negative Other-Presentation. Typical examples of such disclaimers, as we have seen, are Apparent Denial ('We have nothing against foreigners, but . . .'), Apparent Concession ('There are also nice foreigners, but on the whole . . .'), Apparent Empathy ('Of course it is sad for refugees that . . ., but . . .'), and Transfer ('I have nothing against foreigners, but my clients . . .'). We call these disclaimers 'apparent' not because the speakers are obviously or intentionally 'lying', but because the structure of their discourse is such that especially the negative part of the sentence is spelled out throughout the discourse. The positive part thus especially has the function of avoiding a bad impression with the recipients.

Form, formulation and expression

Discourse meaning especially realizes 'underlying' beliefs of speakers, such as their mental models about a specific event reported in the news. But discourse is more than just meaning: meaning must be expressed in concrete words, as we have seen above, and these words make up sentences, with their own syntax, and (in the press) their characteristic expression in different letter type, layout, photos, place on the page, and so on. These various forms or formulation patterns of discourse may themselves emphasize or de-emphasize meanings. Thus violence and crime of minorities will typically appear in (big) headlines, and prominently on the front page, whereas this is seldom the case for other news about them. Similarly, 'active' sentences may emphasize the responsible agency of the subject, whereas 'passive' sentences about the same action may background agency. The same is true for verbs that are 'nominalized', such as using the word 'discrimination' instead of saying who discriminated whom. Much research has shown that this is a well-known device in the coverage of ethnic issues, for instance to mitigate the negative actions of ingroups or 'our' organizations, such as the police (Fowler *et al.* 1979; Fowler 1991).

Conclusion

We see that various levels of discourse (and we shall mention some others below) may be involved in the enactment, expression or inculcation of negative beliefs about immigrants and minorities, and thus contribute to racism. Beyond a superficial content analysis of isolated words, a detailed discourse analysis may provide insight into the underlying mechanisms of how discourse embodies ethnic stereotypes and attitudes, and at the same time, how the minds of recipients are 'managed' by such discourse structures. Overall we have found that both the meanings and the formal structures of text and talk in general, and of news in particular, tend to favour the ingroup and often derogates or problematizes the outgroup.

Example

Let us finally examine in some detail a concrete example of a newspaper text. In light of what has been said above, such an analysis focuses on the ways that events and their participants are being represented in the text, and whether the structures of the text do convey a generally positive or negative opinion about Us versus Them.

The news report we analyse is taken from the British tabloid the *Sun* of 2 February 1989. It is presented as a 'News Special', which suggests not only that it is 'news' but also that the *Sun* probably has done some 'investigative reporting' of its own. It is signed by John Kaye and Alison Bowyer. The article deals with 'illegal immigration' and police raids of various establishments where 'illegal immigrants' were arrested. Given the *Sun*'s circulation, millions of British readers may have seen this article.

The article takes up nearly a whole page, with three pictures of 'raided' restaurants on the left, with a band on the pictures saying 'RAIDED'. In the middle of the article there is a figure with statistics of 'illegal immigration' headlined 'HOW THE ILLEGALS TOTAL HAS SHOT UP'.

Over the full width of the page there is a huge banner headline saying:

BRITAIN INVADED BY AN ARMY OF ILLEGALS

Let us begin our analysis, quite appropriately, with this not exactly unobtrusive headline. Theoretically, headlines express the major topic of an article. In this case, the topic is 'illegal immigration' more generally, and not (as in most news items) a specific event. This is also the reason why this is a 'News Special', and not a normal news report. News specials may deal with an issue, and in that respect are more like background articles.

In our analysis, we shall print theoretical terms in bold italic, so as to highlight what kind of analytical concept is being used in the description. Implications and interpretations are printed in italic, and relate to the structures of news on ethnic affairs dealt with above. Instead of dealing with each phenomenon separately, we study them in an integrated way for various fragments, since they often are closely related. Words used in the article quoted in our running text are signalled by quotation marks.

The most obvious property of this headline is its ***rhetoric***, as is common in tabloid headlines, namely, the ***hyperbolic*** use of ***metaphors***. Thus, entering

Britain is conceptualized as an 'invasion', which is a common negative metaphor to represent immigration, and the immigrants are described with a metaphor of the same military *register*, namely, as an army. Obviously, such metaphors are hardly innocent, and the use of military metaphors implies that immigrants are both *violent* and a *threat*. We have seen that violence and threat among the main properties of the meaning of news discourse on immigrants. However, the violence and threat is not merely that of some individuals coming in, but is suggested to be *massive* and *organized*, as is the case for an army. Moreover, invasion does not merely imply a violent act, but also a massive threat, namely a massive threat from abroad. The target of this threat is Britain, which is *topicalized* in the headline (it occurs in first position of the headline and the article), so that it is highlighted as the victim of the foreign army. On the other hand the *passive sentence* construction emphasizes the 'news' by putting the 'invasion by an army of illegals' as the *comment* of the sentence. Note, finally, that only one dimension of the immigrants is selected in naming them, namely, that they are 'illegal'. This *lexicalization* is adopted also in the mainstream press in most European countries and North America to describe undocumented immigrants. Beside the massive violence of their entry, immigrants are thus also *associated* with breaking the law, and hence implicitly with *crime*.

It needs no further comment that at various levels of the structure of this headline immigrants are being described very negatively according to the third main topic of ethnic issues, namely 'They are a Threat to Us'. But even the notion of Threat is not strong enough, and here further emphasized by stereotypical hyperbolic metaphors used to describe an Outside Threat.

Let us now consider some other fragments of this 'News Special'. The lead, printed over three columns, reads as follows:

1 BRITAIN is being swamped by a tide of illegal immigrants so desperate for a job that they will work for a pittance in our restaurants, cafes and nightclubs.

As usual, leads express the macrostructure of the text, and thus further specify the main topic expressed in the headline. Whereas the headline further abstracts from 'illegals' working in restaurants and other establishments, and describes Britain in general, here further information about the more specific location or targets of the 'foreign army' is given. However, also in this lead sentence, Britain is *topicalized* as the point of focus, the target of the army, and thus not only syntactically marked by the passive sentence, but also further graphically emphasized by the use of *capital letters*.

Then the other standard *metaphor* is being used to negatively describe the arrival of foreigners, namely, that of threatening water, namely, by 'swamped' and 'tide'. The 'swamp' metaphor is well known in Britain, because it was used by Margaret Thatcher in 1979 when she said she understood ordinary British people being 'rather swamped' by people with an alien culture. Again, the actors are being described as being 'illegal', a form of *rhetorical repetition* that further emphasizes that the immigrants break the law and are hence criminals.

There follows an apparent local rupture in the dominant negative meanings in the characterization of the immigrants when they are being described as 'desperate'. Such a description usually implies empathy, and such *empathy* is inconsistent with a description of immigrants in the threatening terms of an 'army' or a 'tide'. However, the rest of the sentence shows that this description is not necessarily one of empathy, but rather explains why the immigrant workers are prepared to work for a 'pittance'. This implies that they are also an *economic threat* to the country, because they thus easily are able to compete against 'legal' workers. This implied meaning is consistent with the current prejudice about foreigners that 'they take away our jobs'.

Finally, notice the first explicit use of an *ingroup designator*, the *possessive pronoun* 'our', thus establishing a clear contrast between Us and Them. That such a use is emphasizing ingroup–outgroup polarization is also obvious from the fact that the rest of the article also speaks about restaurants owned by foreigners or immigrants. That is, the restaurants or other establishments are not literally 'ours', but 'belong to Britain' in a broader, nationalist sense.

> 2 (a) Immigration officers are being overwhelmed with work. (b) Last year 2,191 'illegals' were nabbed and sent back home. (c) But there are tens of thousands more, slaving behind bars, cleaning hotel rooms and working in kitchens. (d) And when officers swoop on an establishment, they often find huge numbers of unlawful workers being employed.

In this first sentence after the lead, other participants are being introduced in the report, namely 'immigration officers', again topicalized in a passive sentence, and again, as in the headline and the lead as victims, but this time of being 'overwhelmed by work'. This verb is a more subdued, but still quite strong, concept of the series established by 'invaded' and 'swamped', and *implies powerlessness* against the force, or in this case, the sheer size of the number of 'illegals'.

The relevance of this implication becomes obvious in the next sentence, which argumentatively provides the statistical 'facts' that prove the amount of work. The same is true for the included figure that literally illustrates the rising number by a steeply climbing line, and the caption how the 'illegals' total has shot up', a metaphor that also is borrowed from the domain of violence (as is 'army' and 'invaded'). Rhetorically, this well-known *number game* of much immigration reporting in the media, does not imply that these numbers are both necessarily incorrect. Rather they signal subjectivity and hence credibility, whereas the numbers themselves imply the size of the threat. And if a modest number like '2,191' should prove to be a weak case for the use of 'invaded' and 'army' and 'swamp', the reporters speak of 'tens of thousands', thus fully engaging in the speculative guesses about the 'real' number of 'illegal immigrants'. Also the last line of this paragraph again refers to 'huge numbers', an obvious *hyperbole* when it later turns out in the article that these numbers barely reach a dozen. In sum, the typical number game of immigration reporting has one main semantic objective: to associate immigration with problems and threats, if only by quantity. This is also why in the examples of raids being mentioned after this paragraph all numbers are printed in *bold capitals*, thus emphasizing again these numbers.

Note also the unexpected use of *quotation marks* for the word 'illegals' in sentence 2b. One might interpret this as taking distance from the use of 'illegals' in the rest of the report, as we do ourselves in this article, but no further evidence exists in the article that the authors take such distance. Therefore the quotation marks should be read as being used to mark the use of the adjective 'illegal' as a noun, and as short for 'illegal immigrants'. Note incidentally, that in sentence 2d another word is being used instead of 'illegal', namely 'unlawful', which also confirms breaking the law, but less harshly so than 'illegal'. In the following examples of raids, all those described as being arrested are repeatedly characterized as 'illegals'.

There is another element of empathy creeping into the article when the authors describe the immigrants as 'slaving'. This totally converts (and subverts) the earlier characterization of the immigrants as active and evil, and not as victims. This use might continue the *thematic line* of empathy, set with the earlier use of 'desperate'. On the other hand, the use of 'slave' presupposes 'slaveholders', and instead of mere empathy, this may suggest an accusation of restaurant owners who exploit their 'illegal' workers, as we shall indeed see later in the text, where employers are explicitly accused.

A numbered description of the raids carried out by immigration officers follows. These examples are being described as 'cases', as in a scholarly or clinical report. This use of *jargon* suggests objectivity and reliability: the *Sun* has concrete evidence. In the next paragraph the *Sun* even claims to have a scoop when it revealed 'exclusively' the previous day 'how an illegal immigrant was nabbed' in the kitchen of one establishment.

Furtive

3 The battle to hunt down the furtive workforce is carried out by a
  squad of just 115 immigration officers.

As is well known for news, and as suggested above, **numbers** are the **rhetorical** device to suggest precision and objectivity, and hence credibility. Also in
this report, we not only find the usual number game to count 'illegal' immigrants, but also other aspects of the operation by the authorities, which in
the next paragraph is said to be carried out by a 'squad of just 115 officers'.
And in the next paragraph it is said that an 'extra 40 men' more are planned
to be drafted.

Note in example 3 also the use of another synonym for 'illegal workers',
'furtive workforce', which also seems a bit softer than 'illegal immigrants',
but which still has the association of breaking the law and crime.

Again possibly in line with the emphatic sequence about the immigrants is
the use of 'hunt down' in example 3, which might show some feelings for the
immigrants, but again the rest of the text seems to belie this interpretation.
Rather 'hunting down' is in the same line as 'battle', and said of a posse after
a dangerous criminal. Rather than the consequence for the victims of such
police hunts, it is the fascinating 'hunt' itself that the *Sun* is interested in.

Just describing migrant workers as being 'illegal' and desperate to work
'furtively' might not impress a lot of readers. So, apart from associating
them with an army, invasion, and other notions (like the word 'battle' in
example 3) in the same metaphorical domain of the military, the *Sun* needs
to be clearer about the negative characteristics of the immigrants. The
tabloid does this as follows:

4 Illegals sneak in by:
  • **DECEIVING** immigration officers when they are quizzed at air-
    ports.
  • **DISAPPEARING** after their entry visas run out.
  • **FORGING** work permits and other documents.
  • **RUNNING** away from immigrant detention centres.

Although perhaps not exactly featuring capital crimes, this bullet list of the
ways immigrants break the law or violate norms, is clear enough to emphasize the overall negative picture of them being represented in this report.
Indeed, apart from breaking the law, the Others cannot be trusted: they are
liars ('deceiving'). The bold caps draw attention and emphasize this negative
characters description, as does the bullet list, which obviously functions as
a mnemonic device for the readers, in case they should overlook and forget
the 'trespasses' of the 'illegals' (now used without quotation marks).

There is only one point where 'people like Us', that is, possible ingroup members, are criticized in this report:

5 They have little difficulty finding jobs, especially in London, because unscrupulous employers know that they can pay rock-bottom wages.
Cash
And they are invariably paid in cash with not a word to the taxman.

Follows a description of the low wages (£60 a week for 60 hours of work – another nice **number rhetoric** example, using identical numbers for money and hours of work).

Usually the *Sun* will not antagonize the business community, so the use of 'unscrupulous' is unexpectedly critical, but the next sentence shows that it is not (only) because poor immigrants are being exploited, but again that the law is broken. This topic fits very well with the law and order orientation of the tabloid, and also the 'illegal' topic of this article. In this sense, 'unscrupulous' employers do not belong to Us. That exploitation is not a primary concern is confirmed by the next paragraph that says that £100 a week is ten times more than a Thai or Filipino would earn at home, *implying* that paying them ten times more than at home is in fact great for them.

Also the next paragraphs continue the **number rhetoric**: how many people were arrested ('nabbed' in the **popular style** of the *Sun*), sent back or voluntarily went back. Keeping the score, apparently, is important when it comes to 'illegal' immigrants, and gives the News Special its hard core, factual character. And if a Thai has overstayed, the number of years he overstayed is printed in bold caps in the next paragraph: **12 YEARS**.

In the rest of the article, we finally get to hear some of the participants. First an immigration officer who comments on the numbers, as well as the military style operation of the 'hunt': 'It is impossible to know how many illegal immigrants there are. But we are certainly stepping up our efforts to track them down.' Then, also employers are quoted, and their violation of the law seemingly excused, as follows:

6 It is difficult for the restaurant trade to work out who is a legal worker and who is not.

As we already surmised above, accusing 'one's own' is not a common element in the overall strategy of Positive Self-Presentation, and example 6 shows that the accusation is *mitigated* by referring to the alleged difficulties of the employers to know who is 'illegal' or not. This is in accordance with the strategy in ethnic reporting that emphasizes Their bad acts, and mitigates those of ingroup members. The quote from the managing director of a trendy cafe, seems to belie these 'difficulties' when he says that checking the passport for a valid work permit is all there is to it. The same quote again returns to the number theme: 'I'd say 1 in 20 people who come here aren't allowed to work in Britain'. A separate side-article, on the other hand, emphasizes again that it is not that easy to find out the status of immigrants, because these often use 'false identities'.

Results of the analysis

Our analysis has shown that reporting on ethnic affairs typically shows the following properties within the overall strategy of positive self-presentation and negative other-presentation:

- Immigrants are stereotypically represented as breaking the norms and the law, that is, as being different, deviant and a threat to Us.
- *We* as a group or nation are represented as victims, or as taking vigorous action (by immigration officials or the police) against such deviance.
- Such representations may be enhanced by hyperboles and metaphors.
- Credibility and facticity of reports is rhetorically enhanced by the frequent use of numbers and statistics.

Conclusion

The New Racism of western societies is a system of ethnic or 'racial' inequality consisting of sets of sometimes subtle everyday discriminatory practices sustained by socially shared representations, such as stereotypes, prejudices and ideologies. This system is reproduced not only in the daily participation of (white) group members in various non-verbal forms of everyday racism, but also by discourse. Text and talk about the Others, especially by the elites, thus primarily functions as the source of ethnic beliefs for ingroup members, and as a means of creating ingroup cohesion and maintaining and legitimating dominance. This is especially the case for media discourse in general and the news in particular. Systematic negative portrayal of the Others, thus vitally contributed to negative mental models, stereotypes, prejudices and ideologies about the Others, and hence indirectly to the enactment and reproduction of racism. Beyond superficial content analysis, detailed and systematic discourse analysis is able to provide insights into the discursive mechanisms of this role of public discourse in the reproduction of racism, and how also the news systematically conveys positive images (mental representations) of Us, and negative ones about Them.

Further reading

Bell, A. and Garrett, P. (eds) (1998) *Approaches to Media Discourse*. Oxford: Blackwell.

Fowler, R. (1991) *Language in the News: Discourse and Ideology in the British Press*. London: Routledge.

McGarry, R.G. (1994) *The Subtle Slant: A Cross-Linguistic Discourse Analysis Model for Evaluating Inter-Ethnic Conflict in the Press*. Boone, NC: Parkway.

Van Dijk, T.A. (1988) *News as Discourse*. Hillsdale, NJ: Lawrence Erlbaum.

Van Dijk, T.A. (1991) *Racism and the Press*. London: Routledge.

Van Dijk, T.A. (ed.) (1997) *Discourse Studies: A Multidisciplinary Introduction*. London: Sage.

WHITE WATCH
John Fiske

Introductory instances and premature conclusions

I would like to begin by recounting some apparently isolated events, in order to argue that they are, in fact, far from isolated.

First, according to polls, African Americans remained solidly in Clinton's corner throughout the Monica Lewinski scandal. Black Americans told me repeatedly how closely they could empathize with him because they thought he was being treated as a Black man.[1] Clinton, in African American knowledge, was Blackened (one man used the word 'niggerized' to me) because

- his behaviour was subjected to intense, disproportionate and unfair surveillance
- his sexuality was made public as widely as possible, because it was 'known' to be a threat to the social order, and thus everyone had a right to know about it
- his sexuality was the means by which his opponents hoped to bring him down.

Time and again they likened his treatment to that of Clarence Thomas, Marion Barry, Mike Tyson, even Rodney King, and, of course, O.J. Simpson (see below). One African American told me that Clinton was the Blackest president he would see in his lifetime, and claimed that many whites were as hostile as they were because of Clinton's coded markers of blackness: he came from the wrong side of the tracks in a poor Southern town, he was brought up by a single mother, his public life had been disproportionately linked with hypersexuality and drug use (even though he did not inhale) and

that, more explicitly, he had been presidentially unusual by frequently drawing the United States' attention to its racial problem, and by appointing significant numbers of African Americans to senior posts in his administration.
Clinton was, he told me, black enough for white supremacy to need to bring
him down.

Second, during a study of the O.J. Simpson events, I interviewed white
and Black Americans about their viewing of the 'chase' in which a flotilla of
police cars followed his white Bronco along the freeways. The whole event
was televised live from media helicopters, and garnered the second largest
TV audience in US history. Not surprisingly, members of each racial group
watched it very differently. Most African Americans were very conflicted
about the experience: few whites were. One African American summed up
the contradictions succinctly: 'My eye was in the helicopter with the police,'
he told me, 'but my heart was in the Bronco with O.J.' Another felt similarly
conflicted: he told me how watching the chase reminded him of how, at some
level, he was always aware of 'the eye in the sky' that was watching him, and
that having this eye made visible justified his feeling of being constantly surveilled, but being able to look through its lens disturbed him deeply by
giving him a taste of the fascination of the panoptic. Watching the white
Bronco from above, he said, 'made me see what I feel I look like' (Fiske
1996).

Third, four young African American men told me that when they visited
a local casino they knew that the security guards monitoring the video cameras watched their every movement. So, on entering the casino, they would
look into the camera, grin and wave. On the third occasion they were
expelled for 'disruptive behaviour'.

Fourth, when the south London borough of Sutton installed video cameras in its streets, it hired a researcher to assess their impact. A Black youth
told how he had been accosted by cops on the street who asked him what he
was doing and said that he had been seen on video 'acting suspiciously'.
Actually, he was waiting for his girlfriend (Polman 1995).

Fifth, a group of African American students in my university have
described how the campus is racially zoned for them by non-technological
surveillance. In computer science, in engineering and in the School of Business white students routinely subject them to a 'what are you doing here'
look that abnormalizes their presence. The look was so intense, so immediately power laden, that one woman had to put her forefingers on either side
of her eyes and point them at me in an attempt to make me experience how
it felt to be on the receiving end of it.

Sixth, a white woman told me how she and a friend gave a Black male
student a ride home after an evening class: he was in the back seat leaning

forward talking to them when a police car pulled them over to check that the women were 'all right'.

Seventh, a Black friend and I were walking home late one night. It was snowing and the pavements had not been cleared so we walked in the tyre tracks on the deserted road. As we passed the gym where he regularly worked out, he commented on how odd it felt to be walking in the road at night. As a white man, I could only look blankly at him, his comment made no sense, it referred to no real or imaginable experience of mine. In daytime, he explained, the pavements are crowded, and when he is wearing his running suit, carrying a gym bag, he notices that some whites are frightened of him and either step off the pavement or press close to the wall as he passes. At night he felt free to use the pavement, but in daytime, as he put it, it was simply more comfortable to walk in the road.

Finally, a number of scholars have pointed to the rapid installation of video surveillance in downtown areas throughout the US and Britain. Polls show consistently that the 'public' want more surveillance, in the belief that it is an effective and unobtrusive mode of policing that operates on everyone in an equal and fair manner.

Other events that African Americans articulate (or link) into the same pattern of sex, drugs, crime and surveillance include the following: Marion Barry, the Black mayor of Washington, DC, was jailed because he had been videotaped accepting drugs from an ex-girlfriend in a hotel room where he had gone for sex; Mike Tyson, the Black boxer, was jailed for the rape of a woman in his hotel room, the details of which were widely mediated; Clarence Thomas, a Black Supreme Court Justice, was accused, during his televised confirmation hearings, of sexual harassment and excessive sexuality; and the Black superstar, O.J. Simpson, accused of the murder of his white wife, Nicole, and a white male friend of hers, had his alleged hyper-sexuality, drug use and violence spread over the nation's media for months. The Los Angeles Police Department (LAPD) officers who beat Rodney King so brutally reported that they thought he was high on a hallucogenic drug and that he had been sexually offensive to one of the white women police officers present at the scene.

A knowledge that is produced by this articulation of events is that white America needs to surveil the Black man continuously because it 'knows' him to embody the main threat to its social order. Black men who have too much power, too much prestige, who have, in effect, got out of place in the social order, have to be brought down, and replaced where they belong (preferably in prison).

Articulated together, these anecdotes and instances lead towards the conclusion that the social experiences of Black and white people living in our society are significantly different, that the difference is qualitative (that is, the Black experience is 'worse'), and that racially differentiated surveillance is one of its constituent factors.

Such a knowledge of video surveillance contradicts its normal characterization as unobtrusive and fair: it knows that the video surveillance of the city functions as a control mechanism directed particularly upon the Black male as he moves through its so-called public spaces, from the neighbourhood store to the suburb, from the shopping mall, the office building or the airport to the public street. It knows that the surveillance that both Orwell and Foucault understood to be essential to the modern social order has been racialized in a manner they did not foresee: today's seeing eye is white, and its object is coloured. Surveillance thus operates differently upon Blacks and whites: surveillance is a technology of whiteness that racially zones both the city space that exists as a matter of physical geography, and the social space that, while more metaphorical, is nonetheless really inhabited in different places by different social groups. In both spaces surveillance draws lines that Blacks cannot cross and whites cannot see. Surveillance enables different races to be policed differently, and it has an insidious set of 'chilling' effects upon the freedoms of opinion, movement and association that cumulatively produce racially differentiated senses of 'the citizen'.

Conclusions, or as I prefer to say, for reasons that will become clear, knowledge, of this sort, can never be objectively proved to be true in the way that would satisfy an old-fashioned empiricist or a contemporary bigot. It can, however, be moved up the scale of credibility to the point at which we decide to treat it as true.

The first step in this movement is to construct a regularity, or pattern, among the instances, and then to show that this regularity extends far beyond them. Arguing that the pattern extends beyond the particular instances is made easier if the instances are from widely different areas of social experience – walking down the street, watching network television, going through legal proceedings, being reported in the media and so on. It helps too if they involve a variety of people, ranging from the ordinary to the important, from the obscure to the celebrated.

We should also look for other studies that evidence this regularity, and we should ask ourselves if we have experienced it. Entman (1990), for instance, has shown quantitatively a pattern of TV news in which stories of crime, particularly, but not exclusively, drug crime, are routinely illustrated with images of African American men. Turning to ourselves, we should check our memories of the media to see if we can recognize such a patterning, and should check our ongoing media experience for further examples. Taking the personal one stage deeper, we should look inside ourselves, particularly if we are white, to see if we can find traces of a deeply sedimented white knowledge that the black man is always, potentially at least, the source of social disorder, and that this disorderliness can be all too easily imagined in terms of excessive sexuality or criminal drug use; to see if, in other words, we find it suspiciously natural to figure the difference of the black man from us in terms of sex, drugs and crime.

If so, we should recognize that we are not personally responsible for this sedimented 'knowledge' (though we are if we continue to live by it). It has a long history; whites have always made sense of racial difference sexually, that is that they have imagined people of a different race to have a different sexuality, and, as sexuality is more readily imaginable than race, that sexuality has been made into a racially defining characteristic.

In particular, the white imagination has been particularly effective in figuring the racial threat to its own social order in terms of the lusting of the male of the threatening race for the white woman. In the nineteenth century, when the racial threat was seen to come from American Indians, there were many narratives of the captive white woman – fictional stories, diaries, and paintings that extended into the movies of the 1950s and 1960s such as *The Searchers*. During the Second World War there were propaganda posters of grinning Japanese soldiers carrying off naked white women over their shoulders, and for as long as the institution of slavery, and possibly longer – think of Othello – the imagined lust of the Black man for the white woman has for whites been a powerful signifier of the racial difference and the racial threat. Most lynchings involved this imagined black sexuality, and its threat to white purity was explicitly encoded in the laws prohibiting interracial marriage in many states. In this imagination, the white woman encodes not only the beauty, but also the vulnerability, of the white social order, and the black male the sexualized threat to it.

Part of the reason why the O.J. Simpson case fascinated white America so intensely and so long was that it appeared to ground this white imagination in reality, to prove that it really was true. The comparatively rare events that can be used to prove the 'truth' of this white knowledge of the black man are granted disproportionately high significance and visibility, whereas the far more common events and experiences that appear to contradict it are relegated to the realm of the insignificant and the invisible.

The black man has thus been made to embody the internal threat to law and order, which are implicitly known to be white. Threats that cannot be eliminated, must be contained. Surveillance must be continuously directed upon him to ensure that he is contained in his place – both geographic and social – or, if allowed out of his place, he must be watched to ensure that his behaviour is excessively normal, by which in this context, we mean white.

Theorizing and knowing

We have to situate both our instances and their regularities into a theoretical frame, so that the explanation we arrive at can be properly extended beyond their own particularities: it will then be able to function as a 'true' example of contemporary racism at work. In this chapter I want to trace some of the means by which this movement towards effective truth might be achieved, and, in doing so, to suggest that this sort of scholarship is necessary in our current historical conditions.

In the industrialized, complex societies of the western world, postmodernity is struggling to displace Enlightenment rationalism as both our defining social condition and our way of understanding it, and that, as a result, we, as scholars and citizens, are living in messy, hybrid conditions in which, for instance, objective truth no longer seems as attainable as once it did, and yet we still make truth claims in ways that derive directly from it. We may no longer, to give another example, feel comfortable with the idea that there is one comprehensive way of knowing the world, a knowledge-in-the-singular, yet, each of the knowledges-in-the-plural (the knowledge-truth system with which some of us feel we now have to work) will often try to establish its truth effectiveness in terms that are disturbingly similar to those of the singular knowledge that has not yet been completely dislodged from its epistemological centrality.

In his voluminous works, Foucault has described our social conditions as ones in which the concept of a singular, objective truth is no longer effective; in which the concept of multiple and situated knowledges is replacing that of a singular, transcendental knowledge; and in which knowledge and truth are to be understood not in relation to an external, objective reality, but in relation to the social operations of power.[2] As the complex societies of late capitalism become more diverse, and as the concept of the 'nation' becomes less effective in organizing a homogeneous society and culture, so we may expect these situated knowledges to proliferate, and the contestations among them to become more intense.

Foucault theorizes a 'regime of truth'. By this he refers to the way in which a certain way of knowing social reality gains enough power to operate as though it were true, in other words, to gain real 'truth-effects'. The white knowledge that the black man is the threat to law and order has truth-effects that can be traced at work in widely dispersed sites in the social order. These range from the imagination of individuals and their bar room conversations, to institutional sites such as the court room, the jury room and the prison, or sites within the policing system including the imagination and conversations of police officers: other sites are the media (including the choice of stories deemed newsworthy, and the conventions of reporting and representation), the educational and political systems, and so on. The discursive regularity across dispersed sites is evidence that this way of knowing the black man is part of the regime of truth.

A regime of truth, as its name suggests, both rules and regiments. It regulates the statements that can be made within it to impose a coherence and regularity among them; it rules in the name of truth and disguises the power upon which its regime depends; and it regiments, or disciplines, social reality to exclude or delegitimate anything that might disorder its regimented order. To achieve this, it has to repress other knowledges from access to power and thus prevent them gaining truth-effects. Ruling truth always represses other truths that challenge it. The regime of truth produces, circulates and grants truth-effects to what we might call 'official' knowledge, while repressing and denying truth-effects to other knowledges which we might call situated, or local. The regime of truth, then, extends its way of knowing beyond the social position where it is produced (in this case white America): situated knowledges, however, are confined to theirs. But while they may be contained, these situated knowledges are not extinguished, and the containment is never total. While excluded from the regime of truth with its socially extensive effectiveness, they still operate effectively in their own spaces, geographic and social, from which they can, at times, emerge to challenge official truth.

The first O.J. Simpson trial provides many examples of these struggles over knowledge and truth. In it O.J. Simpson was found not guilty of the murders of Nicole Simpson and Ron Goodman. Responding to the verdicts, Gil Garcetti, California's District Attorney responsible for the prosecution, spoke for many white Americans: 'Apparently', he said, 'the decision was based on emotion that overlapped reason'. On the jury that reached this decision sat eight African American women, and only one white person, and in the word 'emotion' Garcetti was simultaneously blackening and feminizing the verdicts. Loaded into his opposition between 'reason' and 'emotion' were the social differences between the knowledges of a white, rational, educated male (who, as we shall see in a moment, reads newspapers) who participates in the regime of truth, and of a black, emotional, uneducated female (who watches tabloid TV), and whose truth is excluded from it, and is thus, effectively, not true. But in this case, a situated truth gained real truth-effects, and O.J. Simpson walked out of the court room a free man.

The theoretical framework within which we are working leads us to wonder if what mattered most was not O.J.'s freedom, but the serious disruption to the regime of truth. In this light, the second, civil, trial (in which

O.J. was found responsible for, though not guilty of, the deaths) may be seen as a (successful) attempt to restore the regime.

As this civil trial began, on ABC's *Good Morning America* Arthur Miller (identified as a 'legal editor') argued that the most significant difference between it and the criminal trial was the change of location from Los Angeles to Santa Monica (16 September 1996). In the centre of Los Angeles, he explained, there lived a population of Latinos and African Americans who had frequent, personal and usually negative experiences of the LAPD (that is, a situated knowledge), whereas Santa Monica's population was largely white and affluent (and thus, he appeared to assume, would participate in official knowledge). The jury pool that was drawn from each district would, he argued, evaluate the LAPD's evidence quite differently.

What is significant here is that his argument caused no surprise in his interviewer who seemed comfortable in accepting as self-evident the fact that differently situated jurors would produce a different truth at the end of their deliberations. This is an unusually clear symptom of the messiness of our current social conditions in which a situated knowledge is acknowledged to determine the truth in a court system that is still predicated on the Enlightenment marriage of absolute justice and absolute truth; or, to put it differently, conditions in which the verdict is seen as simultaneously the product of a situated knowledge (and hence jury selection as one of the most critical struggles in the court room) and as the result of the asocial rationality of the Enlightenment. It is also significant that two privileged white men should not wish to comment upon, or even apparently notice, their acceptance that justice was coloured by the situation, both geographical and social, in which it was produced. The court room and, in particular, the jury room have become one of the sites where struggles over knowledge and truth are made explicit and visible, and where our unstable mixture of postmodern and Enlightenment conditions is most disturbingly experienced.

In the jury room, official truth had been knocked off balance even before the verdicts in the first O.J. trial dislodged it, however temporarily. In a *Time* article published shortly before the O.J. Simpson criminal trial, Dan Lundgren, the Californian Attorney General, expressed concern about the effect of television talk shows upon jurors, which he called 'Oprahization' (after Oprah Winfrey, the Black woman talk show host). In the same article Gil Garcetti expressed his fear that the effect of such talk shows had put the criminal justice system 'on the verge of a crisis of credibility' (*Time*, 6 June 1994: 30–1). These two powerful white men were not opinionizing without evidence: Jo-Ellan Dimitrius, a professional jury consultant from Pasadena, has warned that 'talk-show watchers . . . are considered more likely to distrust the official version and believe there are two sides to a story' (ibid.) and

DecisionQuest (a jury consulting firm advising the prosecution in the Simpson trial) found a positive correlation between tabloid TV viewing and the belief that Simpson was not guilty (*Newsweek*, 16 October 1995: 39).

Oprahization (a wonderfully 'situating' label) refers to the process by which the disempowered produce their situated knowledge, oppose it to official knowledge, and speak it on the media in a way that grants it a social extensiveness that the regime of truth would deny it. Tabloid television, with its multiply situated knowledges and its intensely dramatized contestations among them, is, in its very form, disruptive to the smooth way that the regime of truth prefers to work (which is why so many who participate in that regime criticize tabloids so vehemently). In both the print and electronic tabloids 'truth' is always contested or uncertain. Tabloid readers and viewers swing between their knowledge of the official truth (what 'they' say or what 'they' would have us know) and the popular truths (what 'we' know). They know, therefore, that for any one knowledge to gain the status of truth other knowledges have to be repressed; they know the production of truth is a function of power. The power to get a situated knowledge treated as true beyond the situation of its production and its local circulation is one of the most important powers in postmodernity.

Judge Ito, ironically as it turned out, rejected from the jury pool anyone who had read a newspaper during the weeks of the selection process in the belief that the ability to weigh evidence objectively is undermined by previous knowledge of the facts of the case. In so far as the newspapers are generally participants in the official regime of truth, he unwittingly excluded from the jury pool many of those the prosecution would have most welcomed. Tabloids, however, are not, in Judge Ito's definition at least, newspapers. Consequently, of the jurors who produced the verdicts, none read newspapers, whereas two-thirds regularly watched tabloid TV.

Tabloid TV is a hybrid form containing traces of both official and situated knowledges, and of the struggles between them. At its best it makes visible

- the productivity of discourse
- the plurality and thus the social situatedness of knowledges and their truths
- the power relations that determine the different truth-effects of differently situated knowledges
- the unfinished nature of knowledge, that knowledge is not an accumulation of true facts but a system of production that is always ongoing and never reaches a point of closure
- the repressive as well as the productive operation of knowledge: for establishing the truth-effects of any knowledge involves the repression of

others, and extending credibility beyond the situation of the knowledge within which it is unproblematic depends upon the repression of any alternate.

The jury room in each O.J. Simpson trial and tabloid television are sites that make highly visible the fact, unwelcome to many, that knowledge and truth are subject to contestation, and the ability of the regime of truth to regulate the field of knowledge production and circulation is not as completely effective as some would like. And this will be an ongoing problem, or opportunity, depending on how you see it, for as our increasingly diverse societies produce increasingly different life experiences for those situated differently within them, so we should expect increasing contestations over how best to know them, and over which truths about them should be made socially effective.

Surveillance and place

We might consider, then, that the civil trial returned O.J. Simpson to his proper place as a sexualized, narcoticized, criminalized, pauperized black man and, similarly, returned the Black knowledge that momentarily forced another knowledge of him into the regime of truth to its proper place in the excluded 'outside'. Foucauldian theory allows us to trace regularities that link the way that the Black men in the instances that opened this chapter were seen to be in or out of place, and the way that O.J. Simpson was positioned and repositioned in both white society and white knowledge, and the way that the Black knowledge of him was deemed in or out of its place in the current regime of truth. Keeping people and knowledges in their place is crucial to the stability of the social order, and being able to see if they are in or out of place is a necessary prerequisite. So we return to the topic of surveillance.

The young man waiting for his girlfriend on a street corner in Sutton was seen differently by the surveillance system than his white counterpart would have been. So was the Black man in the car with my two white female students. They were seen to be out of place.

Where one's place is, of course, is never defined legally or explicitly in writing, but implicitly by social norms. Norms are what hold the social order in place. And, as Foucault has told us, the power to produce the normal may be the most important power of all. Street behaviours of white men (standing still and talking, using a cellular phone, passing an unseen object from one to another) will be known as normal and thus granted no attention, whereas the same activities performed by Black men will be coded as lying at least on, and often outside, the boundary of the normal. The truth-effects of this knowledge will soon arrive in uniform.

Defining what is in or out of place is central to the power over the normal. In the contemporary US city the image of a Black man 'out of place' is immediately moved from information to knowledge, from the seen to the known. In these conditions being seen is, in itself, oppressive. To be seen to be Black or Brown, in all but a few places in the US, is to be known to be out of place, beyond the norm that someone else has set, and thus to be subject to white power.

To be in place is to be confined to the ghetto. The ghetto is not surveilled, because it is that which the eye of power does not wish to see, the regime of truth does not wish to know. The abnormalized and their knowledge of our society cannot be exterminated, but they can be contained. The ghetto is necessary. It is where the displaced can be held in place. Statistics appear to show that the video surveillance of town centres, of white commercial, recreational and residential areas reduces crime, but some criminologists argue that it does not reduce crime, but displaces it into the ghetto where it is neither seen nor known. The ghetto is the necessary 'in-place' for what is elsewhere out of place. It is the spatial category of the abnormal that is entailed by the relentless production of the normal.

The efficiency of widely extensive surveillance depends vitally upon this active and minutely refined process of normalization. Ubiquitous surveillance produces such vast quantities of information that any knowledge system would collapse under overload if most of the gathered information were not left dormant and inert until needed and activated into knowledge. The boundary of the normal is the trigger that activates information and transforms it into knowledge. Behaviours and social groups who lie on, or over, this arbitrarily inscribed boundary are thus disproportionately the object of surveillance, because inert information about them is routinely transformed into power-bearing knowledge.

The US Drug Enforcement Agency (DEA), for instance, has a set of norms whose transgression allows it to identify a 'likely drug courier'. These norms enable it to stop and search those who can be seen to be outside them at airports, bus stations and on the highways. Ehrenreich (1990) has reconstructed from recent trials some of the video-visible features by which DEA agents can recognize those who are thus abnormalized: they include

- wearing gold chains
- wearing a black jump suit
- carrying a gym bag

- being a member of 'ethnic groups associated with the drug trade'
- travelling to or from a 'source city' such as Los Angeles, Miami or Detroit, or in a car bearing licence plates from a state containing source cities, though New York will do.

The Black activist intellectual Zears Miles read the full list on *Black Liberation Radio* and pointed out that it worked to punish Black expressiveness (in a way that has a chilling effect upon freedom of expression) and that in order to avoid being stopped and searched at airports or on the highways Black travellers must, as far as possible, deny their Black culture and identity, and look and behave like whites. Surveillance is a technology of normalization that identifies and discourages the cultural expression and behaviour of social formations that differ from those of the dominant, and thus chills any public display of difference. It inhibits diversity.

The Panopticon, as described by Foucault, was a machine of normalization.[3] It was designed to monitor abnormal behaviour, to measure its steady progress toward the normal, and to identify the point at which the prisoner could be returned to society and re-enter normality. This early panoptic surveillance was limited, however, for it could monitor only behaviour: its effects could be only corrective and not preventive, it was necessarily *post hoc*. To be preventive, that is, to be proactive rather than reactive, surveillance has to be able to identify the abnormal by what it *looks like* rather than by what it *does*: it needs to abnormalize, or criminalize, by visible social category, not by social behaviour. Nineteenth-century scientists devoted much energy to this enterprise, and the camera was a vital tool in their efforts. They spent long hours poring over photographs of criminals and lunatics in their attempt to produce visibly identifiable categories of the abnormal (the criminal or the insane) that could be subject to corrective action in advance of any deviant behaviour.

Black masculinity may form the first social category that is both abnormalized and visible. And the LAPD have not been slow to take advantage of the fact: In 'Operation Hammer' Chief Darryl Gates instructed his officers to pick up anyone '*looking* suspicious' (Davis 1990: 268, my emphasis). As a result, 1500 young Black men were taken in for questioning. While most were charged with minor offences, such as curfew and traffic violations, some were not charged at all but simply had their names and addresses logged in the LAPD anti-gang task force database: documentation is a necessary component of surveillance. In a similar operation, the Gang Related Active Trafficker Suppression programme, LAPD officers were instructed to 'interrogate anyone who they suspect is a gang member, basing their assumptions on their dress or their use of hand signals' (Davis 1990: 272). Kelley comments on an important subtheme in gangsta rap that protests this criminalization by appearance as part of an ongoing battle for 'free expression and unfettered mobility in public spaces' (Kelley 1996: 133).

This criminalization by visual category is not confined to the ghetto. Michael Eric Dyson tells a searing story of attempting to draw some cash from his credit card in a bank (Dyson 1993: 191–3). He is a Black man, and was wearing a black running suit. He is also an academic and a Baptist preacher, but these characteristics were not visible: his Blackness, his maleness and his running suit, however, were, and were seen to be out of place in a bank. The teller refused to advance any money. Dyson's request to see the manager started an apparently irreversible sequence of events which culminated in the manager slicing his card in two with a pair of scissors. When Dyson protested, the manager called the police.

Patricia Williams, a professor of law, tells a similar story of being refused entry into, ironically, a United Colors of Benetton store because she was Black, and of the editorial censorship she encountered when writing up the incident for a white legal journal (Williams 1991: 44–51). Her black body was as out of place in a white store as was her black knowledge in a white journal.

Racism is the paradigmatic instance of abnormalization by visible and thus surveillable category. The abnormalization of the racial other that enables the DEA to identify drug runners by what they look like, the bank similarly to identify fraudulent credit card users, and the store to identify shoplifters by their appearance rather than their behaviour, is a process without which surveillance cannot work, whiteness cannot work and contemporary racism cannot work.

At the core of this process is, of course, the way that whiteness normalizes itself, and excludes itself both from categorizing and from being categorizable: it thus ensures its invisibility – an invisibility that extends into the widespread white ignorance of such incidents. Whiteness wants to see everything except its own operations. We whites, whose norms are used to abnormalize, categorize and identify the others who are not us, cannot experience directly the oppressive application of those norms, for they are applied *from* our position, not *upon* it. Indeed, we often do not know that such incidents occur, let alone how routine they are. Many African Americans, however, not only feel the oppressive applications of norms, but also see how whites are largely free from the constraints of normalization, and the perception of the difference is part of the experience of discrimination.

Some issues with which to end, but not conclude

In this chapter I have used methods of analysis and interpretation derived from a Foucauldian theoretical framework. In keeping with that framework I must disclaim any implications of totalism: all knowledge is partial (in both senses of the word): no object of study can be known totally or objectively. I have used this framework to make sense of some contemporary events that can, of course, be made sense of differently: no event contains its own meaning, it always has to be made to mean. I have attempted to make the process of making these events mean explicit and thus open to critical investigation and to critical comparison with other theoretical frameworks which would make them mean differently, or that might not even select them as particularly meaningful in the first place.

I have attempted to demonstrate that a productive relationship between theory and the object it is aimed at explaining is a constantly mobile, interactive one in which the specificities of the particular and the generalities of theory are used to explain each other, and that each is modified or secured by this interaction. I hope that the theory of knowledge and surveillance gives a credible explanation of the instances I have recounted. Equally, I hope that the instances explain, modify, test and realize the theory's explanatory power: that they help constitute a terrain upon which its truth-effects can be traced and without which it is incomplete.

I hope I have demonstrated that the absence of a final, absolute, unchallengeable truth leaves us not, as some argue, awash in a sea of relativity in which nothing means anything any more so let's all go back to bed, but, on the contrary, puts the struggle to make things mean right in our faces every morning as we get out of that bed. We cannot avoid the struggles over which ways of knowing our social order are to be granted material truth-effects.

I hope, too, that I have demonstrated that our critical evaluation should not be directed upon how true or accurate a particular representation is, but on how it is put to work within the regime of truth. As scholars we explain and analyse how the regime of truth operates in our society, and as critical scholars, we evaluate that truth and its operation so that we may decide whether we wish to support and continue its truth-effects, or oppose, deflect or obstruct them. In making this decision we begin to blur the line between scholar and citizen, a line, that arguably, should never have been drawn in the first place.

I have tried to show, too, that a regime of truth is socially and historically specific, and thus the situated knowledges that contest for power within it, while multiple, are not infinite: they are limited to the social diversity that the regime of truth is attempting to rule, discipline and control. Situated knowledges are produced by material social formations, not by whim.

I hope, too, to have shown that theoretical or academic concerns and social concerns can be happy bed-fellows, and while the preceding paragraphs are lying on the academic side of the bed, and the following ones on the social, they are nonetheless in the same bed. The relations between them are, at the very least, conjugal and even, we may hope, productive.

The rapid extension of video surveillance over our cities cannot be explained by appeals to a form of technological determinism: we do not surveil simply because we have the ability to. It may be a technological feature of the surveillance camera that enables it to identify a person's race, but it is a racist society that wants that information and that turns it into knowledge: technology can determine only what is seen, it is society and its politics that determines what is known. Surveillance technology is being adopted so widely and rapidly in part because it technologizes and makes more efficient a process by which the powerful maintain the social order of whiteness. Black and white are simultaneously differences of light density in the pixels of a TV screen and social categories. They constitute a perfect match between technology and a racist social order within the field of the visible. The closeness of the match between technological capability and social need is what matters.

As whiteness is put into crisis in both the US and Europe by the transnational flows and national pauperization of those who have been raced as non-white its need to abnormalize and surveil the racialized other will intensify. The racialization of the other is, of course, part of the white process of abnormalization, so the category of non-white may, in different historical and social contexts, include the Turkish and the Irish: blackness is a product of whiteness, not of melanin.

We should dispute, too, any claim for the social neutrality of technology. Although surveillance is penetrating deeply throughout our society, its penetration is differential. The lives of the white mainstream are still comparatively untouched by it. But in Black America, its penetration is deep. The urban scanscape is invisibly mapped, both physically and conceptually, into areas where a Black presence is known to be normal or abnormal, where the Black body can be seen to be in place or out of place.

We should recognize, too, that surveillance is not just a means of gathering knowledge that can then be used to exert power by other means, but that the process of surveillance itself is an exertion of power, a power that is differentiated racially while being spatially universal. Surveillance zones the city in ways that give both spatial and temporal dimensions to racial categories. The norms that define such invisible but very real places, their times of occupation, and the behaviour or dress deemed appropriate to them, operationalize the totalitarian, for they are norms that are outside the control of those subject to them: they are imposed, and those upon whom they are imposed have no say either in their production nor in their application. Such norms, then, are physically experienced by their abnormalized objects as constraints, as divisive and exclusionary mechanisms. For those whose normality has produced them, however, they are unseen and thus unfelt. Norms may be universal in extent, but are they differential in operation?

Surveillance is the information technology of the regime of truth. It disciplines the physical order in the way that the regime of truth polices the discursive order. Surveillance is the operation of official knowledge in the field of the visible. By turning the city into the visible it extends the reach and effectiveness of that knowledge.

Conclusion

Whiteness has the social power to define itself as the normal, as the point where normality can be produced and elided with the orderliness of the social order: whiteness is both the source and the practice of normalization. Under pressure, and it is under pressure, whiteness appears all too ready to resort to increasingly totalitarian strategies. Surveillance makes the city operate as a machine of whiteness. It is the means by which the sense-making system in white heads is externalized into the spatial system of our cities; it is the mechanism that gives a material dimension to abstract or theoretical concepts such as 'situated knowledge', 'social position' or 'social space', for it makes them literal as well as metaphorical. Surveillance gives a physical geography to the socio-political construct of 'race'. Whiteness is cartographic: as it always has, it colours its maps of the world according to its own norms and interests.

Notes

1 I use the convention of capitalizing 'Black' to signal the positive, reclaimed use of the word, and spelling 'black' with a lower case initial to indicate its derogatory use in a white racist discourse.
2 See particularly Foucault's *Discipline and Punish: The Birth of the Prison* (1979), *The History of Sexuality: An Introduction* (1981) and *The Archaeology of Knowledge* (1972).
3 The Panopticon was a prison designed by Jeremy Bentham (but never built). It was shaped like a doughnut with an observation tower in the centre and the cells in the

periphery. Each cell had windows placed so that one observer in the tower could see into it at all times. The prisoners, however, could not see if the observer was watching them, so they behaved as if they were being surveilled even if no one was in the tower. This surveillance and self-surveillance is supremely efficient, and Foucault made it into a foundational metaphor for contemporary western societies.

Further reading

Davis, M. (1990) *City of Quartz: Excavating the Future in Los Angeles*. London: Verso.

Entman, R.E. (1990) Modern racism and the images of Blacks in local television news, *Critical Studies in Mass Communication*, 7(4): 332–45.

Fiske, J. (1993) *Power Plays, Power Works*. London: Verso.

Fiske, J. (1994) Radical shopping in Los Angeles: race, media and the public sphere of consumption, *Media, Culture and Society*, 16(3): 469–86.

Fiske, J. (1996) *Media Matters: Race and Gender in U.S. Politics*, revised edn. Minneapolis, MN: University of Minnesota Press.

Foucault, M. (1979) *Discipline and Punish: The Birth of the Prison*, trans. A. Sheridan. Harmondsworth: Penguin.

4 | 'DREAMING OF A WHITE ...'
John Gabriel

Introduction

In 1988, Richard Dyer wrote an influential piece which he called, simply, 'White' in which he explored its dominance in popular cinema. Since then a number of authors have written more fully about whiteness (see, for example, Frankenberg 1993; Fiske 1994a; Dyer 1997; Gabriel 1998). Why the sudden interest in whiteness? Of course, whites and white culture have always been visible to 'others', and explored in the writings of black scholars, including Frantz Fanon (1986), Walter Rodney (1988), bell hooks (1989, 1994) and W.E.B. Dubois (Sundquist 1996). The difference now is that whiteness is becoming visible to whites! But what is it exactly? And what roles do the established and new media play in the construction, circulation and contestation of 'whiteness'?[1]

Is it a state of being, that is 'being white', or does it refer to a dominant ('white') culture? Is it an ontological state or should it be understood in epistemological terms? The difficulty here is that the answer to both questions is a very qualified yes. If we take the state of being white first, not only do many people fall within the ambiguously 'white' category in terms of skin and/or background but also there are populations such as Jewish and Irish whose racial status has fluctuated over time. I have used the term 'subaltern' whiteness to refer to white ethnicities which, at given times, are strategically distinct from and subordinate to dominant whiteness (Gabriel 1996).

Both Dyer (1997) and Fiske (1994a) have explored the sources of power of whiteness in discursive terms. The specific techniques of exnomination, naturalization and universalization have been identified as key mechanisms in the construction of whiteness in and through the representational regimes of the media. Exnomination refers to the capacity of whiteness not to be named. The widespread tendency to equate ethnic with minority culture as if dominant culture has no ethnicity is one example of this technique. When Hall (1991) says that it is very difficult to get the white English to admit they are just another ethnic group, that is another. Naturalization refers to the means by which phenomena which are the product of social and cultural processes come to appear as just there by force of nature, innate ability or circumstances beyond human control. The common tendency to leave unquestioned the predominance of white men in suits in positions of authority in government, industry, the public sector and the media/arts is one example of this technique, so much so that there is a deep-seated resistance among white men to even see it as an issue. Universalization refers to the ways in which what are in fact white English European values, traditions, practices and beliefs are seen as or assumed to be held by everyone.

Whiteness is not a stand-alone discourse but works most effectively in conjunction with other discourses, notably those of gender and sexuality. Ware (1992) has argued that forms of western femininity are intimately bound up with the construction of whiteness in the colonial experience. Ideas of purity and vulnerability on the side of white femininity and black (sexual) aggressor on the other combined to reproduce both feminized and racialized roles in the Indian context. Michael Radford's film *White Mischief* (1987) is testimony to the continuing significance of these forms of representation. Sibley (1995) provides a powerful illustration of the ways in which the language of the body and sexuality have been intertwined with discourses of race. Ideas of leakage, defilement, contamination and pollution have thus served to police both bodies (in terms of white anxieties surrounding interracial sex) and borders (in terms of immigration paranoias).

The above comments are not meant to suggest that whiteness can be reduced either to a single knowledge/experience or to one group. Whiteness is not a monolithic discourse and whites are not a cohesive, homogeneous, ethnic group. On the contrary, whiteness is both diverse and heterogeneous as recent research has concluded (Bernal 1987). In a way this is the point. The fact that whiteness is constantly threatened by its own heterogeneity and hybridity reveals it for what it is: an intrinsically pathological discourse which has been constructed to create the fiction of a unitary and a homogeneous culture and people (that is, essentialist). The effective mobilization of whiteness bolsters what appears a threatened and anxious, although not yet marginalized, ethnicity.

There are differing levels of consciousness of as well as expressions of whiteness, some of which are more strategic than others. At times whiteness is characterized more by its absence or 'exnomination'. At other times its visibility is its hallmark, as in the case of fundamentalist Christian groups in the US or organizations like the National Association for the Advancement of White People and groups like Combat 18 and the British National Party in the UK. As far as these groups are concerned, naming is part of a strategy of defending and celebrating whiteness and hence for mobilizing political support around a conscious attachment to white ethnicity. Despite import- ant differences between these different forms and expressions of whiteness, there are nevertheless some important continuities, not just between the extreme right and more coded conservative traditions within mainstream politics but also between these and liberal, progressive discourses.

The shifts in white consciousness and forms of whiteness have been accen- tuated by a set of global processes. The sovereign power of western nation- states was challenged initially by the collapse of old colonial regimes, and subsequently by the emergence of international and transnational political and economic blocs including the United Nations, the European Union, the International Monetary Fund and the World Trade Organization. The growth in significance of multinational corporations, allied to financial deregulation of financial markets in the 1980s, strengthened the role of both industrial and finance capital to invest and speculate according to the whims of their investment analysts. Political upheavals in Eastern Europe have pro- voked new power struggles which in turn provoked a series of interventions under the auspices of the UN or the North Atlantic Treaty Organization but which in reality have been executed under the decisive influence of the United States.

Migration, which played such a pivotal role in the early development of capitalism, has played an equally significant role in what Lash and Urry (1987) have referred to its disorganized period, one characterized by the break up of mass production in the west, the fragmentation and decentral- ization of production which has created global production lines and the franchising out of key production processes to small business and firms will- ing to recreate old sweatshop conditions in cities of both the third world and the west.

One effect of such processes has been to dislodge those collective securi- ties, associated with modernity and inscribed and etched into the identity of the white western male, with the result that the growing demands for recon- stituting national and global divisions along multi-ethnic lines has been met with a fierce oppositional backlash. Whiteness has been mobilized in differ- ent guises in response to these developments and not only at the neo-fascist fringe. Even the liberal centre has set out to redefine the limits of multiculturalism, one principle of which appears to be that whites and white political agendas must dominate 'alternative' discourses.

The above processes have coincided with and have been exacerbated by the proliferation of media and information technologies, both electronic and digital, which have spawned everything from satellite television to camcorders to CD-ROMs to the Internet. These developments have further collapsed old boundaries and divisions and forged new communities. 'Space/time compression', which is how such developments have been conceptualized (see, for example, Massey 1984; Harvey 1989) has created the prospect of new ethnic alignments built around global white identities. The very conditions which helped to provoke a backlash, notably new transnational media and information technologies, are now being harnessed to the backlash project itself, as I shall illustrate below with reference to a variety of media forms and the Internet. However, this is not to suggest that whiteness monopolizes such technologies. On the contrary, the democratic potential of camcorders, multi-channel cable television and community radio have not been lost on its opponents either.

The following offer different examples of resistance to and assertions of whiteness in both the US and Britain with reference to the role played by different media. They offer points of contrast as well as convergence within a context which make comparisons between relatively self-contained 'nations' or societies increasingly problematic when set against those processes of globalization referred to above. The chapter is organized around the following themes: backlash culture, the limits of liberal whiteness and white pride politics. Different media appear more or less suited to represent and/or contest whiteness in its liberal and conserative incarnations and part of what follows will seek to identify and begin to explain these patterns of variation in the US and Britain.

White anxieties and the architecture of backlash culture

Globalization, the term intended to capture those cultural, political and economic processes referred to above, has provoked new ways of locating and understanding 'the west'. Questions of difference are being faced in ways at one time thought unimaginable. Ethnicity, according to Stuart Hall (1991, 1992b) has become the means by which the margins are able to speak and by the same token, the west decentred. At one time Britain's global supremacy rubbed off on its white subjects, who inevitably saw themselves as belonging to some master race. The fact is that there are now not one but many epicentres, often pulling in different, sometimes conflicting, directions.

Each of these calls for allegiances to new transnational identities built around such diverse objects of allegiance, from 'the west', 'Europe' and so on to seemingly more trivial attachments, from consumer products and media icons to vernacular languages, which are promoted and reinforced through such media and communications technologies as advertising, news broadcasting, Hollywood film, popular music and the Internet.

Migration has also played an important role in the formation of new ethnicities, cross-fertilizing groups sharing a colonial connection or a relation prompted by forced migration in the case of refugees. Under such circumstances, old ethnic divisions including white ones have been eroded as different styles (built around fashion, music, humour), languages, values coexist alongside or fuse with those promoted at school, work and in the neighbourhood as well as in the press, on TV and the radio.

Anti-discrimination and cultural diversity have also been more consciously promoted through the efforts of black and ethnic minority groups and organizations. Such political activity has included anti-racist campaigning, including demands for greater representation throughout the public and private sectors. Anti-discrimination laws, which are one notable consequence of such politics in the US and UK, may not have substantially changed much but at least they have served to throw down the gauntlet of both greater material equality and cultural diversity.

The response to global processes, new cultural formations and forms of political intervention has been a white backlash. This has been expressed in explicit as well as more coded terms and via numerous cultural spaces and media forms. What follows are some of its key themes. These include the creation of a white victim, the role of black spokespeople, and sex and the orchestration of whiteness.

The photograph used to publicize Joel Schumacher's film, *Falling Down* (1992), is of the lead character, played by Michael Douglas, dressed in a short-sleeved white shirt with a 1950s/1960s crew-cut and set against a desolate urban landscape with the Los Angeles skyline in the background. The effect is to make Douglas appear superimposed on his surroundings, accentuating his sense of displacement and alienation. The latter are key themes in the film's narrative: a Vietnam veteran and now redundant defence worker who has lost both his job and his family (he and his wife are divorced) who spends the duration of the film trying to find his way 'home'. The 'D-Fens' (*sic*) character played by Douglas quickly acquired iconic status as white male audiences in the US reputedly cheered and applauded as he smashed up a Korean-owned shop and attacked members of a Latino gang (Gabriel 1996).

In a similar vein, although in a different context, Lynch's (1989) study

Invisible Victims documented thirty-four more cases of anti-white discrimination and reached the conclusion that white men were angry and alienated by the US policy of affirmative action. Meanwhile, *US News* ran a feature on the plight of the white male under the headline, 'No white men need apply?' It is worth noting the peculiarly gendered slant to US representations of white victims, that is they are predominantly male, whereas in Britain the emphasis has been on white educational and family values.

Moreover while talk radio has played a key role in orchestrating white anxieties and mobilizing around a set of conservative white interests, in the UK the tabloid press has more often than not played this role. Perhaps the public service traditions of radio in the UK have predisposed this medium to a less overtly political role than in the US. In any event white English media *causes célèbres* have tended to originate in the tabloid press. One such case involved the group of white parents in Dewsbury who objected to multicultural developments within their children's school and withdrew them to a local public house where lessons were held (Gillborn 1995). Similarly, the principle of same-race placement in fostering and adoption cases, that is the principle of placing children with parents of the same 'racial' or ethnic background has been roundly rejected by the tabloids and in some instances broadsheet press. In place of the principle of 'race' the press took sides with a succession of prospective white adoptive/foster parents who were seen, in contrast, to offer a 'loving' and 'humane' environment (Gabriel 1994).

The role of key black media spokespeople has been crucial in the legitimation of white knowledge. The advantage of using expert black testimony in defence of white knowledge has been to make the case appear epistemologically neutral rather than reflecting dominant white 'interests'. There are parallels between the roles played by Clarence Thomas and Ward Conerly in the US and John (now Lord) Taylor in the UK. The views of all three have been used to denounce affirmative action and anti-discriminatory policies. Adding the odd black voice to the white backlash seemingly takes race out of the equation. Their 'blackness' would suggest that the attack on affirmative action policies is based on some rational, universal, supra-ethnic logic. Likewise, the opportunity to make political capital out of the research of black intellectuals like Dinesh D'Souza has not been lost on those Republican-leaning foundations and newspapers which have funded and given full and sympathetic coverage to D'Souza's (1992) polemical attacks on affirmative action.

Part of the appeal of whiteness lies in its capacity to resonate with other discourses. Sibley (1995) has argued that discourse of alterity (otherness) have provided a common language for attacks on women, homosexuals and mentally ill people as well as racialized others. The shared language which binds these discourses together is built around the threat of pollution and defilement and corresponding notions of purity of stock. Anti-immigration discourses have been organized around such themes. Hence, the appeal of anti-immigration rhetoric has been partly built around its capacity to play on ideas of race and sexuality simultaneously. Paranoias about bodies have fed paraonoias surrounding the nation-state and vice versa to the mutual enhancement of both.

The case of the police beating of Rodney King in Los Angeles in 1992 offers further evidence of these links. The striking feature of the case was the court's ability to reverse what appeared incontrovertible evidence of police brutality as it appeared to millions around the world on amateur video. Specifically, what made the difference was the evidence of the Los Angeles police officers who retold the incident emphasizing the sexual threat posed by King as he lay on the ground. By freeze framing each shot of the video (a process referred to as disaggregation) the story was transformed from one of police racism to one characterized by black lawlessness and sexual terror. Even as King lay there taking the blows of the long arm truncheon, he was allegedly gyrating in a sexually suggestive fashion (Koon 1992). The fact that the story was told to an almost all-white jury from Simi Valley, a well-known haven of white flight from the City of Los Angeles, also made a difference. In other words the context in which the events were being presented and the audience made all the difference. Finally, the innocent verdict returned in the case of the Los Angeles police officers was only possible given the long-standing common-sense association of racial and sexual fears. In the nineteenth century Jack the Ripper's alleged Jewish identity, at least according to local police sources and the popular press of the time, played on the idea of the defilement of the white woman as it spoke, simultaneously, of the sexual threat of the racialized other. In both cases different media are implicated in what Butler (1993) calls the racial production of the visible, although their impact cannot be fully understood without reference to: the scope of particular media technologies, for example the camcorder; key agencies, for example the police, or to a wider context of racial politics in Los Angeles and the influx of Jewish refugees into inner city London in the nineteenth century and to the forms of political mobilization which emerged around this and other migrations.

The limits of liberal/progressive whiteness

The limits of institutionalized anti-racist politics were exposed in the late 1980s not only by a tabloid press hungry for stories of white victims, but also by black scholars and minority organizations. As far as the latter were concerned anti-racism as practised and preached by left Labour councils had lost touch with those groups who were supposed to benefit from such policies. The language of institutional anti-racism and equal opportunities was mystifying and remote (Gilroy 1992) and the forms of consultation and participation established with grassroots community organizations at best weak and at worst a cynical attempt to contrive consent (Ben-Tovim *et al.* 1986). Moreover, as the critiques of modernity took hold from the early 1990s, ideas of equality and rights became associated with a wider discourse, inherited from the eighteenth-century Enlightenment, which had preached universalism and colonialism almost in the same breath. The limits of equality articulated by well-meaning whites within a western liberal discourse became transparent the more it was juxtaposed alongside discourses of difference as expressed by ethnicities other than the dominant white one.

Popular film provides some insight into the contours of liberal and progressive whiteness. The industry's avoidance of controversy partly in the aftermath of the McCarthy trials and partly because of the financial risks increasingly taken in Hollywood may explain the apparent absence of whiteness in mainstream film. The artistic tradition among film makers and actors also tends to ensure that films which do raise questions of racism do so with a liberal slant. In the 1980s and 1990s a succession of films concerned with civil rights abuses in the US all embraced a simple formula; racism is confined to the actions of a lunatic fringe and not part and parcel of mainstream liberal culture and that liberal whites alone are capable of resolving conflicts and finding solutions. The formula was evident in Costa Gavras's *Betrayed* (1988), Alan Parker's *Mississippi Burning* (1988) and Joel Schumacher's *A Time to Kill* (1996).

Interestingly, British films have adapted their settings and narrative themes while still relying on key aspects of the above formula. Costume dramas have provided opportunities to employ an all-white cast, while the 1980s Raj revivals, for example David Lean's *A Passage to India* (1984), depicted various viewpoints but all in relationship to a dominant liberal discourse. Even films with a strong social commentary, for example Mark Herman's *Brassed Off* (1996) and *The Full Monty* (1997), were by and large about the experiences of white working-class communities in the north of England, this time offering a form of nostalgia for the days of good old-fashioned (white) trade unionism. A very different tale of the role played by black workers in the 1984 miners' strike and in trade unions and dole queues more generally in the 1980s and 1990s was not told. In fact in the case of *The Full Monty*, the original production's focus on the cultural diversity of the group was changed in order to accommodate the sensibilities of its would-be Hollywood backers and audiences. Hollywood prefers its versions of Britain to be oldie worldly and/or pastoral but if it has got to be contemporary at least white and middle class, for example Mike Newell's *Four Weddings and a Funeral* (1994) and if not middle class in the case of *Brassed Off* and *The Full Monty,* at least, as good as, all white.

Some recurrent forms as well as limits of liberal whiteness are also to be found in anti-racist organizations, particularly with respect to their strategic use of the media. For example, there is a widely held view that racism can be fought by appealing to reason. The strategy is thus to attack racism in terms of factual error and to use alternative publications to expose its flaws and inconstancies. This has been the approach of the New York-based media watchdog organization FAIR (Federation for American Immigration Reform). While investigative journalism of this kind is obviously important in one sense, appealing to reason can only go so far in challenging what is something as inherently irrational as racism. The 'truth' is no match for the deep-seated anxieties which the discourse of whiteness plays on (for example, the white victim, the fear of black sexuality).

The second feature of many anti-racist organizations is their white leadership and reliance on white spokespeople often coinciding with a strategy aimed at changing the law. For example, the Alabama-based Southern Poverty Action Group have used the media to publicize their judicial confrontations with the Klu Klux Klan and other extreme right-wing groups. The organization's white leadership thus have sought to expose and destroy the far right using western notions of rationality and jurisprudence on the largely correct assumption that the media would reflect such principles as if they were universal givens. Likewise, in Britain the campaign against the 1996 Immigration and Asylum Act relied on black-led grassroots organizations and those facing deportation at a local level but more on white spokespeople and white dominated organizations (churches, political organizations, Members of Parliament, the media) at a national level. This is not meant to discount the significance of such forms of politics but to acknowledge their points of convergence with discourses of whiteness and hence their limits.

Neo-fascists, music and the Net

The extreme right has always been made up of street fighters and 'respectable' politicians. Internecine disputes between the two have provoked numerous splits, splinter groups and organizational reincarnations. In the UK, feuding over the electoral strategy of the British National Party

(BNP) led to the formation of a breakaway group, Combat 18, with an orientation towards football and music and more generally establishing a niche within neo-fascist youth culture. Not surprisingly, Combat 18 were financially supported by neo-Nazi bands Screwdriver and Razors Edge and promoted by parent magazines like *Blood and Honour* and *Resistance.*

Besides such fringe publications, the Internet has become a particularly important means of communication for neo-fascist groups worldwide and especially between Europe and the US. The Net's significance as a new media technology, particularly for the young, lies in the opportunities it provides for new sources and forms of information production, dissemination and consumption. In fact the distinction between these activities becomes increasingly blurred which increases its scope. These factors and the relative absence of regulation and censorship surrounding the Net has created an important space for extremist views including those of young fascists.

Moreover, the themes taken up in the home pages of such organizations and groups often echo themes taken up in more mainstream media outlets. George Hawthorne, for example, in a piece on the fears of 'race mixing', wrote that 'without the wombs of our women, we cannot reproduce our dwindling numbers. Race mixing spells race death since WHITE PEOPLE are becoming the true "new" minority'.[2] The solution, according to Hawthorne, is to forge a new destiny for white power music (ibid.). Such links have been a means not only of disseminating ideas but also of acting as distribution networks for records of Nazi bands and white pride paraphernalia.

Likewise, the BNP's home page provides access to its monthly newspaper *British Nationalist* with recurrent attention paid to black crime, black sex and white fears. The home pages of organizations based in the US reveal distinct yet by no means incompatible themes including the biblical origins of the white race (Aryan Nations); a commitment to white living space (National Alliance); the imminent collapse of western civilization (American Renaissance); a commitment to the authentic southern legacy (The Southern League of Florida) and anti-government regulation (Christian Patriots).

The mainstream media face something of a dilemma in their coverage of white extremism, as illustrated by the coverage of the riot at Dublin's football stadium in 1995. To probe too deeply into the motives and views of the rioters might well have brought opinions to light which were embarrassingly close to their readers. Consequently, the tabloid press, in particular, concentrated on the mindless violence of the fascists (in this case the National Socialist Alliance) rather than on their views. The fact that the far right groups involved in the riot also had close links with loyalists in Northern

Ireland meant an even greater synergy between the rioters and *Sun* readers who, after all, had been subjected to blanket anti-IRA coverage for over two decades. The tabloid press thus avoided the political dimensions to the riot and concentrated instead on background features on the victims of the violence, lurid profiles of the lifestyles of the hooligans involved and the alleged incompetence of the Garda (Irish police).

The continuities between white extremism and more coded conservative discourses are well captured in the political career of David Duke, who was a one-time member of the Klu Klux Klan and a leading member of the National Association for the Advancement of White People (NAAWP). A brief survey of *NAAWP News* reveals a striking convergence with mainstream media concerns, including white victims of reverse discrimination, anti-government regulation, welfare dependency, and racial threats to law and order. Duke stood and won a term in office in the Louisiana House of Representatives. His attempts to win a seat on the US Senate in Washington and presidency of the US were opposed by the Louisiana Coalition Against Racism and Nazism (LCARN) whose members sought to expose the flaws and 'truths' behind Duke's politics and to drive a wedge between Duke and the mainstream by highlighting Duke's infamous links with fascist organizations and ideas. The strategy was effective, for although Duke himself was exposed and defeated, the views expressed in his extremist organ, the NAAWP, in the early 1990s prefigured those on affirmative action, welfare law and order and immigration which found their way into mainstream political and media debate by the middle of the decade. As history would have it, California's attempts to reverse affirmative action policies, curb immigration and immigrant benefits, and toughen up policing and the judicial system, came to closely resemble the earlier ideas of Duke and others on the so-called 'lunatic fringe'. A combination of astute advertising backed by a crop of sympathetic talk radio hosts helped to mobilize an effective opposition to both immigration and affirmative action (Gabriel 1998: 113ff).

Intertwined histories

The racialized histories of the US and Britain are both specific and related. The US was a white settler society which was marked by the genocide of native Americans, forced migration and enslavement of Africans and the use of immigrant labour from South East Asia, Latin America and Europe. In Britain, such relations were historically experienced by the vast majority of white English at a distance, usually through the reports of writers and colonial administrators as well as tales of white, 'ex-patriot' communities.

In the post-war period, analogous developments in both countries have played a critical role in shaping internal developments and fueling white anxieties. The defeat of the US in Vietnam, on the one hand, and colonial independence from the UK, on the other, served to unsettle assumptions of global superiority. Nostalgia thus predictably played a prominent role in the backlash such events inspired. Popular film, literary classics and television series all reminded viewers and readers of their national heritage and essential characteristics. In the case of the US, whiteness drew on its English history and in particular sentiments and principles of its early Christian settlers and 'founding fathers'. In the UK, TV and cinematic productions, adaptations and revivals of anything from sixteenth-century royal bio-pics to nineteenth-century romances and family sagas act as reminders of a bygone age. Other cultures were invariably introduced as foils, there only to support notions of US/English superiority, reason, civilization, and so on.

Elsewhere the media have been less subtle in their levels and forms of articulating whiteness than cinema and TV which, from the above examples, have worked more through techniques of exnomination, naturalization and universalization referred to above. In the US, talk radio has proved a particularly significant means of disseminating and negotiating a more overt, essentialist whiteness while in the UK the tabloid press has played an analogous role. Both have been particularly adept at appealing directly, over the heads of government, special interest groups and the so-called liberal establishment, to 'the people'. Hence while talk radio hosts in the US invited and sometimes cajoled and berated their daily audiences to side with white victims of affirmative action or to challenge the intrusive and restrictive role played by governments, lawyers, teachers and others, the *Sun* steered its UK readers towards opinions on immigration, transracial adoption and anti-racist education, which it then tested in regular polls of its readers with predictable outcomes.

In some notable instances, the reverberations from 'racial panics' in the US and UK have sent shock waves across the Atlantic, in both directions. For example, coverage of the uprisings in US cities in the 1960s, which were broadcast on British news programmes and in the press, provoked considerable debate in Parliament and were among the factors responsible for the urgency surrounding the anti-discriminatory race relations legislation in the 1960s. Likewise advocates of California's Proposition 187, which aimed to restrict the numbers of immigrants from Mexico by cutting their entitlement to benefits, borrowed directly from the ideas and speeches of the former British cabinet minister, Enoch Powell, who had expressed them some twenty-five years earlier.

The general sense of intertwined and convergent histories developed here confirms the point made by Appadurai (1990) who encourages us not to see cultural flows as one way or emanating from one place as the term Americanization, for example, implies. In the case of the US, there are evidently powerful flows originating on the British side of the Atlantic. At the same time, it should be noted that what has been appropriated from its UK traditions has been very selective. Ideas and images of Britain which reinforce such values have thus attracted support and sponsorship in Hollywood. Not surprisingly, royalty, Regency costume dramas and rural settings have all featured prominently in the spate of British successes at the box office in the 1990s. There are alternative versions of Britain around, but these have been, by and large, reserved for smaller, art-house audiences and rarely receive the backing of big Hollywood producers and distributors. The flows may be two way and multidirectional as Appadurai argues but there is an unevenness which reflects the dominance of white culture.

Conclusion

Does writing about whiteness give it a 'reality' that it otherwise would lack? Is it better for whiteness to remain hidden as it is in its seemingly more benign media forms? Do we, by making whiteness an object of analysis, confer an analytical status on it beyond its due? The charge of reification is analogous to those critiques of the concept of 'race' which argue that, since 'races' do not exist, we are only giving the concept intellectual credence by focusing on it (Montagu 1997). We might similarly argue that whiteness does not exist in a pure form either as 'skin thing' or as a knowledge. On the contrary, despite the attempted construction and mobilization of 'white interests' in old and new media, white culture is heterogeneous with numerous internal fault-lines along axes of class, region and gender and other sources of difference. These are persuasive arguments which are supported by recent academic efforts to challenge the idea of a unitary white culture. Such deconstructions range from attempts to prove the inherent hybridity of European culture in terms of its African origins (Bernal 1987) through evidence of the diverse influences underpinning popular culture (Hall 1992b) to research highlighting the increasingly complex identities of young people growing up in multicultural urban environments (Back 1996).

However, the acknowledgement of the ever presence of hybridity, cultural syncretism and emergence of 'new ethnicities' is not necessarily incompatible with the concept of whiteness as a particular ethnic strategy. On the contrary, the argument here has been that at the very moment that new ethnicities have begun to assert and express themselves, so whiteness has been named, constructed and mobilized as a defensive strategy. And different media have played varying but nonetheless significant roles in constructing white identities and mobilizing around perceived white interests. Possibly, whiteness can no longer afford the luxury of invisibility, or perhaps it has been named by others. This chapter has been particularly concerned to show the ways in which whiteness, named and unnamed, resides across the political spectrum and in a range of media forms.

In neo-fascist and some conservative discourse, white people as whites have been celebrated or as is increasingly the case perceived and defended as victims. Elsewhere the defence of whiteness is more coded. Attacks on 'welfare moms', opposition to immigration defence of national identity and so on have been about defending a version of white interests in all but name. In the case of liberal and progressive discourses whiteness is mobilized via a defence of humanistic and/or socialist values necessarily fronted by white men. Hence, both the problems continue to be set within the terms of dominant white discourses and the solutions kept in white hands. The examples from popular film are testimony to such forms of representation.

Anti-racism is a case in point. According to a recent survey (Law 1997) anti-racism has become a much more common form of press reporting than it was in the 1980s when the hostility to anti-racist initiatives was at its peak. Might this be because in its institutional forms, anti-racist politics are more often than not couched in local authority-speak, invariably spoken by white policy and decision makers and within a framework of legal, policy and service provision which is rooted in liberal welfare traditions of the nation-state? Politicians and their media sympathizers have been quick to spot the advantages using prominent black spokespeople to speak out against anti-racism or affirmative action. Such interventions have seemingly drawn on a logic which has gone beyond the particularities of ethnicity and hence underlined the assumed universalism of whiteness.

The media forms have been shown to vary both between the US and UK, notably in the popularization of a backlash discourse which has relied heavily on talk radio and the tabloid press in the US and UK respectively. Popular film has played an important role in coding whiteness under the guise of rural nostalgia, period costume dramas and an unprecedented fascination with British royalty. Multi-ethnic/racial themes are possible so long as the principle of liberal yet white superiority remains intact. The proliferation of communication technologies at increasingly affordable prices has provided the basis for an expanding network of fascist groups across Europe and the US. Websites provide opportunities to peddle nuanced versions of the crisis of white masculinity as well as a distribution means for fascist music, T-shirts, literature and so on.

The articulation of racialized discourses to those of sexuality and gender has played on white paranoias, particularly in media discourses concerned with population control/immigration, interracial sex and crime, each of which have attained heights of newsworthiness across the range of popular media, partly because of the capacity of ideas of sex, race, population and defilement to resonate and feed off each other. In both the US and UK immigration debates have been laced with linguistic themes of moral defilement and pollution. In the case of Rodney King, the setting for the trial, in conjunction with the role of the white police officers and the reworking of the amateur video, transformed the story from one of police racism to that of a black sexual predator. Such narratives send shock waves through what are already highly charged white cultures on both sides of the Atlantic. The resultant ethnic strategies, varyingly aimed at defending, bolstering and self-consciously celebrating whiteness, have formed the subject matter of this chapter.

The fact that whiteness is socially constructed, rather than an expression of some agreed set of essential characteristics of white culture, means that its forms as well as its strategic significance change over time. And the media have played no small part in securing such shifts. The idea of subaltern whiteness illustrates this. In the US, the Irish became distanced from their African Americans, and hence 'became' white, as a result of political manoeuvrings within the Democratic Party and their political allies and reports in the press (Roediger 1991; Ignatiev 1995). Likewise, in Britain, the stereotypical reporting of the Irish and Irish issues (see Curtis 1984) including the conflict in Northern Ireland (see Hillyard 1993 on the use of the Prevention of Terrorism Act) has been complemented by the non-reporting of other issues in for example the incidence of mental illness among the Irish (Greenslade *et al.* 1997) and the widespread absence of any acknowledgement of the extent of an anti-Irish racism (see, for example, Hickman and Walter 1995). Such studies confirm that it is indeed possible to be white and not to be part of the dominant white culture and that media culture articulates with political developments to effect changes around white subaltern status.

Overall, however, such complications and qualifications should not dissuade us from naming whiteness, so long as its dominance is taken for granted both in terms of its knowledge/power and the near monopolistic hold that white men continue to have over the world's leading institutions. In this analysis the media have been seen to play an important role in representations of whiteness in all its guises, from its more unashamedly neo-fascist to more coded and liberal forms. New syncretic forms of representation serve to undermine the fictional unity of white interests and identities. In the mean time, the analysis of whiteness, rather than reifying it, can be seen as a necessary stage in its 'abolition' (Ignatiev 1995).

Notes

1 This chapter draws on ideas developed more extensively in Gabriel (1998).
2 Resistance records at http://.resistance.com/

Further reading

Dyer, R. (1997) *White*. London: Routledge.

Gabriel, J. (1998) *Whitewash: Racialized Politics and the Media*. London: Routledge.

Hall, S. (1991) The local and the global: globalization and the media, in A.D. King (ed.) *Culture, Globalization and the World System: Contemporary Conditions and the Representation of Identity*. London: Macmillan.

Hall, S. (1992) The question of cultural identity, in S. Hall, D. Held and T. McGrew (eds) *Modernity and its Futures*. Cambridge: Polity.

Sibley, D. (1995) *Geographies of Exclusion*. London: Routledge.

Ware, V. (1992) *Beyond the Pale: White Women, Racism and Identity*. London: Verso.

Part II
CHANGING CONTEXTS OF PRODUCTION

THE PARADOX OF AFRICAN AMERICAN JOURNALISTS
Clint C. Wilson II

Introduction

African American journalists in the United States exist in a professional paradox rooted in circumstances that date back more than 100 years. In 1896 the US Supreme Court ruled that segregation of the Black and White races was constitutionally valid and that 'separate but equal' was acceptable public policy. Although many have written and spoken about the effects of the ruling in *Plessy v. Ferguson* on race relations in such areas as voting rights and discrimination in housing, employment, education and public transportation, few have addressed its influence in the subsequent practices of newspaper and other mass communications media. But it is clear that following the *Plessy v. Ferguson* court decision, the Black press grew and flourished under the impetus of racial injustice and social degradation suffered by African Americans. At the same time, the daily 'mainstream' press pursued a policy of general indifference to the concerns of Black people and supported the status quo regarding race relations in the United States. The 'separate but equal' doctrine persisted until 1954 when the US Supreme Court reversed the policy in its decision in *Brown vs. (Topeka, Kansas) Board of Education*. During the nearly 60 years that elapsed between the two landmark court cases, African American journalists were almost exclusively confined to working in their own racial newspapers which, with only a handful of exceptions, were published once per week. The Black press, in fact, was extremely influential in getting the *Plessy* ruling overturned as part of the widespread civil rights movement. One key African American editor, Enoc Waters of the Chicago *Defender*, said of the era that 'We were not only black newsmen but we regarded ourselves as a specialized division of a vast black civil rights crusade' (Waters 1977: 20).

Despite the legal dismantling of 'separate but equal' doctrine, the decade following the *Brown* decision saw little improvement in the plight of Black Americans and the US Congress had to pass a Civil Rights Act in 1964. During this period the mainstream press devoted significant attention to the civil rights movement and exposed discrimination in various areas of American life. However, it paid little attention to its own shortcomings as the middle years of the 1960s brought a series of racially tinged civil disturbances fuelled by inner city Black residents who had been frustrated by social, economic and political inequities. In response, President Lyndon B. Johnson issued an executive order in 1967 that created the National Advisory Commission on Civil Disorders. Because the commission was directed by Otto Kerner, a former governor of the State of Illinois, the investigative body became known as the Kerner Commission. The commission's task was to determine the cause of civil disturbances or 'riots' by Black Americans which had occurred in more than a dozen US cities since 1964. Among the key findings was that mass communications media, including the journalistic press, played a role in the discontent of Black Americans. The commission determined that it needed to look beyond merely how the press had reported news of the riots, but 'to consider also the overall treatment by the media of the Negro ghettos, community relations, racial attitudes, urban and rural poverty – day by day and month by month, year in and year out' (Kerner 1968: 363). Moreover, the commission found that the press reported 'from the standpoint of a white man's world' and reflected the 'biases, the paternalism, the indifference of white America' (Kerner 1968: 366).

Among the solutions offered by the commission was to train and hire more African American journalists and editors into positions within the mainstream journalistic press. The commission believed that increasing the numbers of Black and other minority newsroom personnel would, over time, bring more equitable coverage and perspective to the daily newspaper press. It noted that in 1968 fewer than 5 per cent of persons employed as journalists in the United States and less than 1 per cent of the nation's newsroom supervisors were Black (Kerner 1968: 384). What made these meagre percentages more striking is that they included persons who worked within the Black newspaper press. At that time African Americans officially constituted more than 11 per cent of the total US population, a figure the commission noted was probably less than the actual count because of inadequate census-taking procedures used in Black communities by the census bureau.

In the intervening decade between 1968 and 1977, it became evident to the American Society of Newspaper Editors (ASNE) that the Kerner

Commission's call for dramatic increases in hiring of Black journalists and editors was not being met with deliberate speed. The organization established a goal of attaining minority journalist employment equal to the percentage of minorities in the US population by the year 2000. Thus, in 1978 it began its annual survey which is designed to track the hiring of African American and other ethnic 'minority' editorial employees in the daily newspaper industry.

The first survey released in 1978 revealed only 3.95 per cent of 43,000 newspaper editorial employees was comprised of 'minority' group members – a term including not only Black Americans, but those of Asian, Latino (Hispanic) and Native American origin as well (ASNE 1998). Approximately half or 1200 of those minority journalists were Black (Wilson 1991: 110). Twenty years later the 1998 ASNE survey revealed the minority employment figure had increased to 11.46 per cent but by that time the minority population in the US had increased to 26 per cent with Blacks comprising more than 12 per cent of the total. Yet, only 2946 Black journalists were found in 1998 from among the total daily newspaper workforce of 54,700. Although the American Society of Newspaper Editors will fall short of its year 2000 population parity goal, expectation was created among Black journalists that the Kerner Commission's premise of increased Black employment in daily newspapers would result in more accurate, complete and sensitive coverage of African Americans in the newspaper press. But, the experiences of the three decades since publication of the Kerner Commission report have proven otherwise.

Martindale's (1986) study found slight improvement in daily newspaper coverage of Black Americans but that white readers were 'being encouraged to think that most problems of blacks have been solved by the advances secured during the civil rights movement . . . What seems to prevail, however, is an "us–them" kind of mentality, a notion that white America has done all that could be expected of it' (Martindale 1986: 147). Equally disturbing as the slow rate of increase in the hiring of Black journalists is their rate of attrition from the industry. Researchers Pease and Smith (1991) found that this was due in part to a perception that daily newspapers marginally or poorly cover issues of concern to the Black community. Therefore, the issue for current consideration is the nature of paradox for Black American journalists who believed their recruitment into careers in mainstream daily newspapers would bring their cultural perspectives to the product. Also, what factors prevent them from affecting the changes envisioned by the Kerner Commission?

Answers may be found in the nature of newsroom organization, journalistic values and related policies and how journalists are socialized to conform to them. Several researchers have undertaken the study of social group dynamics in the American newsroom. For the most part, they have been interested in factors that determine news story selection and the role of newspaper publishers in influencing content. A seminal study by Swanson (1949) found that editors and writers shared policy beliefs. Furthermore, he found that members of both groups had been selected for employment by executives and publishers on the basis of certain social criteria, which accounted for the consensus they shared concerning general philosophical values and objectives of the newspaper. Sociologist Warren Breed, himself a former journalist, conducted perhaps the most significant work in this area. Breed's (1955) study on social control in the newsroom attempted to explain how socialization processes work to maintain normative standards in a newspaper organization. While later studies have been critical of Breed with respect to his reliance on subjective premises, the study remains the seminal work in its topic area. Although Breed's work did not specifically address the effects of socialization and newsroom control on Black journalists in White news media *per se*, it does provide a basis for overlaying what has since been learned about their experiences.

To establish the conceptual framework, a synopsis of the subject study by Breed is necessary. The study involved interviews of at least one-hour's duration with 120 journalists, mostly in the north-eastern quadrant of the United States, who worked for mid-sized daily newspapers (circulations of between 10,000 and 100,000). The research was based on the premise that all newspapers have policies, whether openly admitted or not. Breed also brought to the study his own experience as a professional newspaper journalist. He identified the principal areas for policy consideration as politics, business and labour, much of which stems from socio-economic class concerns. Because of the atypical nature of news enterprise in the United States, that is its First Amendment constitutional protection and the ethical norms of the journalism profession, the policies are covert and not written or codified. Breed found that policy is determined by publishers and executives and he cited examples of how they invoke both long-term and immediate policy decisions on matters such as which political candidate to support, whether to feature or bury a labour trouble story, or how much 'free' space to give 'news' of advertisers' doings.

The views of other scholars on this point, however, provides additional perspective. For example, Swanson (1949) found little policy of this nature needed direct involvement of the publisher/executive because persons selected for news management positions were chosen partially because they already shared social and ideological beliefs with their employers. At the same time, another researcher, Bowers (1967) found that when publishers wanted to be certain that policy was followed, they gave direct instruction:

> Although Breed reported that his investigation indicated many indirect pressures on a news staff from the publisher, the respondents to this questionnaire felt that most of the time any directions that were given were expressed rather than implied.
>
> (Bowers 1967: 49)

Bowers, who surveyed more than 600 daily newspaper managing editors about the activity of their publishers in directing the use or non-use of stories and their content and display, found that expressed policy direction was given very infrequently and then only under specific conditions. Those conditions included issues which could conceivably affect the newspaper's revenue. On stories pertaining to racial issues, the geographic proximity to Black population centres correlated highest to publisher issuance of policy directives. Bowers (1967) also found that when publishers did provide policy direction, it was most often in the area of story display rather than in use, non-use or content. However, media critic Ben Bagdikian (1987) maintains that the influence wielded by news media corporate executives is immense and is often motivated by their complicity in interlocking directorates with other industrial enterprises and international banking interests. In his book *Media Monopoly* Bagdikian observes that fewer than 30 corporations control more than half of the sources of public information and expression of opinion disseminated in the United States. Bagdikian argues that while the degree to which parent corporations control content of their media subsidiaries varies, the potential for conflicts of interest are pervasive.

> What is the proper behavior of a banker who is a director of General Electric, owner of NBC, if he hears that the network is about to produce a documentary highly embarrassing to the banking industry? It could be to the best interests of NBC News to attract an audience with a documentary on what could be a compelling public issue. Yet such a documentary might not be perceived as being in the best interest of the banks.
>
> (Bagdikian 1987: 25)

Bagdikian goes on to cite numerous examples of corporate intervention in news and public information for purposes ranging from influencing public policy to the waging of private feuds to the manipulation of public communication for personal profit.

It is clear, therefore, from other research on the topic that news organizations operate within a framework of institutional policy which originates at the highest level. Breed (1955) maintained that much of it is covert; Swanson (1949) suggested that covertness is facilitated because of the homogeneous social characteristics shared by executives and the editing-writing staff; Bowers (1967) reported that policy is directly expressed by publishers under certain conditions; and Bagdikian (1987) provided the *raison d'être* for most corporate intrusions into the sanctity of newsroom independence. Perhaps the issue was best summarized by social scientist Herbert Gans (1979) in his book, *Deciding What's News*. Gans wrote: 'The values in the news are rarely explicit and must be found between the lines – in what actors and activities are reported or ignored, and in how they are described' (Gans 1979: 89). It is these non-explicit, yet operational, values from which arise what Breed termed 'covert policy' that provide clues to the nature of paradox for Black journalists in the daily US newspaper press.

How journalists learn policy

Breed (1955) found that although philosophical policies were not written or even discussed formally, all but the newest staff reporters knew what policy was. None of the newspapers involved in his research provided a training or orientation programme for newcomers involving policy matters. Numerous reporters whom Breed interviewed remarked that they had never been told how to 'slant' a story. Many news organizations provide staffers with a 'style book', which outlines literary style and copy processing procedure, but none address specific policy concerning philosophy of coverage and content. While respondents to Breed's research questions often said that they learned organizational policy 'by osmosis', in sociological terms each learned policy by discovering and internalizing job and performance expectations according to the normative standards and values of the organization. The norms and values are supported by a system of rewards and punishments within the social system of the newsroom. Newspaper newsrooms, and by extension, television and radio newsrooms, operate much as do other occupational social systems. A socialization process envelopes all who are part of the group and fosters the dynamics of 'belonging' and a sense of pride that one works for the *Times* or the *Post*. Breed (1955) cited the ways in which journalists learn policy and assimilate into the group dynamic:

1 *Reading and observing the product* Journalists in Breed's study, as is the case today, were often required to read their newspaper every day. The absorption of content provides the news reporter with a ready reference

for learning policy parameters. Again, by extension, electronic newspersons learn from listening and watching their organization's newscasts which types of stories get the most air time and 'play' as well as those which do not. Interestingly, Breed noted how a reporter in the American South learned policy regarding political and racial stories in his newspaper by writing that the reporter observed that Republicans were treated in a 'different' way from Democrats, and that 'news about Whites and Negroes is also of a different sort' (Breed [1955] 1960: 182).

2 *Editing of their stories* Journalists who find their stories edited or 'blue pencilled' consistently for policy rather than for stylistic or professional reasons are given strong lessons on their newsroom's norms and values. Thus, the editing process is a means of enforcing and maintaining policy conformity.

3 *Reprimand* When stories are seen as serious violations of policy, the offending reporter may be called in by the senior news manager and subtly reprimanded. The deed is most often done with a gentle admonition such as: 'We don't write about —— this way in the *Chronicle*'. The advice is usually followed by an explanation as to how the policy is not an encroachment upon journalistic ethics but, rather, is a part of the organization's tradition. This occurs most often in instances where a journalist has undertaken a story on his/her own initiative without knowledge that a particular type of story or 'angle' is not consistent with organizational policy. Nevertheless, the circumstance illustrates the unique aspects of the journalism profession in that most occupational social systems have no inherent means for independent work assignments.

4 *Characteristics, interests and affiliations of executives* Here, Breed lists five ways in which new reporters acquire a sense of values held by those in the uppermost levels of the organization. Knowledge of personal tendencies of superiors helps the journalist obtain perspective and context for policy. Newsroom neophytes may overhear or be part of a discussion about executives at the office water cooler, or at an after-hours tavern. This communication, often in the form of gossip, gives insight at least into how co-workers view the publisher or senior editors and their ideological perspectives. Another source of personal information about superiors is the observance of how executives position themselves on various news issues during story conferences with staff. Also, the organization's house organs (company newsletters, employee magazines, and so on) often reveal the external interests and affiliations that executives maintain. Finally, Breed noted, a reporter may get an impression of executive attitudes through either personal observation or by listening to them give direct expressions of personal opinion.

Why journalists conform to policy

It is probable that most laypersons think of journalists as independent, strong-willed and sceptical observers of society and its institutions. A natural question arises as to why such individuals would accept the limits of socialization in the organizations for which they work. Breed, a sociologist, sought to explain this phenomenon in sociological terms with reference to 'institutionalized statuses' and 'structural roles'. He wrote that reporters must be viewed in terms of their own status and aspirations within the context of newsroom organization and of the larger society. Breed (1955) proposed six reasons why journalists maintain professional conformity in the workplace:

1 *Institutional authority and sanctions* Although news media in the United States are unique business enterprises because they enjoy constitutional protection and uphold a tradition of public service, they are, nevertheless, businesses with a bureaucratic organizational structure. As such, the corporation, publisher or other designated officials have the power of authority. That is to say, the right to hire and fire rests with them. The authority to sanction by employment termination, although rarely invoked, provides a strong incentive to conform especially when linked to other incentives cited below. More likely, however, than the happenstance that a policy-violating story will result in firing the reporter is the chance an editor will alter or 'kill' the offending story before it ever comes to the attention of executives.

2 *Feelings of obligation and esteem for superiors* Since journalists in news organizations ply their professional skills to earn a living, they naturally harbour a grateful allegiance to those who hired them. Even if individual reporters aspire to leave their present job for a better opportunity, they would not want to risk the good will of superiors. In many instances, according to Breed (1955), reporters hold certain superiors in esteem or admire them as role models and mentors. Thus, a natural desire to conform to perceived values and policy is developed. Breed found a correlation between the obligation-esteem factor and staff morale and performance. On newspapers where senior editors were highly respected, their subordinate staff members performed with enthusiasm and the news gathering and production process was efficient and of good quality. However, newsrooms in which reporters lacked esteem and respect for editors and news managers demonstrated low staff morale and a climate conducive to hostility toward policy.

3 *Mobility aspirations* Breed's study found that the younger news staffers

whom he interviewed all indicated a desire to advance their careers. All agreed that violating policy would seriously hamper their personal ambitions and the salary rewards that go with them. A major means seen of achieving recognition that might lead to promotion was to get 'big' stories on Page One. A reporter who ran foul of policy would lose that opportunity. We should note that research (Institute for Journalism Education 1985) has shown that Black journalists are more interested in advancing to management levels than their White colleagues and that desire is linked to the motivation to affect change within and without the journalism profession.

4 *Absence of conflicting group allegiance* Breed noted that no other formal organization existed among journalists which would provide opposition to covert policy within newsrooms. He cited the American Newspaper Guild as the leading journalists' organization. At the time of his study (*c.* 1955) Breed observed that the guild was a labour union primarily concerned with interests outside the newsroom. In the late 1990s, the guild is even less a factor as increasingly more news organizations (as have other American industries) are moving away from unionization. Today's journalists are more inclined to membership in professional groups such as press clubs or the Society of Professional Journalists that are active in freedom of information and First Amendment issues as opposed to internal policy matters. Even professional groups interested in the role of ethnic minorities and their relationship to the press, such as the National Association of Black Journalists, have avoided direct confrontation over internal matters with major White-owned media institutions that employ the vast majority of their members. Thus, no concerted and organized effort exists among journalists to contest internal policy.

5 *Pleasant nature of the activity* In this category Breed cited three aspects of the journalism profession which appeal to the individual's self-satisfaction. First, was what Breed termed the 'in-groupness in the newsroom'. Although reporters are on the lowest level of the newsroom hierarchy (excluding college interns and editorial assistants) they are treated as executive co-workers. Editors, and occasionally an executive, may freely discuss stories with a reporter on a give-and-take basis. It is not uncommon for news managers to leave their private offices to visit with reporters in the newsroom. The newsroom atmosphere, therefore, is friendly and a sense of teamwork rather than hierarchal bureaucracy prevails.

Second, the required operations of journalistic work are interesting. Breed found that few reporters whom he interviewed for his study expressed complaints about their jobs when given the opportunity. The elements of news work, including witnessing events, interviewing sources, considering the meanings of events, checking facts and writing, were seen as interesting activities.

Third, journalists enjoy several non-financial perquisites. Their work entails a variety of experiences which include eye-witnessing significant and interesting events; being among the first to know about issues and occurrences; being privy to 'inside' information not accessible to the general public; and meeting and possibly befriending persons of social and/or political stature who often must treat newspersons with deference. In addition, journalists are close to those making major decisions without having responsibility for making the decisions themselves. Their role and the organizations they work for are important to society, and personal status accrues to journalists.

6 *News becomes a value* News is a commodity and its production is the focal point of the newsroom. Even if, in the parlance of the profession, 'it's a slow news day', the newspaper must be produced. Breed believed that because getting the news was the focal point of all activity in the newsroom, reporters understood any performance rewards resulted from those efforts as opposed to activity directed against internal policy. Consequently, he surmised, 'instead of mobilizing their efforts to establish objectivity over policy as the criterion for performance, their energies are channeled into getting more news' (Breed [1955] 1960: 187). He likened this phenomenon to what social scientists term the 'displacement of goals'. This is a process whereby journalists direct their energies toward getting news instead of seeking ways to get *better* news. Sociologist Robert K. Merton (1949: 154–5) wrote of this concept as being a social 'dysfunction' because society's need is not for increased quantity of news but for better news quality. In the newsroom, however, the production of news is the central value and the executives, editors and reporters share it as their common interest, making it an instrument of conformity.

Social control in the 1990s

Because Breed conducted his research in the 1950s, it is reasonable to question the extent of its validity in the 1990s. At least one scholar attempted to assess and draw upon Breed's work during the 1970s. Garvey's (1971) doctoral dissertation at Stanford University sought to determine whether social control was operative in television newsrooms. As an approach to his own study, Garvey challenged both the notion of the existence of social control and Breed's concept of policy. Garvey criticized Breed's work as 'impressionistic' and described his conclusions as 'inherently subjective' (Garvey 1971: 4). Despite those caveats, however, and using his own refined definitions of policy and social control, Garvey's study of selected California television station newsrooms generally supported Breed.

> In general, the findings of the dissertation indicate that social control, such as Breed described it, does exist at some American television stations. The staff does absorb policy and converts that policy into content.
>
> (Garvey 1971: 395)

Since Breed's study, television has become the medium by which most Americans get their news. Garvey's work, therefore, is significant in that it establishes the validity of social control and policy as factors in the determination of news content in that medium. In addition, subsequent work (Gans 1979; Martindale 1986; Pease and Smith 1991; Wilson 1991: 152–4) strongly suggests that basic newsroom dynamics have changed little over time since Breed conducted his study.

Why have there not been more dramatic gains in the nature and quality of news stories about African American culture although there has been an increase in the numbers of Black daily newspaper journalists since the late 1970s? Perhaps a hypothetical illustration will provide some insight into the issue. Let us suppose that for many decades a manufacturer had been producing 'square widgets' (an object designed to meet the needs of a predominant 'square' marketplace) utilizing workers and methods dedicated solely to that purpose. A small minority of triangles are ignored in the marketplace population. Over time, however, the marketplace demographics change toward a triangular orientation and a concern for pluralism and/or government-mandated employment regulations prompt the company's executives (themselves all square-oriented) to hire a few triangular workers for the assembly line. The triangular workers become adept at their task and the newly integrated workforce continues to produce square widgets with a high degree of proficiency. Problems arise as it becomes clear that the market for square widgets is headed for a rapid decline in an increasingly triangular marketplace. Because the nature of the marketplace is changing, the square widget executives begin to fret over how they might save their business. They wonder why the addition of triangular workers to help produce square widgets has not effectively increased their ability to attract a larger share of the triangular marketplace. We learn that merely placing a few triangular workers in the production line to perform square-oriented tasks is not sufficient to meet the needs of the new marketplace environment. The solution, of course, is that the plant must retool and change its product to meet the needs of a different marketplace.

The performance of the triangular-oriented workers in our hypothetical manufacturing plant was based on their ability to meet existing expectations, procedures and policies as defined by the values and mores of the square-oriented workplace. If we apply our hypothetical case as a simile for American news media, the basis for answering our question about the news coverage of Black America becomes evident. When the Kerner Commission challenged the news media to racially integrate their staffs, it failed to realize the limitations of newsroom integration as a tool for putting into effect a fundamental change in the product of the American press. What the commission desired was a major content change in the news product that would utilize the perspective and input of Black Americans which had been historically ignored and abused. However, the term 'news' has – by covert policy definition – come to stand for content that is restrictive of the Black perspective.

At this point we must be mindful of the corporate context in which American news media operate. The ability to show a successful 'bottom line' is directly related to a medium's proficiency at delivering a desirable audience to its advertisers. Advertising income is the fuel that powers corporate media. A great deal of media effort is directed toward attracting and holding the young, affluent segment of society which has expendable income to purchase goods and services. Unfortunately, until very recent years almost as much energy has been spent by media to exclude unwanted segments of society from their audience. Much of the African American population falls into this category. As Bagdikian (1987) noted:

> Broadcasters cannot keep the nonaffluent and elderly from watching or listening to their programs, but they design the content to attract younger, affluent viewers. Newspapers control the readership by not reporting significantly on neighborhoods of low-income and elderly populations and by promoting their circulation in affluent neighborhoods with the desired characteristics.
>
> (Bagdikian 1987: 199)

The reason that this approach has appeared to change in recent years has more to do with demographic shifts in the US population than with media desire to serve a more culturally pluralistic society. The fact is that African American and other non-White cultural groups are collectively becoming the fastest growing economic force in American society. Census and demographic data reveal that portions of the Black, Latino and Asian American populations are becoming more affluent and are in the younger age groups preferred by advertisers. While some news media executives have foreseen where their corporate economic futures lie and have increased hiring of non-White reporters, the constraints of institutionalized 'business as usual' in coverage and content hinders change toward cultural pluralism in the product.

Placing Black journalists in the almost total racial and cultural isolation of the newsroom where operative news values, procedures and policy have been long ingrained to exclude the African American perspective obviates their effectiveness as agents for change. Their survival on the job depends upon how well they conform to newsroom policy expectations and how they 'fit in' with fellow workers. One Black male reporter at the *Washington Post* said that the newspaper 'frequently seems to interpret equal opportunity as meaning that if minorities and women work hard and follow directions, they too can become white men' (Coleman *et al.* 1986: 4). Black journalists who take seriously their role as adding African American cultural perspective to the news product face a personal and professional paradox of considerable proportions. One result of this paradox is the ponderable often discussed whenever Black journalists congregate: 'Am I a journalist who happens to be Black, or am I a Black journalist?' This issue is not a new one for African Americans and has been publicly debated for many years. In 1942 sociologist Horace Cayton discussed its Second World War variation, 'Am I a Negro first and then a policeman or a soldier second, or should I forget in any emergency situation the fact that . . . my first loyalty is to my race?' (Cayton 1942: 267). Implicit in this question is the dilemma that Black journalists face in seeking to reconcile their desire to fulfil personal professional ambitions by gaining acceptance of peers and superiors with the responsibility to fill a void in the informational needs of society. While many may assume the two objectives to be compatible and complementary, history and tradition have shown they are not. For we now know that the perspectives, values and direction of journalistic information and commentary are culturally exclusive of non-White vantage points.

Consequences of paradox

The consequences of Black journalists' frustration in the daily newspaper workplace is the probability of their abandoning the profession. In a study of *The American Journalist in the 1990s*, Weaver and Wilhoit (1992) warned that 'a serious problem of retention may be just over the horizon' and that 'more than 20 percent of those surveyed said they plan to leave the field in five years, double the figure of 1982–83' (Weaver and Wilhoit 1992:

1). Although Weaver and Wilhoit's data address all journalists' views of job satisfaction, it is clear that the news industry can ill afford to lose any percentage of its already too small pool of Black journalists. Although entry-level hiring of Blacks has grown at a slow but fairly steady pace since the late 1970s, their overall percentage increase in the workforce has been tread-milled because of the rate of departures.

The following excerpts from Pease and Smith (1991) *The Newsroom Barometer* are instructive:

- 71 per cent of minority journalists said that their papers covered minority issues and concerns marginally or poorly; 50 per cent of whites agreed.
- Minority journalists (63 per cent) were twice as likely as whites (31 per cent) to believe that race plays a role in newsroom assignments, promotions and advancement.
- 72 per cent of minorities and 35 per cent of whites said that managers and supervisors doubted the abilities of minority staffers to perform their jobs adequately.

Pease and Smith summarized their study by noting that 'These results paint a picture of newsrooms in which journalists of color feel themselves besieged because of their race. It's a picture few whites are aware of.' This lack of change in apparent newsroom policy is reminiscent of the Kerner Commission's observation in the late 1960s: 'Many editors and news directors, plagued by shortages of staff and lack of reliable contacts and sources of information . . . have failed to recognize the significance of the urban story and to develop resources to cover it adequately' (Kerner 1968: 383).

Another measure of the Black journalist's paradox during the post Kerner Commission years was evident following civil disturbances in Los Angeles when the Rodney King police brutality case verdict was rendered. A task force report on news coverage of the unrest in Los Angeles was issued by the National Association of Black Journalists (1992). The NABJ report found a 'simmering frustration among many black journalists – about how they were utilized, about how they were regarded, about the slow pace of racial change in newsrooms. In relatively few cases did Black journalists direct coverage or participate in front-page decisions' (NABJ 1992: 1).

Conclusion

With the approach of the year 2000 the hiring issues raised by the Kerner Commission have largely become fodder for a repetitive cycle of panel discussions on newsroom 'diversity' at major professional journalism conventions and conferences in the United States. But, attention still leans too heavily toward entry-level hiring at the expense of rectifying problems that are causing African American journalists to leave the profession. They are the problems of inclusiveness of perspective in news coverage and of advancement into decision-making ranks. The slow but gradual tendency toward adding non-whites to daily newspaper staffs (in 1998, 42 per cent still had none on their news staffs) belies the fact that white editors still want them to think and report from the white perspective some 30 years after the Kerner Commission admonition.

Further reading

Ainley, B. (1998) *Black Journalists, White Media*. Stoke-on-Trent: Trentham.
Bagdikian, B. (1987) *The Media Monopoly*, 2nd edn. Boston, MA: Beacon.
Pease, T. and Smith, J.F. (1991) *The Newsroom Barometer: Job Satisfaction and the Impact of Racial Diversity at U.S. Daily Newspapers*. Athens, OH: Ohio University Press.
Wilson, C. (1991) *Black Journalists in Paradox: Historical Perspectives and Current Dilemmas*. Westport, CT: Greenwood.
Wilson, C. and Gutierrez, F. (1995) *Race, Multiculturalism, and the Media: From Mass to Class Communication*, 2nd edn. Thousand Oaks, CA: Sage.

6 | A ROCK AND A HARD PLACE: MAKING ETHNIC MINORITY TELEVISION
Simon Cottle

Introduction

There is more to British television than the problem-oriented, racializing discourses of news, or the stereotypical and simplified characterizations of popular entertainment forms identified by research (and reviewed in Chapter 1). Given the historically embedded nature of the mass media, as well as its changing relationship to the surrounding play of social and cultural power, the nature of its 'representations' can change through time and these often exhibit internal complexity. Today, as in the past, British broadcasting literally and institutionally 'mediates' the politics of 'race', ethnicity and cultural identity and gives expression, albeit in unequal ways, to this contested field. Across the years 'race' has variously been constructed and/or challenged in terms of 'assimilationist', 'integrationist', 'pluralist', 'multiculturalist' and 'anti-racist' positions and agendas, with further recent infusions from varieties of 'feminism', ideas of 'new ethnicities' and 'the end of the essential black subject' (Hall 1988) – all pointing to a surrounding field as contested as ever.

Broadcasting itself, of course, is not historically static nor institutionally fixed but subject to sometimes powerful forces of change. Across the 1990s, for example, the British television industry was shaped by a combination of three such forces:

1 *Political deregulation*, which was principally embodied in the 1990 British Broadcasting Act that released commercial operators from former public service obligations, exposed the British Broadcasting Corporation

(BBC) to increased competition and financial pressures, created 'lighter touch' regulatory bodies, and imposed a statutory obligation on all broadcasters, including the BBC, to commission at least 25 per cent of their original production from independent producers.

2 *Technological developments*, especially the development of cable and satellite delivery systems, digitalization and processes of technological (and industrial) convergence.

3 *Increased market competition*, as part cause and part consequence of regulatory and technological developments, that led to further industrial concentration, proliferation of channels and exposure of programme makers and broadcasters to the forces of the marketplace. A marketplace, moreover, that increasingly reaches out across national and international borders towards global penetration.

Institutionally positioned in between, and buffeted by, the forces of regulatory, technological and economic change on the one side, and the shifting sands of ethnic minority cultural-politics on the other, stand the television producers. By force of circumstance, then, producers have much to contribute to our understanding of the forces that bear down on, and are condensed within, the moment of programme commissioning and production – insights that are too often ignored or only guessed at when interpreting media texts. Empirical studies of media producers and production contexts serve to remind us of the often 'messy' contingencies of cultural production as well as the pragmatic accommodations that producers may feel obliged to make in their bid to survive in difficult institutional and culturally contested times. The theorization of media representations approached in terms of enacted cultural politics thus needs to incorporate a sharper sense of the complex of determinations often condensed within the 'moment' of cultural production. These too are 'at work' and variously combine to shape and facilitate, condition and constrain the practices of media/cultural producers and their representations.

This chapter is based on recent research into the production of ethnic minority programming, that is, programming made by, for and about ethnic minorities by programme makers working inside the BBC and outside in the community-based and commercial independent sectors (Cottle 1997, 1998). The findings presented here help account for the 'cultural containment' of ethnic minority programme production within both the public service and independent sectors of British television and identify a complex of dynamics and constraints that inhibit and constrain minority television production and output. This is so notwithstanding the 'positive' aims of multicultural programming in contrast, say, to news and other conflict-driven genres, public statements by various television institutions in support of multi-cultural programme aims, and even the best intentions of ethnic minority programme makers themselves. Despite the pressing need for enhanced multi-ethnic representation and the exchange of understanding both within and across different cultures (see Husband, this volume), ethnic minority programmes all too often fail to give robust representation to the diversity and difficulties of minority communities, cultures and identities. This research helps to illuminate why.

Inside the 'rock' of public service broadcasting: BBC producers

The BBC is often thought of as the bedrock or cornerstone of public service broadcasting; for ethnic minority producers working inside the BBC the metaphor of rock or stone, as we shall hear, can take on an entirely different meaning. The BBC has produced programmes aimed specifically at ethnic minority communities since 1965. Early programmes were produced by a special 'Immigrants Unit' and were designed to help integrate newly arrived Asian people into British society and act as a link with the Indian subcontinent through performances and interviews (Morar 1995). Programmes for the British African Caribbean population were first produced in 1992 with the setting up of the *Ebony* production office. The history of the separate, combined and, more recently, separate again BBC production arrangements for targeted Asian and African Caribbean programmes has proved controversial (Cottle 1998). Across the years early assimilationist aims and outlooks have given way to a more multiculturalist programming ethos. By the mid-1990s the managing editor of the Multicultural Programme Department, for example, claimed that his department was 'no longer simply a vehicle for educating ethnic minorities or a hammer with which to bludgeon society's racial problems' and that the department 'had the freedom to move in any direction and to encompass any genre it feels suitable' (Morar 1995: 8). This view seemingly bears out public statements of corporate intent:

> For many years, the BBC has been publicly committed to serve its ethnic minority audiences properly, both through targeted programmes and services and through fair representation in mainstream radio and television output.
>
> (BBC 1995: 163)

When examined close-up with the help of the producers involved, however, we find contrary to official BBC views disseminated in glossy brochures that the picture at the BBC is decidely less rosy. BBC reluctance to release any but the bluntest of data about its ethnic minority workforce, notwithstanding its own equal opportunities policy which, like all such policies, proves meaningless without adequate monitoring and means of verification, does not help to clarify matters. The latest data provided to the author by the BBC simply state that ethnic minority producers comprise 4 per cent of all producers though the situation is said to be moving towards the BBC's target of 8 per cent (Britain's ethnic minority population is currently 5.5 per cent). These data though 'promising' do not reveal, of course, the exact composition of different ethnic minorities or where they are found in the corporation hierarchy.

BBC conservatism and 'Byzantine bureaucracy'

The corporate context and programme making environment of the BBC, according to ethnic minority producers, is relatively exclusive, staid and unadventurous and populated predominantly by white, middle-class males. A senior producer describes:

> You're kind of dealing with very well established, white, male middle-class attitudes and you can feel you don't belong to that club. It's hard to break into it, and that's a major problem. And I would go so far as saying, that's not just a major problem for minorities, it's a major problem for white working-class people.
>
> (Producer/director)

Rigid bureaucratic structures also hinder the flow of communication and impact upon producers' capacity to innovate and push forward new programme ideas with confidence and a sense of institutional support.

> In the BBC you have such an intense sort of *Byzantine bureaucracy* in operation that it is deemed totally outrageous to pick up the phone to anyone who isn't your immediate superior because it is seen as disrespecting your head of department . . . As an executive producer I need to know what the person who is buying my programmes thinks of it, and I need to know what he's got in mind.
>
> (Executive producer)

Lack of communication, inhibited by 'Byzantine bureaucracy' and rigid hierarchy, is thus said to impact upon the commissioning process, with the programme producer forced, in the absence of engaged dialogue, to guess the latest senior decision maker's thinking on programme requirements.

Lingering racism, contrary to BBC equal opportunity objectives, though not felt to be widespread, nonetheless continues to be experienced in regard to technical support staff and this too impacts on production decisions and processes, prompting for example, use of technical services outside of the corporation.

> There's still a lot of institutionalized and underground racism, especially from technical staff . . . Personally, because of 'Producer Choice' I'm very glad that we can go outside. I don't want to go outside, I want to stay and cut all my items, to use BBC resources . . . But when you're faced with that situation.
>
> (Producer)

Generally, however, the problem confronting BBC producers is not that of crude racism but the prevailing corporate ethos of BBC conservatism inhibiting programme ideas, design and production.

> The major thing really is that air of defensiveness which creates conservatism which means when people [producers] jump up and down and they're excited about an idea that sounds a bit iffy, a damp sponge is applied, and they're told to calm down. That robs people of a lot of enthusiasm and again it's quite a demoralizing atmosphere to work in.
>
> (Executive producer)

Confronted by a corporate ethos of conservatism that inhibits producer creativity and innovation in matters of programme subject matter and form producers, understandably perhaps, develop a pragmatic response that safeguards personal survival and career prospects within the BBC.

> The most important thing for minority ethnic programme makers is to get a good job in television and don't worry too much about being part of something that you perhaps don't fully approve of . . . But you've got to stick in there doing enough to get up the greasy pole. Get the experience, bite your tongue and do what every other programme maker does which is get the experience under your belt. Then, when you've got pips on your shoulder, then you can start calling the tune. Obviously, try and make programmes you are proud of. Obviously, say your piece but don't feel you can carry the burden of representing your community on your shoulders because you can't, you can't, you won't survive.
>
> (Executive producer)

With increased exposure of the BBC to market forces, both externally and internally, BBC producers are not unlike independent producers discussed later – both are dependent upon programme commissioners or key gatekeepers who, in turn, it seems are compelled to commission programmes according to schedule priorities – priorities generally acknowledged to be increasingly market driven. As a producer explains, they have little option other than to provide what is thought to be expected of them.

> You're trying to find all the best ways of getting the commission, because it's become a market orientated programme making style; we no longer have a set budget to make whatever we want. It's no longer like that. It's like what do we bid for. It's like an auction where the Controller decides what he or she wants A, B, C and D. And if you've given them all E's you can forget it. So in all, I'm afraid that's what we call a market economy.
>
> (Producer/director)

BBC professionalism and cultural-politics

The corporate context and institutional position occupied by minority BBC producers generates a contradiction at the heart of professional practices and thinking. On the one hand, producers feel intensely the need to be perceived by their BBC colleagues as 'professional' producers and afforded the due status and opportunities that accompanies the production of high profile, high production value, 'mainstream' programmes. On the other hand, they also maintain that they alone have the specialist expertise, knowledge and contacts to make programmes deliberately targeted at the needs and interests of ethnic minority audiences. While no doubt some programmes can indeed fulfil this double mission, with programmes appealing to both minority ethnic and 'mainstream' audiences, it is also the case that some minority programmes, by definition, are unlikely to have less than 'mainstream' appeal – especially if broadcast in minority languages. In the corporate climate of BBC professionalism the pursuit of 'mainstream' appeal and professional status have become, however, deeply infused within the production culture of ethnic minority producers who struggle to overcome corporate marginalization as 'ghetto programme makers'.

> [The department's] first priority should be to make high class production value programmes which anyone in the media would be pleased to have made. That's the bottom line. If you don't make good programmes, we'll be seen as a ghetto, and we cannot afford that sort of label.
>
> (Producer/director)

In recent years the phrase 'the burden of representation' has been used to describe the situation of black film makers who, confronted with so few opportunities to create and produce films, feel that they must use each and every opportunity to 'represent' black interests and viewpoints and counter dominant mainstream images (Mercer 1994). This burden is often experienced as creatively constraining, if politically unavoidable, and places an inordinate pressure on producers to make ideologically engaged films – films expressly challenging, but also thereby constrained by, the terms of reference of dominant cultural representations. Interestingly, then, the producers interviewed at the BBC for the most part do not feel unduly weighed down by a felt 'burden of representation'; their corporate and professional circumstances do not permit, let alone encourage, an engaged and championing stance towards the contested terrain of 'race', ethnic minority cultures and identities. Their position is not entirely divorced from concerns of 'race', however.

> I think you have to be careful because there's a lot of ignorance. You don't want to compound the ignorance. You don't want to confirm people's worst suspicions. So you've got to do something to say, 'here's a problem' and find a way of contextualizing which doesn't make all the old ladies in middle England buy another bolt for their door because they think black people are coming to get them.
>
> (Executive producer)

This professional stance, pragmatic in the corporate context of the BBC, declines to champion in any explicit way a particular community politics other than a general 'middle-ground' (Kumar 1977) debunking of racist myths – a stance, in other words, directed principally outwards towards the wider white community. Producers seeking mainstream audiences and recognition as 'mainstream' producers are inevitably obliged to counter dominant myths and racist assumptions, and their programmes will be shaped accordingly. In all other respects, however, the producers are professionally disinclined to adopt a partisan or engaged position on the cultural politics of 'race' and proclaim a position of professional detachment and objectivity – always a useful strategy in warding off criticism from potential critics (Tuchman 1972) whether inside the BBC or without. Producers, for example, are wary of becoming too closely involved with a particular community and its representatives since this could be interpreted as compromising their claim to professionalism. This is important because the pursuit of professional detachment distances producers from those communities and groups who could otherwise serve to keep them in touch with, and to some extent accountable to, community interests.

Perhaps related to this stance of 'professional detachment' some BBC producers also entertain a very wide view of 'multiculturalism' indeed or, to turn it around, a less than committed stance to any one community group, minority faction *or* informing politics. In-house producers express interest in pushing beyond the conventional BBC identification of multiculturalism as more or less confined to Asian and African Caribbean groups and cultures. This position, though laudable as a generalized future multicultural aim, fails to acknowledge the particular circumstances and conditions of existence of many Asian and African Caribbean minorities. The term 'minority', after all, is not simply a numerical designation but refers to imbalances of economic, political and social power – inequalities often forged in relation to a colonial past, diaspora histories, and contemporary patterns of disadvantage, discrimination *and* unfair access to the means of cultural representation. Multicultural television has to pursue more than a celebration of difference if it is to engage with the lived experiences of minority groups. Many of the producers interviewed nonetheless appear to entertain a view of *multicultural equivalence*, where the imbalances above are rendered more or less invisible in a celebratory pursuit of 'multiculturalism'.

Programme conservatism and community difference

For BBC producers the cultural politics of multiculturalism is not simply an abstract idea but is also, fundamentally, a practical affair. How they respond practically to complexly differentiated, ethnic minority communities and interests also shapes the nature of their programme output – often in the most decisive of ways.

> I just feel sometimes that we cop out and that we water down, we are just not aggressive, perhaps that's the wrong word, but we're just not progressive in exploring the issues facing our community purely because we are scared of the backlash we would face . . . And also, you know, we work for the BBC as well. We have to be very careful.
>
> (Producer)

Here the producer states clearly how programme design is informed by a certain timidity in anticipation of potential reaction both from the minority audience and the BBC itself. Problems are also encountered, however, in relation to the differentiated and sometimes factionalized nature of ethnic minority communities. While community complexity helps fragment any lingering sense of the 'burden of representation' by dispersing obligations across a wide range of community groups and factions – so many in fact that it may prove unrealistic to entertain expectations that they could all find adequate representation – community complexity and differences also present producers with a challenge, especially if some communities are more geared up to the ways of the media than others.

> The key problem is breaking down the Asian community within itself. I think the Muslim community, especially the Bengali and to some extent the Sri Lankan community, feel they have really been left out. They feel it's dominated by Hindi/Indian against Pakistani/Muslim. I have to admit last year's *Network East*, though we tried to balance out Hindi or Islamic/non-Islamic stories, when it comes to doing stories about the Bengali community in this country, there are very few stories there. The Bangladeshi community are not experienced in dealing with the media.
>
> (Producer/director)

Not only are there complex differences of religion, language and region of family origin to address, but also there are generational differences and continuing political animosities – animosities the producers decide, pragmatically, to ignore.

> So we've always been very, very careful, especially in our coverage of Muslim/Pakistani affairs because of the trouble it can lead to. For example, with our editor and our department, we feel we can't cover specific religious events. The reason being that if we covered one which falls in our programme span which is October to December, how do we cover Ede which falls in April when we're not on air?
>
> (Assistant producer)

Here we see how lack of overall programme volume, measured in terms of seasonal programming, plays a part in the BBC programme silence that attends certain festivals or major events that occur outside of ethnic minority programme seasons. A graphic example of this concerns how the disorders in Bradford involving Asian youths were covered only by mainstream news programmes (driven by news values) and not by any of the producers' (more knowledgeable) ethnic minority programmes, since they were off air at that point in the year. And we have already heard how producers' concerns about possible audience *and* corporate reactions to programmes about 'difficult' subjects also curbs their willingness to represent these. This response can be interpreted as professionally pragmatic when contextualized within the corporate environment of BBC conservatism already described.

Perhaps it is no surprise, then, that producers often experience a less than enthusiastic response from minority communities and groups when seeking to involve them in their programmes. The reputation of the BBC, which normally proves useful to producers in 'opening doors', gaining interviews and securing programme information and insights, clearly cannot be relied upon when it comes to the production of ethnic minority programmes.

> It means that you don't walk into a room and when you say BBC everyone's eyes light up and they go, 'Oh brilliant you've come to make some programmes!' They say, 'Oh, the BBC. What do they want?' . . . And so it takes persuading.
>
> (Executive producer)

If we are to move beyond the colourful but safe 'steel bands, saris and samosas' approach to multiculturalism and engage with some of the tough issues confronting our multi-ethnic society, institutions like the BBC must provide a programme making environment where programmes have teeth, and where programme makers are not afraid to make them bite. Unfortunately, as we have heard, the confluence of competitive, corporate *and* professional forces currently at work in the BBC – the 'rock' of public service broadcasting – today combine to undermine the production of politically engaged, culturally challenging representations. Perhaps independent producers, as the name implies, fare better?

Making programmes in a 'hard place': independent producers

This second discussion turns, with the help of independent ethnic minority producers, to an examination of community-based and commercial production companies and their experiences of television production. Given the highly fluid nature of independent production and organisations, whether commercial and/or community-based as well as the regrettable lack of monitoring by bodies such as, for example, the Producers' Alliance for Cinema and Television (PACT), Channel Four or the Independent Television Commission (ICT) again it is difficult to determine the numbers of ethnic minority producers involved. At the time of the research over 600 independent production companies were officially listed (Peak and Fisher 1996) though these do not indicate how many or to what extent production companies are involved in the production of programmes aimed specifically at ethnic minorities. Producers working in the field and interviewed for this research estimate, however, that a handful of production companies at most are regularly involved in the production of such programming, though new and

aspiring independents working in and around community-based organisations are more numerous (and transitory).

Little has been published about the production of minority ethnic television, though an area of related interest concerns the black independent
film and video sector of the 1980s and the work of a number of high-profile
collectives and workshops including *Sakofa Film and Video, Black Audio
Film Collective* and *Ceddo Film and Video.* This vibrant black cultural
development, subsidized for a short period by, among others, Channel Four
and the British Film Institute, produced politically engaged and often experi-
mental and innovative films, which unleashed academic and theoretical
reflection on the distinctive aesthetics and politics of these black films (Hall
1988; Mercer 1988, 1994; Snead 1994). In the 1990s the erosion of public
subsidies and grants, as well as changing television funding and general logic
of the marketplace, however, all appear to have taken their toll (Keighron
and Walker 1994).

Today minority ethnic producers based in independent commercial and
community-based enterprises confront a situation characterized by limited
funding opportunities and a television industry increasingly led by market
logic. The director of a small production company that has successfully produced BBC dramas in the past indicates perhaps the key dilemma that must
be grappled with.

> We have to come up with mainstream ideas that reflect our reality and
> it isn't being done at the moment. That is why I say it is quite a serious
> thing – I mean nobody is giving us pocket money to make ghetto pro-
> grammes any more, and anyway I don't want that. The only thing you
> can do is compete with the mainstream.
>
> (Producer/director)

Established commercial producers, understandably perhaps, develop a pragmatic stance; they have to produce programmes for the 'mainstream' if they
are to survive commercially, while nonetheless seeking to minimize the
extent to which creative programme ideas are compromised. Through force
of commercial circumstance the professional focus here tends to look
inwards to the survival needs of the independent company itself while nevertheless trying to hold on to distinctive cultural aims.

A more outward looking stance, informed by collectivist ideals, characterizes many less well-established, 'community-based' independents.

> It's difficult for black people to break into the larger organizations like
> the BBC, like ITV. If we're given the opportunity to develop ideas here
> and get them shown on the small screen or in the Arts cinemas then I

think that's a way forward. The initial reason why this project came about was through training . . . we are still committed to giving people the opportunity to train, learning about the business, about the industry.

(Coordinator)

Here concerns of 'representation' extend beyond the pursuit of programmes that 'reflect our reality' to increasing access to the world of television and production via training. A more explicit cultural-political agenda and commitment also informs many of the community-based independents.

Our broad aims are to raise people's confidence who we involve in making these programmes with us and to develop skills, media skills, and also to get people to question, not to accept the white media that comes in at every pore, and try to empower people.

(Artistic director)

My aims in this company are to reach out to minority, to help minority groups to see themselves as important, to give them some form of self-esteem and self-worth, to help them fit in within society, and make positive role models. In the long run it is mainly to develop self-esteem and self-worth in these minority groups.

(Producer)

A stated aim across many community-based organizations, then, is to enhance the confidence of minority ethnic individuals *and* communities in order to increase access to, and active participation in, media production – a view that for some appears to be grounded in the idea that the problem is one of lack of self-esteem or self-worth. While some community independents seek to counter dominant white media views that stigmatize and racialize minority communities with the production of 'positive' images, others entertain a more differentiated approach to the complexities of minority ethnic communities, experiences and the politics of representation.

Our aims are to treat these black kids, young people with the understanding that they themselves are contributors to society . . . to show them that they are not all thieves and drug pushers and liars and persons who would steal cars, or the aggressors, the oppressors, the inferiors – no, they are somebody, a person.

(Producer)

All I can do as a black producer, or a black director, or a black artist is do what I think is truthful to my experience. The essence of a rich culture will be enormous diversity – as much diversity as there are individuals to express a vision.

(Producer/director)

A sense of being part of a 'community' and responsive to shared problems is probably easier to sustain by newly formed, locally based and small-scale production companies than established companies producing programmes aimed at national television audiences. That said, claims to 'represent the community' by small independent collectives are equally hard to verify – which is not to deny statements of genuine commitment nor their sense of moral grievance and solidarity with 'their' communities. More tangible here is the evident concern with television 'representation' – in the double sense of enhancing access both on and behind screen – that provides the *raison d'être* for most community-based organizations, a line of continuity that stretches back to the black workshop movement of the 1980s.

Cultural-politics and the 'burden of representation'

Reference has already been made to the 'burden of representation' often said to be felt/experienced by minority cultural producers. Here, however, the producers themselves need not always experience this as a 'burden' if, for example, they themselves identify with the need to counter dominant images and see this as the political *raison d'être* of their practice.

So I think as a film and video producer, black people recognize that I've got an important tool in my hand to make a change. And black people know that the kind of shit that they see on TV is not them at all, so they expect me, as a producer, to produce accurate documentary programmes to dispel all the rubbish that is put out about us.

(Director)

Other producers, however, undoubtedly feel the 'burden of representation' and point to a double-sided complexity involved.

The problem with the burden of representation is that it comes from both sides. You get it from the black community and you get it from out there, from people who are not black. They already have a whole load of preconceptions, preconceptions about who you are and what you're going to say . . . You know, it really, really worries them, especially among white commissioning editors, or the power structures that give money for production to happen . . . If as a black film maker I want to

make a film that has no black subject in it at all, they will look at me
and they will defy my capability to do so.

(Producer)

This provides an unusual insight into the so-called 'burden of representation' drawing attention to the pressures and expectations placed upon
black film makers and programme makers by white commissioners, an
aspect explored further below. The producer next outlines what he experiences as the other side of the 'burden of representation', as exerted by the
black community.

> On the other side, in the black community, there is a burden about posi-
> tive representation. You're not allowed to be just a film maker. If some-
> body feels that within the film the representations of black people are
> not good, they will use that to beat you over the head with . . . So, much
> of the work can really run into trouble with the black community even
> though so much of the work is up-front politically, up-front about chal-
> lenging these assumptions within the narrative structures, within the
> visual language.
>
> (Producer)

The producer's reference to 'challenging assumptions' within the 'narrative
structures' and 'visual language' of television points to the complexities of
representation and the difficulties encountered from members of the black
audience when seeking to move beyond simple oppositions of 'negative' and
'positive' images – audience expectations may, according to this account, lag
behind the creative intentions of programme makers in matters of form as
much as political content, creating further difficulties for the cultural producer.

Structural disadvantages of scale, funding and location

Independent producers, whether community based or commercial, confront
not only the competing cultural-politics and communities expectations but
also, of course, practical difficulties. Unlike producers at the BBC, however,
these principally relate to organizational scale, funding and location.

> It is always difficult for small companies because you tend to be funded
> on a project by project basis and there is the danger that because the
> production fee is being squeezed by certain large organizations, you
> haven't enough money to survive in between times; you are always on
> the basis of putting all your energies into getting one production going

> . . . A lot of companies are very tiny, like myself, and that makes it very difficult to survive.
>
> (Director/producer)

Small companies that cannot benefit from the efficiencies of scale and the specialist division of labour enjoyed by the large production companies now dominating the independent production sector are at an obvious disadvantage by virtue of their size alone. The general squeeze on production fees also impacts more heavily on small independents; whereas the bigger companies can aim to stagger production and commission bids in a constant flow, cross-subsidizing different projects, such flexibility is denied the small independent. They must also seek commissions in competition with other independents, many of whom may previously have been colleagues of the commissioning editors before setting up as independents, resulting in unfair so-called 'sweet-heart' deals.

Funding from grant awarding bodies has also become increasingly tight across recent years as mentioned earlier. Moreover, seeking out funding from grant awarding agencies and institutions often places the receiving organization in a double-bind. When funding, as is often the case, is only partial other sources of finance, including commercial revenue, have to be sought. This, however, can then jeopardize continuing support from the grant awarding bodies.

> Should we be so reliant on these organizations [the Regional Arts Board, local authority] to actually keep us going, or should we be more reliant on ourselves in developing projects that can be commissioned, developing ideas and touting our own business instead of being reliant on these people? But then again, if you start doing that, they look at you and say, 'Oh, these guys are making money on their own, so we've got to cut this umbilical cord that we have with you and you've got to deal with it on your own.'
>
> (Coordinator)

The television industry's commercial focus in London also causes independents based elsewhere difficulties in terms of access to funding, networks and programme commissioners.

> I think nothing exists outside of London when it comes to film and video. Really and truly. It's just the way it runs. If you live in London you tend to get more access to funds. London is where it's at. Everywhere else is kind of slightly provincial and slightly not really happening . . . Wherever I went, people automatically assumed I was from London.
>
> (Producer)

Commissioners and programme deals

Independent producers seeking programme commissions are, of course, dependent upon commissioners and senior corporate decision makers. These gatekeepers occupy a pivotal role in determining which programme proposals get considered, developed and made, and those which do not. They also respond to the surrounding forces of competition and must deliver programme schedules in line with corporate market aims. Some of the institutional hurdles confronting the would-be programme maker seeking a commission are spelled out as follows:

> The nature of the way the commissioning happens in the TV industry: they don't have the capacity to see everybody. They tend to go with the people that they know and people that they know can deliver the products. At the end of the day they are on a commercial footing so they have to think about those things . . . The mechanisms by which you can begin to try and unlock the doors are skills that have to be learnt. There's all this language that has to be learnt to begin to talk with the Arts Council and to talk to people like the BFI [British Film Institute]. You have to learn a certain language to do that. Some of the organizations like the BBC or the BFI, it's like you have to understand how their system works and you have to sus out what kinds of things to say, you know it's their buttons that you have to push and they're not really that interested in what you've got to say or your films. It's becoming so slot driven these days: you've a great film but no one's going to make it unless it fits in with their slots. They're just not going to make it.
>
> (Producer)

Entry into the world of commissions evidently is not a straightforward matter. It's highly competitive, commercially informed (if not driven), and it involves established networks. It also requires the acquisition of a new language, the language of television deals based upon a knowledge of how television commissioning works and the sorts of things the commissioning institution is interested in, particularly in relation to predetermined schedule slots. As the producer says, these are considerable skills, skills that the experienced practitioner may more readily be able to deploy than the inexperienced newcomer. And, as we have heard above, it is not simply a matter of experience alone; considerations of company scale come into play, as can established networks informed by tried and trusted professional relationships. In all these ways, then, independent producers whether working in community-based independents or commercial production companies, inhabit a 'hard place' and must negotiate a combination of formidable obstacles in their efforts to make challenging, and innovative television programmes.

Conclusion

The above paints a depressing picture of the state of ethnic minority television production in Britain and the forces that currently combine to 'culturally contain' this. Producers working inside the BBC daily confront a corporate context and programme making environment that constrains their programme practices and output. Marginalized within the corporation, as we have heard, producers pragmatically adopt the mantle of BBC 'professionalism' – a disinterested programme-making stance that disengages from the surrounding field of 'race' and minority ethnicity and which seeks to avoid community backlash and corporate censure by avoiding 'difficult' issues. Independent producers, both community based and commercial, are no less subject to conditioning forces than BBC producers; here, however, an array of forces serve to marginalize and contain programme ambitions in line with commercial institutional requirements and the programme commissioners' schedule priorities and available 'slots'. In both production arenas, then, the cultural-politics of representation has in fact been subject to, and deeply conditioned by, the 'mediating' forces of the marketplace, institutional culture and professional and producer practices. When politically and culturally engaged 'multicultural' programmes are made and shown on British televison, as occasionally happens, this is indeed then a testimony to the creative energies, determination and tenacity of the producers concerned and cannot be interpreted as indicating everything is rosy in the television garden. Behind the screens, as we have heard, BBC producers and independent producers confront, respectively, 'a rock' and 'a hard place'.

Acknowledgements

This chapter draws upon research conducted under the Ethnic Minorities and Television Research Programme directed by Professor J.D. Halloran at the Centre for Mass Communication Research, University of Leicester, supported by Leverhulme and Channel Four. Interviews for the BBC part of the study took place at the Multicultural Programme Department, Pebble Mill Studios, Birmingham in October 1995, and involved an executive producer, producer/director, producer, assistant producer, two programme researchers and a trainee researcher. Interviews with independent producers were conducted in late 1995 and early 1996 by myself and my colleague Patrick Ismond and involved the following community-based and commercial organizations: Black Pyramid, Black Scorpio, Hall Place Studios, Indigo Productions, New Image, Non-Aligned Communications, Orchid Productions, Truth, Light, Action, and Wave Nation. Sincere thanks to all the above.

Further reading

Cottle, S. (1993) *TV News, Urban Conflict and the Inner City*. Leicester: Leicester University Press.

Cottle, S. (1997) *Television and Ethnic Minorities: Producers' Perspectives*. Aldershot: Avebury.

Frachon, C. and Vargaftig, M. (eds) (1995) *European Television*. London: John Libbey.

Givanni, J. (ed.) (1995) *Remote Control*. London: British Film Institute.

Hussein, A. (1994) Market forces and the marginalization of Black film and video production in the United Kingdom, in C. Husband (ed.) *A Richer Vision*. London: John Libbey.

Ismond, P. (1997) From Asia vision to Asia net, in S. Cottle *Television and Ethnic Minorities: Producers' Perspectives*. Aldershot: Avebury. pp. 167–92.

BLACK REPRESENTATION IN THE POST NETWORK, POST CIVIL RIGHTS WORLD OF GLOBAL MEDIA
Herman Gray

Introduction

Much about the world of American network television has changed in the years since I completed *Watching Race* (Gray 1995). I ended *Watching Race* with the 1992 television season. Although I was disappointed with the cancellation of several of my favourite programmes, I remained hopeful about the prospect of black representations on American network television. Black-oriented shows like *The Cosby Show* and *It's a Different World* moved from premiere network schedules to the financially lucrative world of reruns and syndication. Although a perceptible shift from a focus on the middle class to urban youth appeared for a while, they were replaced in the network schedule with black shows preoccupied with domestic families, parenting, and social relationships. Fox Television continued its quest for legitimacy and financial profitability with black shows like *New York Under Cover* and a staple of hip-hop youth oriented comedies.

Two new networks – Warner Brothers (WB) and Paramount (UPN) – joined Fox in challenging the dominance of the three major networks. To do so the new networks used black-oriented programming to anchor their evening schedule. This use of black-oriented comedies to get a scheduling toehold in a network's formative years continues the programming strategy that the Fox News Corporation used in its formative years. With the least to lose financially and reputationally, Fox Television took greater (aesthetic and marketing) risks by pursuing urban and youth audiences interested in black-oriented programming (Zook 1994; Gray 1995; Watkins 1998). Today new networks like Warner Brothers and Paramount operate in an environment transformed by cable and satellite delivery systems and niche marketing (Burrough and Master 1997; Sterngold 1998b).

By 1997 black cast and black theme oriented shows were still confined largely to the genre of situation comedy and entertainment variety. The major networks scheduled a mixture of night-time drama featuring black lead characters. These included *NYPD Blue*, *ER*, *Law and Order*, *Chicago Hope*, *Homicide: Life on the Street*, *Touched By an Angel*, *413 Hope Street* and *Players*. The network also scheduled the usual fare of black-oriented situation comedies with identifiable black actors like Bill Cosby, Gregory Hines, LL Cool J and Jaleel White.

There is little news here. These developments are quite unremarkable. The network strategy of offering programmes that feature all black casts and themes accompanied by a smaller number of shows with a sprinkling of black cast members continue a pattern that began in the early 1970s following the urban rebellions of the previous decades. But I do remain curious, even intrigued by the excessive and persistent dwelling by journalists and some scholars on the ebb and flow of black television representations from season to season.

For instance, according to a 1998 *New York Times* piece, the prospect for black television representations seemed considerably more dismal than prior seasons (Sterngold 1998a). Indeed, it seems that the hour-long drama has finally delivered the goods by staging programmes with multiracial casts, devoting story-lines to complex depictions of black life, and locating such programmes in integrated workplace settings. Apparently this has not been the case for television's construction and representation of the intimate domestic spaces of home and family. For not only does the representations of blacks remain largely confined to the genre of situation comedy, but also there seems to be a general apprehension (if not outright fear) on the business side about the financial risks involved in pursuing racial crossover dreams. As interesting to me is the discursive frame through which journalists, critics, industry observers, network executives and television makers talk about television representations and race. The conventional wisdom seems to be that black and white television viewers like and watch different programmes. The financially risky and culturally pressing question is whether or not white viewers will watch shows about black life that feature predominately black casts?

The structural and financial circumstance of the US television industry continue to evolve including the fact that audiences are migrating in record numbers to other forms and sites of service delivery (Burrough and Masters 1997; *The Economist* 1997b). In such a context, the racial politics of audience composition, viewing preferences and financial risks articulated by the stability of data on the racial basis of audience preferences may well be the cultural expression of a crisis. In this instance television is the pre-eminent space of the public sphere. I want to suggest that this crisis is cultural and structural. That is, that the structural transformations in the global media industry are articulated culturally and that the racialization that structures audience preferences in US network television are expressive of the developments. Moreover I want to ponder what this circumstance means for black television programming and black media representations, both in terms of possibilities and limitations.

Black television representations are shaped by shifting conditions of possibility that include new global markets, larger and more powerful interlocking structures of ownership, newer and more complex relations between products and means of distribution and circulation, and less and less regulation by local, national and international governments. Among the most far-reaching and consequential transformations affecting American television are passage of the 1996 Telecommunications Act, the changes in corporate ownership of media conglomerates, the emerging structure and global reach of entertainment/media/information companies, and rapid advances in new technologies and programme delivery (Andrews 1996).

In the years since the close of the 1992 network television season (where the concluding episode of the year's most popular programme, *The Cosby Show*, was broadcast opposite news coverage of the flames of the Los Angeles rebellion), a new industrial logic has emerged. Within this logic, larger and often more nimble corporate entities have formed ensuring access to larger and larger capital resources that afford bigger and bigger shares of the global entertainment/information/communications market. Through joint ventures, buy-outs, mergers, and new investments, global companies like Fox, Warner, TCI and Microsoft have solidified their positions as global players. These companies acquired television stations, film studios, cable operations, satellites, publishing houses, record companies, theme parks and communications infrastructure. While remaining large complex bureaucratic organizations, these global media corporations are organized into smaller and more efficient administrative (and creative) units, designed to strategically and efficiently deploy precise methods to identify markets, generate products, control distribution, and move them anywhere on the globe. Larger and larger, yet nimble and more flexible administrative and financial units are structured to generate and distribute a diverse range of entertainment and information products. The goal is to establish greater access to and control of global markets.

In this new mediascape, distinctive creative, technological and financial entities and activities – computers, cinema, telephony, broadcasting, pub-lishing, satellite, theme parks, cable, music and electronics – are organized to form giant global media firms like TCI, Time Warner, Fox News Corpo-rations, Disney and Seagram. While this kind of reconfiguration was antici-pated in the late 1970s and early 1980s, one of the immediate political and legal factors that facilitated its realization was, of course, the passage of the 1996 Telecommunications Act (United States Government 1996). The Act restructured major aspects of the telecommunications industry. These included the scope of federal regulation and oversight, the size and compo-sition of firms, the assignment of broadcast frequencies for television, radio, and cellular telephones, the upper limit on the operation and ownership of broadcast stations, the control of delivery systems and the complementarity between various media technologies.

The 1996 Telecommunications Act sharply deregulated the telecommuni-cations industry. This gave major US corporations like Time Warner, Gen-eral Electric, Fox News Corporation, TCI, Microsoft, Seagram and Disney the green light to pursue mergers, joint ventures, new research and develop-ment, and worldwide expansion with the blessings (and supposed oversight) of the US Congress. So profound and far reaching was the 1996 Tele-communications Act that no aspect of American (and to a lesser extent global) telecommunications was left unaffected.

As the major corporate players acquire new properties, enter joint ven-tures, and otherwise pursue the globe as one giant market for media, infor-mation and entertainment newer more powerful and diverse corporate entities appear. Microsoft the computer software giant is suddenly in the television business, Fox News Corporation is in the sports and satellite busi-ness, General Electric is in the sports arena business and Time Warner owns news, cable, film, publishing and music entities (Auletta 1997). Television production companies, television stations, television networks and cable operations all represent components of these global media giants.

In the new environments of global media, companies must maintain con-sistent sources of content or software that can be moved efficiently through multiple delivery systems (such as computers, television sets, CD players or movie screens) aimed at markets across the globe. The technological dis-tinctions, organizational partitions and cultural meanings that once defined technologies, delivery systems or media are no longer meaningful in any pro-ductive sense. Media content moves just as easily from novel to cinema screen to television to video to theme park and programming (Davis 1997).With such a voracious demand for content to fill markets worldwide, telecommunications companies must contend with increasing production costs, greater consumer choices, and more varied delivery systems all of which are intended to exert control over production, distribution, and markets.

Through joint ventures, multiple ownership (TCI for instance owns controlling interests in the black cable network operation Black Entertainment Television) and cooperative development agreements covering hardware and software, the major corporations extended their control (Auletta 1997). As consumers we experience these forms of control at the point of our most familiar and mundane encounters with the telephone receiver, the cable box, the computer screen and the television set.

Where have all the black shows gone?

The 1997 autumn season of American network television indicates a pattern with regard to black television representation. In the autumn television schedule, black television shows are still present, however they are concentrated largely among the programme offerings of the newest television networks. They were also mainly situation comedies. Of the six commercial television networks, Warner Brothers (WB), Paramount (UPN) and Fox News Corporation (Fox) have a combined total of sixteen shows that can be identified as black or black oriented prime time programmes. Of the traditional majors, CBS programmed three and NBC one. ABC did not schedule a single black show for the 1997 season. Fox scheduled three (including the only night-time drama), WB scheduled four and UPN placed a total of five shows on its autumn schedule. Most of the scheduled programmes are returning from the previous several seasons; of these the most popular and well known black show on Fox is *Living Single* starring Queen Latifah. *Living single* was initially cancelled, but quickly revived by Fox after a successful letter writing campaign by the show's fans. The often-controversial *Martin* and the popular *New York Undercover* were not renewed for the 1997 Fox line-up.

In addition to Queen Latifah, familiar stars like Bill Cosby, the members of the Wayans family, Jamie Fox, Brandy (Moesha), Steve Harvey, Jaleel White and Malcolm Jamaal Warner all returned to the prime time television schedule. It should come as no surprise that situation comedy is the dominant genre and households and workplaces are the dominant setting for shows this season. Stories about adolescent maturation, relationships, friendships and room-mates provide continuing story-lines and narrative action. This season's televisual black Americans are drawn largely from the middle and working classes and it includes both students and retirees who range in ages from small children to elders. Characters live in various domestic arrangements including extended families, shared living spaces, marriages and nuclear families. All of the situation comedies fall within the predictable conventions of the genre – medium shots, light-hearted dramas, everyday difficulties and relationship tensions. These genre conventions move characters through predictable experiences and situations that provide momentary transformation. The action and emotional cues are pumped up and pushed along with laughter provided by enthusiastic studio audiences and laugh tracks. Contemporary music, fashion, language and information give the shows the feel of being steeped in contemporary urban black popular culture and style that is made explicit with regular guest appearances by entertainers and athletes. Recognizable figures – mostly athletes and musicians – regularly find their way to the small screen. Similarly former television personalities like Will Smith (*Fresh Prince of Bel Air*) and Martin Lawrence (*Martin*) have moved from the weekly grind of sustaining a weekly series to the more lucrative world of film.

While not particularly remarkable aesthetically, the fact is that these shows help blacks to sustain a presence, albeit separate, in the media-scape of American network television. This stubborn separate (and not always equal) racial representation on American commercial network television remains the source of continuing frustration and concern, especially on the part of media activists, journalists and scholars. Upon closer inspection it is apparent that the most integrated casts and story-lines take place on hour-long dramatic programmes like *ER*, *Homicide* and *NYPD Blue*. These shows are often set in the public spaces of work. However, the genre of situation comedy – long associated with intimacy, family, romance and domesticity – is a site of some of the most benign but persistent segregation in American public culture.

Furthermore, while the television industry continue to maintain what many see as a minimal commitment to black presence on commercial network television, the shows that do survive are located, least structurally anyway, in the least risky part of the network schedule (and the low investment sector of corporation). WB, UPN and Fox – all among the newest networks – use the principle of narrow-casting and the strategy of niche marketing to target their start-up markets: youth. Even though ABC, NBC and CBS still enjoy a considerable share of the commercial television market, when cable and the new networks are factored in the traditional network share is below 50 per cent. Traditional networks like NBC have also adopted niche marketing strategies by positioning their operations as name brands that appeal to white middle-class professionals with shows like *Friends*, *Seinfeld*, *Frasier*, *Cybil*, *Suddenly Susan*, *Third Rock from the Sun*, *ER* and *NYPD Blue*. As with cable, the newest networks have made the greatest inroads into the traditional network share by targeting youth and urban markets. That is, these new networks pursue such programming strategies until they establish a logo or product identity with advertisers and key sectors of their market.

From the culture of the television business and financial interests of media corporations, what appears on the social and political radar as segregation and containment of black shows, may, be the articulation of the new industry logic. Since the television environment is no longer dominated by three major networks, the force of various new delivery systems, global media operations and marketing clutter is felt ever more immediately and directly. This means that in order to remain competitive, television programmers must be more focused, efficient and explicit about their audiences, their programmes, and their so-called product identity. Despite their claims to the contrary, to remain competitive networks long ago abandoned the strategy of aiming the least objectionable programmes at the widest possible audiences. Cable operators, upstart networks and some majors have made explicit marketing decisions to use programming to target and reach various demographics. Black shows may not be contained so much as they are developed and deployed by networks to gain a specific market advantage in an increasingly cluttered schedule.

This segmented programming strategy suggests that Fox, UPN and WB are modelled explicitly after cable (Carter 1998; New York Times Magazine 1998). Together with cable the modest success of the new networks in such a short period is helping to reshape the scheduling, marketing and programming of the US television industry. These operations are after smaller, more sharply defined demographics. They schedule relatively inexpensive shows (including reruns, films, game shows and reality programmes) with identifiable stars and personalities. They combine various forms of programming and service delivery including cable wire, the traditional broadcast signal and satellite service.

The cultural politics of black representation

These powerful structuring conditions are constitutive and productive. They are structuring forces expressed culturally. But social choices and cultural frames saturate these structuring conditions. Cultural meanings shape the organization and use of media products and representations. Where black representations are concerned, therefore, the very conception of a black show or black programming (even as an expression of local, regional and national sensibilities and identities) must be theorized in relationship to these structuring conditions and cultural meanings. Given these circumstances, black television makers and programmers face the very real prospect that the circuits, meaning(s) and uses of blackness are accelerated and more dispersed than ever before. (The sign of blackness as always circulated discursively, historically and geographically.) Moreover black American intellectuals and cultural workers have always exercised, to the extent possible, a measure of control over how and what blackness signified. In light of the new technologies, sophisticated means of circulation and reconfigured systems of production, the contemporary challenge is not just to consider the narrative of assimilation versus separation of black Americans in network television, but how blackness means, what it means and where.

Just what exactly is a black programme and what does it signify? Discursively the emphasis on the local conditions of production, the specific social circumstances in which they are received and the particular cultural meaning that they express will continue to shape what such representations mean in the US. Its encounter with and circulation in the new global media environment will mediate the cultural meanings of blackness. I still want to insist on the cultural significance and historical specificity of black television programming that emanates from the US. The cultural significance of black images generated from the US rests with how they function as cultural sites for the articulation of specific meanings, relations, histories and struggles. At the same time the significance of this programming can no longer just be limited to local and specific meanings and politics in the US. Programming constraints (especially American commercial networks) shapes these very local and particular meanings and cultural encounters that are neither local nor specific to the US. It is very clear that American network executives remain deeply ambivalent and suspicious of black shows to do any more than generate short-term profits in US television markets. But new technologies or exhibition, circulation, and delivery make it possible to broaden the field of vision and play for the first time.

Now (black) programme makers and buyers can ask, for perhaps the first time, how will black television programming play in the distant reaches of the vast corporate marketplace made possible by satellite, cable, the Internet and other forms of global delivery? Will the demands of distant markets rob locally based black programming of its specificity and historicity? Is the prerequisite for black television shows (and cinemas) that they travel well? That they speak in a universal language? And if so, what is that language(s) and what is the embodied representation(s) through which it is expressed? Is it the naturalized (racialized) athletic and dancing black body? Perhaps it is the body endowed with musical prowess? Is it the black corporal body of liberal civil rights? Perhaps it is the neo-nationalist sub-ject of hip-hop discourse? As the American television experience seems to suggest, the desire for blackness articulated in the public spaces of inte-grated workplaces is preferable to that which threatens the intimate spaces of the family and domesticity. This narrative is, of course, a very old story in the American racial imagination.

Shows that finally make it to a network schedule (or a cine-plex screen) now more than ever are required by the structure of new corporate owners, delivery systems and global markets to speak in a universal language recog-nizable across (or perhaps through) the particularities of history, circum-stance, experience and geography. Black shows now mean in relation to a rapidly changing political and cultural field of finance, production, exhi-bition and circulation of media software that includes sports, film, music, games, fashion and style. The travels of media representations of blackness also provides an occasion to grapple directly with the role of media and tele-vision in the cultural production of the US as a structured racial and national formation. The meanings, pleasures and identifications we generate from black television representations, no matter where and how it travels, still bear the perceptible traces of the specifically American circumstance in which blackness is constructed and operates.

Black representation and the post-civil rights public sphere

While liberal journalistic discourses about segregation and integration, crossover and separation persist in the US, the shifting global media environ-ment may well provide the occasion for asking a different kind of question about the racial politics of American network television and its program-ming practices. They may present the opportunity for making sense of tele-vision's representations and audience reception patterns as the expression of the breakdown even irrelevance of a conception of (a mass mediated) public sphere organized by the discourse of civil rights. The persistence of racial-ized programming patterns and viewing preference may well suggest the presence of a post-civil rights public sphere (Lipsitz 1994).

The new logic of television broadcasting in the US may well have two seemingly contradictory social implications for television representations of blackness. In purely economic and marketing terms television shows about blacks will continue to appeal to (network) programmers to the extent that they can compliment and heighten the product identification of their pro-grammer (networks). This means that as traditional network identities – expressed through their logos and stable of programmes on a given evening, across the schedule and throughout the season – become more focused and explicit the defining market characteristics and aesthetic parameters of a network will drive the demand for programmes. The genre, star power, programme conventions and scheduling strategies cannot help but remain constraining as they continue to guide programme suppliers. While it may well fulfil demand within identifiable genres designed to attract a particular market niche, this strategy, developed to reduce market uncertainty, will mean that the programme offerings that do manage to find their way to a networks programme schedule will remain safe and conventional. As buyers and schedulers of programmes, network executives continue, indirectly at least, to shape the range, look, content and style of a show that it seeks to programme. All of this is with the explicit aim of matching advertisers with the ears and eyes of those guaranteed by the networks.

A broader range of service delivery options and the rising importance of television programmes as sources of product identity for global media companies may well mean greater possibilities for black and minority representations to circulate more widely within and across various market niches. Indeed, a stable and persistent finding in the US indicates that blacks and whites like and view different programmes (Sterngold 1998a). Black oriented programming that enjoys wide reception in black households, seldom if ever register with white viewers. As I have already noted, rather than see or read this finding as a failure of the ideal of integration in the post-civil rights public sphere, perhaps the finding can be read as an opportunity to register black tastes, interests and pleasures. The real question is whether or not programme makers and buyers will respond to these expressions of tastes and preferences. Though the range of difference within a given market niche will perhaps be reduced, the proliferation of niches – the 500 channel model touted for digital television – could mean more programming outlets for black film, video and television makers. (The hegemony of corporate control of television means that even with the proliferation of channels and new delivery systems, this proliferation may well mean that these 500 plus channels will look more alike than different.)

If this is true, then the most immediate implication is the appearance of programming that is driven less by the demand for intelligibility and relevance by broad audiences who may speak a given language or know the intimacies of a particular cultural experience. Though relatively small, the success of ethnic programming on low cable stations and low power operations is but one example. Story-lines, cultural assumptions and social context may be more directly assumed and thus easily negotiated under such conditions than those that presently exist. Politically this situation makes for some interesting possibilities for engaging memories, histories and stories that are particular and specific at the same time as they have global implications. Directed at specific audiences in particular places, such stories also require information and understandings rooted in identifications, loyalties and interests that transcend such specificity and particularity.

Of course imagining such possibilities for the new broadcast environment assumes that the global corporate entities remain open to identifying and serving such niches (and that they are profitable). Make no mistake about it, at this point American television broadcasting is a buyer's market. Giant entertainment/information/media companies control the libraries, film holdings, book lists and software around the world. With their vast financial resources and through their control of telephone lines, satellites, broadcast stations, publishing houses and software, there is little doubt but that they are the major purchasers and schedulers of programming content around the world.

Nonetheless, in the changing climate of global broadcasting, the logic that drives this global structure still must respond to and organize the uncertainty that still exists at the local level. Even as it continues to structure identifications and alliances that can be realized through the new technologies of communication, it can never completely discipline nor absolutely control such possibilities. Thus it would appear that blacks, Asians, Latinos, gays and lesbians can get a small toehold into an industry whose hallmark is packaging our desires and identifications. While it is true that the control which these global entities exercise over the programming options available to us all is increasingly hegemonic, in the end they must still be able to reach the eyes and ears of real people if they are to survive.

Conclusion

The immediate problem for black programme makers is no longer the challenge of making black programmes, they are available perhaps as never before. The problem of making a greater variety of programmes – and getting them to desirable audiences – may well be the more urgent challenge. In addition, negotiating the logic of the market as a terrain on which forms of community, identification and association are constructed and structured is as tricky as it is potentially productive. Programme makers will face the competing demands of generating programmes that speak to the specific concerns of particular and local markets. By the same token these programmes must travel to distant markets and audiences with different histories, traditions, languages and experiences. The meanings (and politics) of blackness will have to be negotiated with the terms of these competing aesthetic and economic demands.

How does one speak with confidence about what such shows mean and how, when the audiences and the markets they organize do not always share particular histories, identifications and experiences? To be sure, in a global media world such as ours, neither immediate experience nor shared identification is required for a given programme to produce meaning and pleasure. (Indeed, I suppose one might argue that our modern global media-scape itself – whether the Internet, cinema, music or satellite – constructs identifications and shared histories through its very existence.) However, representations, no matter where they circulate or how they are generated, are more than free floating signifiers cut loose from the social and historical mooring that make them intelligible in the first place. Though media representations do obviously mean at multiple levels and in different times and places, they continue to bear the traces of their conditions of production and the historicity of their time and place.

Further reading

Davis, S.G. (1997) *Spectacular Nature: Corporate Culture and the Sea World Experience.* Berkeley, CA: University of California Press.

Gray, H. (1995) *Watching Race: Television and the Struggle for 'Blackness'.* Minneapolis, MN: University of Minnesota Press.

Herman, E. and McChesney, R. (1997) *The Global Media: The New Missionaries of Corporate Capitalism.* London: Cassell.

Lipsitz, G. (1994) *Dangerous Cross Roads.* London: Verso.

Sreberny-Mohammadi, A., Winseck, D., McKenna, J. and Boyd-Barrett, O. (eds) (1998) *Media in Global Context.* London: Edward Arnold.

Part III
CHANGING CULTURES
OF IDENTITY

8

IN WHOSE IMAGE? TV CRITICISM AND BLACK MINORITY VIEWERS
Karen Ross

Introduction: research, 'race' and audience

Although two of the four main British television channels have discrete departments dedicated to producing and/or commissioning programmes for black minority viewers, the attitudes and beliefs of those putative viewers have never been canvassed in any systematic way.[1] Unlike in the US, where concern over the representation of non-white Americans (see, for example, Fisler and Lowenstein 1968; Brasch 1981; MacDonald 1992; Dates and Barlow 1994; Campbell 1995; Wilson and Gutierrez 1995; hooks 1996; Dennis and Pease 1997; Gandy 1998) provoked a number of studies into the views of minority communities (Fife 1987; Gray 1989, 1995; Ziegler and White 1990; Jhally and Lewis 1992), private and piecemeal public protest among black minority viewers in Britain has not been followed by institutional concern. The research project on which this chapter is based, therefore, represents an unprecedented exploration of a great diversity of black minority voices articulating a variety of views on the ways in which 'race' and ethnicity are represented, but whose views nonetheless cohere in consensus around a number of highly significant and important aspects of black minority representation. While black actors and performers have been given some space to articulate their views and experiences in the past (see, for example, Pines 1992), those of the more 'ordinary' black minority viewer have scarcely been listened to, let alone acted upon. It is thus precisely the fact that these viewers' opinions have *at last* been canvassed that makes the study on which this chapter is based so interesting and important – this *is* cutting edge.

This discussion takes as its starting point a straightforward acceptance that diversity in/and difference exists, as both rhetorical device and lived reality, and also acknowledges that audience and reception studies are valuable, meaningful and capable of providing considerable insights into the *collective* experience of 'groups' of viewers, as well as capturing individual actors' experiences and assumptions about their social worlds. In the past few years, work on the audience has seen a return to some of the more problematic aspects of audience effect, revisiting and challenging some of the old orthodoxies which have grown up around concepts such as involvement, negotiation and 'reading off'. In some ways, the reinvention of the 'couch potato' would seem to return us to early theories of viewer passivity, but the crucial difference now is that viewers are assumed to be much more sophisticated in their ability to read off meanings from televisual texts. Not for them/us an unthinking and uncritical ingestion of mass mediated products but rather a Pandora's Box of possible meanings, meanings moreover which we make, which we choose, depending on our own personal and individual textual reading, our own background, experiences and beliefs.

But in their zeal to promote the viewer as a fully autonomous being with total control over the production of meaning, what many of the new individual-centred models of the audience (see, for example, Corner 1995; Nightingale 1996; Reeves and Nass 1996; Croteau and Hoynes 1997; Edelstein 1997; Webster and Phalen 1997; Dickinson *et al.* 1998) tend to overlook is the way in which (some) real *audiences* (as opposed to media *theorists*) still believe that television sends out powerful messages whose meanings are accepted uncritically by most of their recipients. I am talking specifically here about black minority audiences in the context of white majority media and this chapter will consider the ways in which black minority viewers think about the image and presentation of their various selves on television, drawing on the findings of a qualitative research study carried out for the BBC in 1995.[2] It considers the way in which black minority audiences interact with television images and explores the perceptions which different black minorities hold towards televisual output.

Researching the audience

It is notoriously difficult, if not completely invidious, to try to identify 'representatives' of any group, let alone attempt to locate 'typical' black minority viewers; indeed, part of the explicit strategy of the study was precisely to explode the notion of a homogenous 'black' community and to speak instead of diverse and multiple identifications. The research team, together with the BBC, therefore decided to advertise for participants in the ethnic press (the *Voice* and the *Asian Times*), thus ensuring that respondents self-identified as fitting the criteria for inclusion – the advertisements called for 'black' and 'Asian' viewers to take part in a study about television and 'race'. In addition, we used census data to identify ten locations which had significant concentrations of Britain's predominant ethnic minority groups and were geographically spread and approximately 150 community groups and associations were contacted in these areas.[3]

These two recruitment strategies generated a sample of 353 people who were interviewed in 35 focus groups, mostly in England; one group of Chinese women were interviewed in Scotland. The ethnic mix of participants more or less reflected the demographic profile of Britain's black minority populations, with slightly more than half the sample claiming Indian, Pakistani or Bangladeshi backgrounds and slightly less than half claiming African, African Caribbean or other black African minority identities. The total sample was spread more or less evenly across all age ranges and employment categories, including individuals who identified as unemployed and 'housewife', but what united all these respondents was an interest in watching and talking about television.

Those individuals who initially responded to the invitations to participate in the study were asked if they would be willing to organize a local focus group who I would then go and interview; discussion groups were thus set up to run in a mix of community centres and private residences. All participants were paid to take part in the study, all completed a short questionnaire and most also kept a television diary for the seven days prior to the group discussions, which were tape-recorded. The combination of questionnaire, diary and taped interview yielded an abundant and rich data source, although such was the excitement with which television programmes were often discussed that the taped material was sometimes indecipherable with several people speaking at once. What follows is a discussion of the main findings of this study, together with some thoughts on how the reactions of black minority audiences towards television might be usefully incorporated into broadcasting policy in the future. It should be noted that although the study attempted to explore the views of different black minority audiences in order, *inter alia*, to challenge the hegemonic strategy of essentializing 'blackness', it has not been possible in a chapter of this length to give full expression to the diversity of black minority views. Thus my intention to give voice to the previously voiceless is somewhat undermined by the demands of brevity, and the distinctiveness of different voices has been unavoidably consolidated in order to explore those perspectives which most viewers *shared*. I note this here since it could be seen that I am pursuing a contradictory claim: on the one hand arguing against essentialism and on the other constructing an imaginary black 'collective'. However, the views that black minority media consumers share around portrayal issues are important and multiple and if this chapter seems to be saying apparently contradictory things because of the elision of those views, then it is still important for black minority viewers, albeit artificially constructed to comprise a single 'audience', to be heard.

Methodological reflections

Before discussing the principal findings from the audience study, I would like to spend a little time reflecting on the process and methods employed in the study, in an effort to problematize (without necessarily arriving at any hard and fast solutions) the conduct of cross-cultural research, of which this study is a good example. In particular, what lessons, if any, can be learnt which could inform similar research programmes in the future?

In many social policy contexts, black minority communities in Britain are, understandably, somewhat cynical and 'surveyed-out', as one team of researchers after another have attempted to find out what their lives are *really* like. Apart from questionnaire overload, individuals and communities have little positive to show for their good-natured participation in these studies, other than a growing certainty that nothing ever changes. There was therefore a strong desire, on the part of the research team, that the project should not offer what it could not deliver – for example, there could be no guarantee that the BBC's policy on 'race' and portrayal would change as a result of viewers' comments – but would be as unexploitative as possible.[4] To this end, we paid everyone to participate and we also recruited an African Caribbean and an Asian researcher to the project to co-facilitate some of the focus group discussions. Interestingly, when I contacted potential participants by telephone, no one thought to ask if I was black or white (I look 'Anglo' enough although I do not have a white European background) and my subsequent embodied appearance did cause some initial antagonism with some of the focus group participants who were very obviously expecting a black researcher to lead the discussion.

So, are there problems in general with carrying out cross-cultural research? The answer to this question is, as far as I am concerned, both 'yes' and 'no' and it is useful to note that at least researchers are beginning to ask this basic question (see Walton 1986; Larbalestier 1990; Bell 1994, 1996; Essed 1994; Edwards 1996; Russell 1996), largely as a result of much feminist scholarship which has looked at the racist assumptions inherent in much work which purports to relate to the condition of 'women', but which priv-ileges exclusively the experiences of *white* women (Lorde 1981; Carby 1982; Cannon *et al.* 1991; Luttrell 1992; Bhavnani and Phoenix 1994). The issue is, broadly, about who speaks for whom, with what right and in what voice? Describing the very particular situation of researching women subjects, Edwards (1996) asks (and answers) the question: 'Can, or should, white middle-class women academics, such as myself, research and represent in writing the voices of black, mainly working-class, women? For me, the ques-tion has always been another way round: can I possibly be justified in leav-ing them out?' (Edwards 1996: 168).

During the conduct of the study, I found myself thinking about how I would represent the views of participants without having to 'speak' for them but, ironically, found myself agreeing to 'tell the BBC what *we* think' on their behalf anyway. One of the perceived problems of white researchers working with black minority 'subjects' is the former's lack of understanding, empathy and sensitivity for the latter: white people can never experience 'being black'. While this is undoubtedly true, to pursue this argument to its logical end is to say that all researchers and all subjects must be identically matched for every possible characteristic in order for any authentic data to emerge, which is clearly nonsense (see Griffin 1996), not least because it sup-poses that there is an authentic and singular 'truth' out there to discover. What seems to be much *more* relevant in the cross-cultural research context is the ability of researchers to demonstrate their command of the subject and thus to allay the fears of participants that this is just another routine job. Speaking from my own experience of working with black minority viewers, what enabled interviews to progress well in sometimes hostile (at least initi-ally) circumstances was my comprehensive knowledge of the subject, not only in my own right but also in relation to the knowledge base of the vast majority of participants. That I was able to discuss fluently the various plot-lines involving black minority characters, the 'real' and fictional names of favourite soap stars and the titles and broadcast details of discontinued shows all contributed to my standing as an interested scholar for whom this was not just another job but who had a real enthusiasm for and knowledge of the topic and was willing to justify why she was involved in the work at all.

To push this point a little further and to suggest that matching ethnicities among researcher and subject does not guarantee a 'better' dataset (merely a different one), I would offer the following observation. Both the women researchers who were recruited to the project to co-facilitate some of the groups – an African Caribbean woman and a South Asian (Hindu) woman – had difficulties with the groups with which they were involved. 'Carol' has a degree and is of mixed parentage but was not 'black enough' for some of her subjects and was seen as a 'sell-out' and 'traitor to her race' because she straightened her hair and spoke with an educated accent. 'Parminder' spoke fluent Hindi and Gujerati but was pointedly ignored by the male members of the Asian groups she worked with. These are very crude analyses, admittedly, but the point I want to make is that *other* cross-cutting characteristics such as class, religion, gender and generation can and do have a significant affect on the outcome of interviewer–subject interactions, and that sharing, apparently, the same ethnic or 'racial' background is no guarantee of success. There is no easy answer to the almost inherent problem of how to avoid 'othering' one's research subjects by appropriating their voices and experiences even as we try and make them 'theirs', simply because we can speak and they cannot. But to acknowledge that tension is, at the very least, an important first step.

An audience with the viewers

The original research study covered viewers' attitudes towards both mainstream programming and specialist targeted shows for black minority viewers. However, space does not permit a discussion of all the findings so, for the sake of brevity, the remainder of this chapter will consider audience views on mainstream popular programming, where soaps and drama were the dominant genres which viewers discussed. In any case, very few viewers wanted to talk about minority broadcasting: what they *did* want to talk about were popular mainstream shows, especially soaps and dramas. A number of key themes emerged early on in the data collection stage which seemed to come up consistently and these emergent themes took on a stronger significance as each subsequent group generated the same issues and concerns. These can be broadly categorized as, in no particular order: racial/ethnic stereotyping; marginality of black minority characters; dominance of 'racism' themes when programmes feature black characters; cross-cultural relationships; and the impact of negative images on both white and black audiences.

The same old story: stereotyping 'race'

While most viewers in the study acknowledged that the current crop of black minority characters on TV were more favourable than those who were portrayed in less 'enlightened' British shows such as *Mixed Blessings* or *Love Thy Neighbour* (see Daniels 1990; Pines 1992; Ross 1996; Bourne 1998) there was still dissatisfaction with the range and largely stereotypical nature of many black minority characters, in particular their almost invisible presence in shows situated, geographically, where black minorities are highly visible in real life. For Asian audiences, there were considerable and strong differences of opinion over 'Asian' characters in soaps and the crucial variables at play seemed to be those of gender and generation, between older South Asian viewers who believe that characters are often too westernized and younger people who feel, on the contrary, that such characters represent more realistic portraits and show clearly the synergies between different cultural communities in more naturalistic ways. Gillespie's (1995) work with young Punjabis in London found exactly the same contradictions in play between her interviewees and their parents. Many of the younger South Asian participants liked watching soaps for precisely the reason that they could be used to rehearse possible strategies in their own lives, looking to soap narratives to gauge the bounds of 'acceptable' behaviour. Some mentioned wanting their parents to watch soaps with them so that they could understand some of the complexities of their own lives without having to raise them as actual personal problems. An example of these differences in perception is captured in the dialogic sequence set out below.

> I don't like those attitudes because programmes have very negative effects. We are Asian and our culture is very different and those stories go against our culture. In *EastEnders*, something happened to the Asian family which doesn't happen in all families and this might be an encouragement to teenagers. Television shouldn't show that because it is a medium which should be giving us good programmes with moral values.
>
> ('Shireen', Birmingham)

> With Gita and Sanjay, they are very westernized and we're nothing like that. They are trying to change us into westerners which we're not. They shouldn't do that. They should leave us to be ourselves. In that way, the message gets across to people that they have their ways and we have ours.
>
> ('Sula', Leicester)

> I think Gita and Sanjay are quite realistic. Their stories really describe what it's like. But Gita can be a bit dull sometimes.
>
> ('Sourayya', Birmingham)

Much of the criticism around black minority characters related to what viewers believe to be the lack of fit between the ethnicity of characters and that of writers, producers, editors and other members of programme production teams, as well as a more vaguely articulated view which could be loosely described as institutional racism. To put it rather crudely, if most people working in television are white, then there are necessarily going to be problems in developing credible black minority characters because productions will be shaped and informed by the cultural baggage of a colonial history and by writers' lack of experiencing black minority communities in real life.

> I think it's a bit sinister. People know how powerful the media are. They know how to send out subliminal messages, even through the simplest scenes on the telly. They know exactly what they're doing.
>
> ('Hyacinth', London)

> I cannot think of a single TV programme from this country where I have seen the major role taken by a black person and this is a problem. They use television in a racist, stereotypical way to keep our people down and flood us with sad and bad news.
>
> ('James', London)

Out at the margins and over the edge

There were a number of specific criticisms made about black minority characterizations, including that they are never properly integrated into the community they inhabit, are rarely perceived as realistic and are mostly peripheral to the main action. When the viewer *is* allowed a glimpse into a black character's home, there is rarely the signification of something alluding to an African or Asian background, no ornament or decoration or picture which suggests the personality of its incumbent, no signs of a provenance (or even contemporary reality) deriving from a place other than the normative cultural environment of 'white' Britain. What often irritated was a lack of 'cultural' authenticity, where Muslim characters had Hindu names or where a Caribbean elder was seen eating the 'wrong' food or where characters behaved in culturally inappropriate ways.

> Where's the Caribbean food, the rice and peas? They've got Jules Tavernier, the grandfather, eating beans on toast. They don't eat that in Trinidad.
>
> ('Shirley', London)

Many viewers argued that black minority characters are rarely shown with other members of their family so they are never allowed to develop as fully rounded characters: they are trapped in stereotypical roles, mostly invented by white writers, which do not reflect the diversity of black experiences.

Where are the black doctors, lawyers and accountants in small screen visions of black life? Where is *that* reality reflected? The exception to black minority characters' isolation is when an entire family is introduced into programme narratives, but even here they are never allowed to be an ordinary family, but must always be the *black* family. There is always something distinctive about them, something deviant and they are never allowed to stay very long.

> They [black minority characters] are always shown as extremes. A normal, everyday person is never shown. They produced an Asian drama [*Family Pride*] but hardly anyone lives that way or could have related to the characters. So one extreme is these very rich families who are very westernized and their lifestyles are completely different to reality. And then you have the other extreme, where people cannot speak English properly, or are always going on about arranged marriages.
>
> ('Farida', Birmingham)

There was a strong belief among participants in nearly all groups that writers simply have no idea about the lives of black minorities and have even less interest in finding out. It was often the case for these viewers that attention to detail was missing, for example, writing a part for a Hindu character and then showing her or him on their way to the mosque. Although it seems a small inaccuracy and highly unlikely to be understood by many white viewers, it signals among black minority audiences a disregard and disrespect for cultural veracity which in turn reflects the low value attached to the portrayal of authentic and credible black minority characters. For some viewers, though, being black was not essential to writing an authentic 'black' character: what was more important was their ability to write *well*.

There are at least three substantive issues to consider from the discussion above. One relates to cultural authenticity, one to memory and one to the constantly shifting television landscape. Debates over what is 'real' culture are rarely capable of resolution because the protagonists often occupy firmly entrenched positions on the real–imaginary continuum, with 'traditionalists' on one side and 'anything-goes' radicals on the other. There is not the space to enter that particular fray here but it is important to note that for every viewer who believed that Jules Tavernier was 'wrong' to eat beans on toast in the 'caff' was another who thought that this was a 'real' portrait of a Jamaican elder living on his own who did not bother to cook 'traditional' food just for himself. It is also true, to which most media researchers will testify, that what the audience *believes* to be portrayed on television is often not what is actually being *broadcast* at the time. Rather, what seems to happen is that viewers have particular beliefs about TV content and continue to hold those beliefs despite actual changes to and shifts in programme content and orientation. This relates to the third point on the fluid nature of the TV land-scape where innovative and challenging work *is* being broadcast in pro-grammes which *do* subvert and rupture the old orthodoxies around race and representation. The problem is that these programmes are seldom broadcast in prime-time slots, so audiences do not always get round to watching them and appreciating that small, incremental progress *is* being made, no matter how slowly.

The 'race' is the thing

As well as criticisms around specific characters and character types, there was also a general concern over the variety (or often lack thereof) of story-lines in which black minority characters feature. Unsurprisingly, 'racism' is regularly used as a suitable topic in soaps, driven as they are by controversy and melodrama. While many viewers were reasonably satisfied with the use of these kinds of themes within programme narratives, believing that the introduction of such themes in story-lines enables the issues to be played out in ways which are 'safe' for the majority audience, there were resentments about the way in which black minority characters are often made to deal with situations.

> You remember when they [*EastEnders*] had that problem with the skin-heads and all they did was to have Alan, Steve and Sanjay getting drunk? That's not very positive. It really irritated me. Waiting around until midnight with a baseball bat. That was a very negative portrayal of how black people handle racism, getting out a bottle of Cinzano bianco and knocking it back. It was really bad.
>
> ('Claudine', London)

Among African Caribbean viewers, there were very strong criticisms that in popular police and crime series like *The Bill*, the black minority characters were nearly always criminals of one sort or another. When black police officers *do* figure prominently, it is usually because 'race' is a theme in a par-ticular episode or else they have been drafted in to deal with a problem in the black community, bringing with them their first-hand knowledge of 'their own' people and having to run the usual gamut of abuse from the black criminal fraternity. But as discussed earlier, the actuality of black police officer roles in prime-time drama series *is* changing, with more com-plex characterizations becoming more routine in some of the more recent police drama series such as *Cops* and *The Thin Blue Line*.

The sex/race nexus

In most mainstream shows, and especially in entertainment genres, black minority characters most usually have white partners. On the few occasions when black male actors are 'allowed' to have black female partners on screen, the woman is usually so light-skinned and European-featured that she could be read as 'white'. While it might seem rather distasteful to interrogate and criticize black minority characterizations to this degree of detail, black minority viewers see such casting strategies as deliberate rather than accidental devices which contribute to their subordination through privileging 'whiteness' as the ultimate goal. There are two main reasons which viewers believe underlie decisions to pair black minority characters with white (or near white) partners. First, because the possible 'threat' of their blackness is neutralized and domesticated by their involvement with a white partner, which makes them more acceptable to white viewers. In addition, there is a belief that most (white) scriptwriters have no idea about black-on-black relationships, so they script stories based on what they *do* know and write story-lines for white couples and hope that they will fit. While this may well be the case, it is also true that black minority scriptwriters such as Hanif Kureishi and Gurinder Chadha have been criticized for their interest in exploring cross-cultural relationships in their work. In some ways, viewers seem to want to ignore a growing experience – for example, 50 per cent of British-born Caribbean men and 33 per cent of British-born Caribbean women have a white partner – which the media at least are treating realistically.[5] However, it would require a completely different study to explore the reasons behind such reluctance to acknowledge this very real shift in social relations in Britain.

Although such black–white relations were generally regarded negatively, this was not the only reading as the following sequence shows, generated during one of the London-based discussion groups. The two speakers are both women and there are a number of important issues which come out of the exchange. The point about putting white audiences off by seeing a black couple is not borne out by the evidence but is clearly something that the speaker feels is important.

> I think they've got Alan and the white woman in *EastEnders* because if you look at the East End, there are a lot of mixed relationships and that's what they're trying to show.
>
> ('Marcia', London)

> They can show mixed relationships, OK, but they should also have black on black relationships as well.
>
> ('Beverley', London)

But that could put people off watching. I mix with a lot of real East Enders. Some are all right but a lot are racist.

('Marcia', London)

Affect and effect: the power of telly

The great majority of viewers in the study believed that white people are overly (and inappropriately) influenced by the way in which 'race', ethnicity and black people generally are portrayed on television because they have such limited first-hand knowledge of African, Caribbean, South Asian or any other ethnic minority community. This perception is, to some extent, borne out by a number of studies which have looked at white audiences and black images (see, for example, Broadcasting Standards Council (BSC) 1992; Ross 1992). For black minority viewers in this study, the largely stereotypical portraits which emerge from both fictional and factual programmes, from soaps to news, serve to reinforce the prejudices that pervade the white consciousness already and impact on viewers who are often a little too ready to believe the worst.

> Television reinforces their prejudices. They have been socialized into thinking that black people are inferior, less intelligent. They shouldn't bias the white majority against us, but that's what they do.
>
> ('Sam', London)

> When something terrible comes on the news, a mugging or a rape, I'm only listening for what colour the assailant is. If he's black I think, oh no. If he's white I breathe a sigh of relief. I think we all do.
>
> ('Mary', Nottingham)

Of particular concern to respondents in this study was the way in which television has a tendency to elide ethnic difference into a homogenizing blackness. If distinctions *are* made between different black minorities, they are generally made between the crude categories of 'black' and 'Asian' (of which I am mindful of compounding here, but see note 1). Members of the Hindu and Sikh groups in the study were especially keen to define their own specific cultural context and were highly critical of the way in which the boundaries between different South Asian cultures were constantly blurred if not rendered completely invisible. For them, the crucial issue was that they did not want to be associated with Islam and what they considered to be extremist and fundamentalist actions and views. Similarly, the African groups were depressed with the way in which 'black' was increasingly taken to mean Caribbean and that Africa was only ever invoked in the context of disaster, corruption or killing. They did not want to be associated with Jamaica and Yardie culture and were dismissive of 'Caribbean' comics who constantly poke fun at Africans. While it is easy to understand the anxiety which some groups display around television's homogenizing tendencies, it is nonetheless the case that the medium is a very blunt instrument, casually blurring ethnic and racial distinctions in order to make a broader point about, say, race relations. This is not to say that programme makers should not concern themselves with accuracy but rather an acknowledgement that several different agendas may be being served at any one time.

Fast forward . . . where next?

Many viewers believe that the way in which black minorities are portrayed on television not only has a negative effect on white viewers, but also affects black communities in very unhelpful ways too. The lack of positive role models and the way in which black minority characters are routinely stereotyped contribute to feelings of low self-esteem and failure, especially among black minority children. Almost without exception, black minority viewers did not feel that they were valued as a specific viewing public, they did not feel that their viewing needs were being met, and they did not feel that they were getting value for money from the licence fee. Because most black minority children in Britain were born in the country, their knowledge of 'home' is very limited, gleaned from what their relatives tell them and, of course, what they see on television. Viewers reported sadness at the reaction of their children to their homelands of Africa, India or Pakistan which, because the media's particular slant on the developing world tends to be negative, is one of shame at the 'backwardness' of their countries of origin.

> My children were born in this country and don't know anything directly of Africa. What they see of black people on TV forms a bad picture in their head about the country where I was born.
>
> ('Yaba', Manchester)

For so many people in this study, 'multicultural' has come to mean cultural homogeneity, a proliferation of uni-cultures into which all their disparate and diverse voices, interests, views, identifications and practices dissolve into a formless mass of stereotypical essences; this is what *Caribbean* people are like, this is what *Asian* people do. What participants in this study want, then, is an acknowledgement of not only their similarities and differences to white Britons, but also those which exist among and between themselves, to mark out their own distinctiveness from all the others who might be bracketed together under the generic term 'black' or 'Asian'. There is an aching desire for black minority experiences to be created, reported, discussed and interpreted in ways which recognize their humanity, not simply their blackness (Daniels 1990). It is precisely because there are so few black minority characters in mainstream programming that each one must be subject to an unbearable scrutiny by black minority audiences who criticize each one for what it is not, each one forced to stand as emblem of a generalizable 'blackness' for white audiences who lack any counter-intuition to combat the stereotypes. If, as Kellner (1990) suggests, television stands at the centre of our symbolic universe, providing repetitive and mythical celebrations of dominant ideologies, then ways must be found to rupture, subvert and challenge that hegemonic orthodoxy in order to release the exciting possibilities of diversity and difference: this really is the future for our multicultural world.

Of crucial concern is, who has control over televisual images and in whose likenesses are those images constructed? It is everywhere the complaint that representations of one 'category', say Pakistani women or gay men or older people, are imagined from the second-hand experience of an entirely other category, say English men or straight women or young people. This is not to argue that, say, a white writer is incapable of constructing a credible black minority character, but rather to suggest that such constructions will necessarily be informed by a perspective and experiential standpoint which is intrinsically different to that of a black writer. It is not necessarily worse but it *is* different. The rise of various types of ethnic minority media around the world demonstrates a clear demand by minority communities to see alternative images (of themselves) to those provided by mainstream, majority media (see, for example, Riggins 1992; Dowmunt 1993; Husband 1994a). However, what is of equal importance is the value placed by *all* writers/producers/directors on cultural authenticity and diversity.

Conclusion

Most of the dissatisfactions expressed by black minority viewers in the study discussed above will find a resonance with viewers in many other so-called multi-ethnic societies: they are not merely British anxieties but mirror the cries of diaspora communities around the globe whose lives are routinely constructed by the mainstream majority media out of nothing more concrete than their own imaginings. What black minority viewers want is not something huge and extravagant but something small and relatively easy to provide: the opportunity to see themselves, in all their diversity, portrayed credibly on that most powerful of media – television.

I feel cheated. They're asking for £90 a year and either you just sell out and watch the mainstream all the time or you pay more to get cable and see the American stuff. It's much better for ethnic minorities, they've got better talk shows, better programmes for children. They've got things from the West Indies. On English TV, I don't mind watching Catherine Cookson on a Sunday afternoon or tuning in to *Emmerdale* now and then, but I wish there was a bit more for us.

('Geraldine', Coventry)

Notes

1 The terms 'black minority' and occasionally 'black' and 'Asian' are used through-out this chapter as inclusive (and political) terms to describe viewers who are not part of the *white* majority and who feel marginalized because of this basic fact. Elsewhere, the terms 'African Caribbean' and 'Asian' are used as shorthand to describe individuals in this study from those two (albeit crude) broad ethnic groups. It is for reasons of brevity alone that these clumsy and essentially mean-ingless terms are used here and I accept their limitations while at the same time believing that they nonetheless convey some sense of the 'us' and 'them' dialectic which I wish to convey when considering the broader question of white media and black images, particularly in Britain.

2 The study on which this chapter is based was commissioned by BBC TV's Equal Opportunities Department and undertaken by Professor Annabelle Sreberny and myself at the Centre for Mass Communication Research, University of Leicester. The audience sample comprised 353 black minority viewers from across England and a group of Chinese women in Scotland: members of Britain's most significant black minority populations were all represented in the study, although their views remain their own and are not necessarily generalizable to all black minority people everywhere.

3 The ten locations were Bedford, Birmingham, Bradford, Coventry, Glasgow, Lan-cashire, Leeds, Leicester, Manchester and Nottingham.

4 Interestingly, though, as a consequence of the original study, I was subsequently asked by BBC TV's Equal Opportunities Department to write a training pack on 'race' and portrayal to be used with their own staff which has now been published but which is not available outside the BBC.

5 The Fourth National Survey of Ethnic Minorities carried out by the Policy Studies Institute contains some fascinating insights into the lives of contemporary Black Britons (Modood *et al.* 1997).

Further reading

Dickinson, R., Harindranath, R. and Linne, O. (eds) (1998) *Approaches to Audiences: A Reader.* London: Edward Arnold.

Griffin, C. (1996) 'See whose face it wears': difference, otherness and power', *Feminism and Psychology*, 6(2): 185–91.

Jhally, S. and Lewis, J. (1994) *Enlightened Racism: The Cosby Show, Audiences and the Myth of the American Dream*. Boulder, CO: Westview.

Mullan, B. (1996) *Not a Pretty Picture: Ethnic Minority Views of Television*. Aldershot: Avebury.

Ross, K. (1996) *Black and White Media: Black Images in Popular Film and Television*. Cambridge: Polity.

9

ETHNICITY, NATIONAL CULTURE(S) AND THE INTERPRETATION OF TELEVISION
Ramaswami Harindranath

Introduction

Much of the academic debates concerning 'race', ethnicity and the media
have been around issues of representation, power and identity, the constraints restricting minority broadcasting, and the aesthetics of resistance.
While these provide various interrogations of the notions of 'race' and ethnicity, and are necessary interventions into the politics and economics of
media representations and their hegemonic role in society, this chapter shifts
the focus, attempting to explore a few of the current debates regarding both
media and 'race' from the perspective of the audience, through the discussion of two studies which examine the interpretations of television programmes by ethnically and/or culturally diverse audiences. We will
encounter, *en route*, the pertinence of 'tradition' in the explanations of
understanding and interpretation in philosophical hermeneutics; developments in post-colonial studies and their relevance to notions of 'race' and
ethnicity in the international context; and finally, a plea towards the need to
revise the questions regarding the nature of cultural imperialism.

Ethnicity, audience and interpretation

The first study I want to discuss is Liebes and Katz's important research on
the audiences of *Dallas* published as *The Export of Meaning* in 1993. Their
intention was to examine the reasons for the worldwide popularity of *Dallas*,
and to interrogate the issue of cultural imperialism: in other words, does the

fact that the serial was watched by audiences across the world imply that American values were being disseminated by *Dallas* and accepted uncritically by audiences? To achieve this, they surmised that 'the actual interaction between the program and its viewers must be studied. In the case of *Dallas*, the challenge is to observe how the melodrama of a fictional family in Texas is viewed, interpreted and discussed by real families throughout the world' (Liebes and Katz 1993: 4). The actual empirical investigation was conducted predominantly in Israel, whose 'ethnic composition' enabled the researchers to examine the 'interaction between the symbolic resources of the viewer and the symbolic offerings of the text' (Liebes and Katz 1993: 6). To this end, they chose their respondents from ethnically diverse communities within Israel: Arabs, Russian Jews, Moroccan settlers and members of a kibbutzim, apart from among American and Japanese viewers, organizing 'ethnically homogeneous' groups who were then asked to discuss episodes of *Dallas*. Various aspects of this study have been examined at length elsewhere (see Tomlinson 1992; Barker and Brooks 1998). What we are interested in here, however, are Liebes and Katz's conclusions regarding the interpretations of the episodes of *Dallas* by ethnically different audiences.

Despite the richness of their data there are significant questions which need to be addressed with regard to the epistemological assumptions that underlie Liebes and Katz's conclusions, and which are specially pertinent to discussions of 'race' and ethnicity. Their 'findings' appear to sit comfortably within the boundaries drawn around strict ethnic groupings – the interpretations of the *Dallas* episodes by their respondents are remarkably consistent in their conformity with ethnically or racially marked categories. However, while these appear to support the initial hypothesis, by treating the respondents' accounts as evidence of culturally diverse appropriations of the text, the researchers reinforce a certain degree of ethnic or racial segregation which is problematic. Their conclusions, and more significantly the theoretically inadequate explanation of them, leave them open to the danger of reproducing racial stereotypes, while their ready acceptance of aspects of respondents' 'cultures' as influencing their interpretations indicates a rather reductionist and crude notion of culture – the various ethnic groups appear preordained to respond in particular ways to the serial and by extension to reality, mediated or otherwise.

In her account of the differences in the retelling of the episodes for instance, Liebes (1988) claims:

> The two more traditional groups, Arabs and Moroccan Jews, prefer linearity [retelling the story in 'sociological terms']. They select the action-oriented subplot for attention, defining the hero's goals and adventures

in trying to achieve them . . . The Russians speak of the episode in themes or messages. They ignore the story in favour of exposing the overall principle which is repeated relentlessly and which, in their opinion, has a manipulative intent . . . Americans and kibbutzniks tell the story psycho-analytically . . . Their retellings are 'open', future oriented, and take account of the never-ending genre of the soap opera.

(reprinted in Dickinson *et al.* 1998: 279–80)

This quote illustrates the interesting but theoretically flawed conclusions of the study: it confirms the interpretation of television, and by extension, other forms of behaviour and patterns of belief, to be determined by the ethnic community to which the respondent belongs. On the face of it, this conclusion might appear unproblematic, even fairly obvious. So why is it conceptually inadequate? One of the main problems with Liebes and Katz's analysis is that while they make straightforward connections between ethnicity and responses to *Dallas*, there is no attempt to provide an explanation for these connections. In other words, *how* does ethnicity affect interpretative behaviour? Without an acceptable elucidation, the entire study becomes problematic, especially in the context of contemporary Israeli politics, and given the value judgements which are inherent in some of the study's findings.

Liebes and Katz (1986, 1993) conclude that 'the more "modern" groups are less involved in the programme, knowing the mechanisms of distancing and discount, while the more traditional groups are more "involved" ' (Liebes and Katz 1986: 169). It is tempting to concur with this conclusion since it offers a seemingly straightforward explanation of the different interpretations. However, while *prima facie* feasible, on reflection their modern–traditional dichotomy appears simplistic and a little cavalier, and is illustrative of the social and political debates surrounding the use of such categories in research involving different ethnic or racial groups. Used without proper investigation these concepts come inscribed with the evaluative connotations of racial or cultural superiority. Primarily, Liebes and Katz's conclusion that the degrees of involvement in and distanciation from mediated communication correspond to degrees of modernity reinforces the perception of the west (on whose terms modernity is conceptualized) as the repository of modernity and 'progress', as well as of all its positive connotations. The term 'traditional', which they use to label the Arabs and the Moroccan Jews on the other hand, contains the negative assessments seen as characteristic of pre-modern cultures. The modern–traditional dichotomy was intrinsic to the values system which, for instance supported the creation of a hierarchy of cultures and races during colonialism. Their finding that the Russian viewers were more critical than the other groups is interesting, but their conclusion that Russians were somehow innately critical seems tautological, and certainly begs the question.

We are faced with two problems here: first, the potential danger in conceptualizing racial or ethnic difference in terms of cultural difference; and second, how to avoid this danger when faced with different responses to media from ethnically different audiences. The first, eliding the difference between race and culture while essentializing the notion of race/ethnicity (in other words, claiming that race determines behaviour), is central to the political and philosophical positions inherent in many contemporary debates concerning the apparent diversity of human races. Liebes and Katz quite rightly foreground ethnicity in their analysis of the popularity of *Dallas* and its potential power as a vehicle of cultural imperialism. Many of the arguments which are covered under the broad rubric of globalization – homogenization of cultures, immigration and diaspora, multiculturalism and identity, and so on – have as their central focus the concept of race. However, conceiving of race as self-enclosed, hermetical communities, marked by their 'traditional' or 'modern' world-view, and by implication resistant to cross-cultural dialogue or dialectical alteration is to conceive it in absolutist terms.

The political implications of such a stance in contemporary Israel are too complex to go into in the present context, but Said's (1986) observations regarding the use of ethnicity in ideological terms are instructive.

> The principal paradigm in mainstream Israeli social science holds the Arab in a psychocultural vice. Such supposedly real and stable objects as the Arab mind, the Arab temperament, and Arab cultural weakness predominate, while little attention is devoted to foreign domination or, for that matter, to developments within Arab history.
>
> (Said 1986: 43–4)

Admittedly, *The Export of Meaning* does not make such claims explicitly about the Arab communities. However, the absence of a sufficiently sophisticated theoretical explanation for the apparent differences in interpretation of the episodes of *Dallas* apart from a problematic use of the traditional–modern dichotomy indicates a form of ahistorical essentializing of Arab culture.[1] This bipartite distinction echoes directly the principle underlying the hierarchization of cultures during colonialism, when the intervention of the progressive, modern west was justified as a civilizing mission, helping the more 'traditional', backward colonies attain a greater degree of enlightenment. As Said (1986) argues in his essay, the maintenance of the ideology of difference plays a crucial role in contemporary Israel, and by not going beyond the initial labelling of the Arab and Morrocan viewers as 'traditional', Liebes and Katz (probably unwittingly) contribute to this ideology, to the politics of exclusion and inclusion.

In nineteenth-century colonial discourses, biological difference was held to be the basis for racial diversity in humans, 'scientifically' determined through the measurement of skull sizes and the like, and given further fillip by Social Darwinism. In the discourse of race the reification of cultural differences as unitary, essentialistic and immutable categories has taken over from biological determinism, collapsing 'race' into culture. As Malik (1996a) argues, the assumption that cultural differences are static and fixed, that for instance,

> the 'race' of a child determines the 'culture' in which he or she should be brought up – reveals a view of culture as a predetermined, natural phenomenon . . . [The] concept of race arises through the naturalisation of social differences. Regarding cultural diversity in natural terms can only ensure that culture acquires an immutable character, and hence *becomes a homologue for race*.
>
> (Malik 1996a: 150, emphasis added)[2]

Comparisons between different ethnic or racial groups in terms of, for instance, their interpretative practices therefore require a highly nuanced theoretical framework which is sensitive to the potential danger of considering ethnic or racial categories as *determining* behaviour.

Television audiences and contexts of interpretation

The problem we are faced with is how to theoretically link the gap between interpretative practice and socio-cultural context. Liebes and Katz's (1993) study exemplifies some of the difficulties fairly typical of relatively recent work on television audiences, especially that which falls under the broad rubric of 'reception studies'. These (for instance, Morley 1980; Jensen 1986; Livingstone 1990) have demonstrated with sufficient clarity and sophisticated data the undeniable connection between textual interpretation and the social situation of the viewer. Although attempts at drawing a causal link between specific socio-economic groups and constructed meanings have not proved successful, such studies do serve to underline the situatedness of interpretative practices – they *demonstrate* the links between socio-cultural context and interpretation, even though they provide insufficient explanation for this connection.

I would argue that given the concern with the relationship between television and the viewer, the actual practices by which meaning is appropriated

by differentially situated viewers needs special attention. There is no denying the support data generated by these studies provide to the concept of
active audience, and to the corollary underprivileging of the tyrannical hold
of the text over the audience – the idea that the text contained one meaning
which 'influenced' audiences in different ways. And yet the audience, though
loosened from the bondage to the text, are not completely free – they are
herded, as for example in Morley (1980), into class-oriented strait-jackets,
or as we saw in the case of Liebes and Katz (1993), the collapse of racial
difference into cultural difference. As Silverstone (1994) points out, despite
contributing to our improved understanding of audience activity,

> none of these reception theorists and researchers has provided entirely
> satisfactory explanations of the relationship between sociological and
> psychological variables in the audience's relationship to television. The
> elements of the dialectic of the socially situated yet individual reader
> and his or her relationship to texts and social structures remains prob-
> lematic.
>
> (Silverstone 1994: 151–2)

Members of an audience certainly do not function in a social vacuum, as
the earlier effects studies with their behaviourist orientations suggested.
Their socio-cultural situatedness can and must be assumed. They function
as social subjects of a particular class, society or culture, as family members, and it is not difficult to see their behaviour, including media consumption and interpretation, being shaped by this membership. The
question here is how rigid are these compartments, divided along 'classic'
sociological variables, and are there, as Corner (1991) argues, other areas
operating within and between these variables which have to be considered
if a theory concerning interpretative practices is to be meaningfully articulated? More significantly, can audiences who have been acknowledged to
inhabit several intersecting social spaces simultaneously (Silverstone 1994)
be unproblematically reduced to just one variable or position? It follows
that the subjectivity of the audience member who confronts the text is
shaped by all these intersecting identities, and to privilege a socio-
economic position, or in the present case, race/ethnicity over the others is
to be reductionist. As Dyer (1977) contends, it is doubtful whether the
knowledge of a person's class, age or gender is enough to predict their
interpretation of a text. It could be argued, following Bourdieu, that this
socio-economic position is fundamental, transcendentally shaping the subjects' horizons of knowledge and behaviour, but even to do that is to
reduce a complex web to a relationship of linear causality. We are therefore faced with a dilemma: how to conceptualize the audience and its

socially motivated interpretative activities without subscribing to deterministic, cause–effect notions?

Attempting to answer this question involves the examination of the notion of understanding: how do we understand or interpret texts, and what is the relationship between the act of interpretation and socio-cultural contexts? It seems to me that the place to start is contemporary hermeneutics, especially the work of Gadamer (1975, 1976). While nineteenth- and early-twentieth-century hermeneutics pursued the elusive goal of fashioning the perfect method of interpretation which would lead the reader to reach across any temporal or cultural divide to understand the 'real' meaning that the author intended to communicate, Gadamer's hermeneutics undermines this entire project, arguing that such reconstruction of the author's intended meaning is impossible. The fundamental 'thrownness' of human life – that is, our ordinary, everyday situation – its temporality and historicity, is also the situation in which understanding is inescapably embedded. In other words, the interpreter's category of historicity, their specific socio-cultural context, is crucial to their understanding of a text.

In stressing the context-dependence of the interpreter Gadamer stresses the inevitable historicity of understanding itself, which no amount of methodological rigour can possibly overcome. Crucially, he considers this historicity to be the result of a combination of both a biographical past as well as a cultural past, which fashions the 'hermeneutic situation' of the interpreter – the context of understanding. Regarding the hermeneutic situation as a combination of culture (or to use Gadamer's term, 'tradition') and biography allows for the reassessment of the concept of socio-cultural context, providing the scope for rescuing it from conventional strait-jackets.[3]

To Gadamer, however, this 'boundedness' of understanding by specific socio-cultural conditions is not a negative phenomenon but quite the contrary: it is the very fertile ground that makes understanding possible. He gives this enabling condition the name 'prejudice' or 'prejudgement', perhaps one of the most controversial aspects of his philosophy:

> It is not so much our judgements as it is our prejudices that constitute our being. This is a provocative formulation, for I am using it to restore to its rightful place a positive concept of prejudice that was driven out of our linguistic usage by the French and the English Enlightenment. It can be shown that the concept of prejudice did not originally have the meaning we have attached to it. Prejudices are not necessarily unjustified or erroneous, so that they inevitably distort the truth. In fact, the historicity of our existence entails that prejudices, in the literal sense of the word, constitute the initial directedness of our

whole ability to experience. Prejudices are biases of our openness to
the world.

(Gadamer 1976: 9)

Gadamer uses the concept of prejudice in this modified sense to push forward his theory of understanding in two ways: first, to demonstrate the
impossibility of 'objective' understanding of an historical phenomenon –
understanding can occur only within a set of prejudgements, therefore the
Enlightenment ideal of a context-free subject is not only a misconception,
but also unnecessary. Prejudices and prejudgements are both inevitable and
indispensable to understanding, fashioned by the 'tradition' to which one
belongs – a tradition that is bound up with history. 'Understanding is not to
be thought of so much as an action of one's subjectivity, but as the placing
of oneself within a tradition, in which past and present are constantly fused'
(Gadamer 1975: 258). Thus understanding is a 'fusion of horizons'
(Gadamer 1975: 273) – the horizons or prejudices of the interpreter, and
those of the text.

The second contribution that Gadamer makes that is relevant here is his
idea that understanding involves the anticipation of meaning of the whole
text based on prior knowledge of the nature of its constituents, as in, for
example, its generic features. He refers to this as 'the horizon of expectation'
a set of assumptions which we take to the text. Crucially, however, these
assumptions are not fixed – they undergo modifications as we encounter the
text. In other words, we constantly revise our expectations of the meaning
of the whole text on the basis of our understanding of parts of it. It is useful
to remember that this idea can be applied at other levels: the culturally, historically situated set of prejudices also undergo constant revision. To put it
another way, we constantly revise our cultural resources as we encounter
new experiences in the form of real events and/or textual depictions. As
Gadamer (1975: 272) points out, the biographical-cultural situation of the
interpreter which both limits and facilitates his/her understanding is flexible,
not a fixed set of opinions and evaluations.

For Gadamer therefore, while all understanding is a projection of a horizon of anticipation, the prejudgements that underlie these projections themselves undergo changes as a result of the act of interpretation. By repudiating
the notion of 'proper' understanding of a text as the reproduction of auth-
orial intentions, and undermining the concept of objective understanding,
Gadamer's theory also points towards the presence of multiple meanings in
a text. The reader, acting from within his or her socio-historical context,
understands a meaning which is coloured by his/her experience in that

context. The life-world shapes world-view, which in turn fashions the understanding of an act, an expression, or a text. The reader as a social agent undermines the idea of the text as the carrier of a single (set of) meaning: the 'fusion of horizons' depending as it does on the prejudices or pre-judgements of the reader, could in effect differ from one reader to the other, connected as it is to their historicity.

Although Gadamer emphasizes his concept of 'historicity' to make a case for the impossibility of an 'objective' understanding of a historically different period, the ontological foundations of this idea can also be seen to support a similar impossibility of understanding a different culture. The historicity of the reader/viewer, his or her specific socio-cultural context acts as a force operating 'from behind his/her back', unnoticed and unacknowledged, but nevertheless potent and inevitable. The past can be looked at only through the eyes of the present; texts from the past are always interpreted from the perspective of the present. But the same constraints that militate against the bridging of the temporal divide, a time-conquering act which would enable the understanding of a text from its contemporaneous position, can be seen to be equally effective in restricting the bridging of the spatial distance which would facilitate the 'perfect' understanding of a different culture, and consequently, the texts of a different culture. I use the terms 'objective' and 'perfect' here to mean the approximation of the meaning that a text has for the people of that period or culture, in other words, the replication of their interpretative practices.

Such a stance has the potential danger of not just relativism, but more insidious, the sealing off of different cultures and races (indeed, any form of collectivity) into mutually incomprehensible camps – a stance that is intellectually unacceptable and politically suspect. As we saw in our discussion of *The Export of Meaning*, an inadequately theorized demonstration of ethnic difference reifies the notion of immutability. Gadamer's idea of 'effective history' as being not just a putative notion of culture, but also, and more significantly, the reader's biographical situation rescues it from the charge of essentialism. It is crucial therefore, that a project which sets out to compare interpretations of media across different 'traditions' or cultural contexts *goes beyond mere display of evidence suggesting a plurality of reading to interrogate constituents of these 'traditions'*. It is imperative that we attempt, in Geertz's (1973) terms, a 'thick reading' of what such differences in interpretation reveal not only in terms of the audiences' responses to the particular film or television programme, but (perhaps more importantly) also with regard to the unequal relations of different cultures or ethnic groups in global politics.

Recommendations from an Indian case study

I shall illustrate my theoretical project by referring to some of the aspects of a research study comparing the responses to documentaries by audiences in India and Britain (Harindranath 1996). The respondents in both countries were selected from a university setting, and comprised academics, students and non-academics (technicians, secretaries and other support staff, who had no university education), who were shown two of four documentary films, two each from India and the UK. One of the basic frameworks adopted for the analysis of the respondents' accounts of their interpretations of the documentaries were the categories of 'transparency' and 'mediation', as set out in Corner and Richardson (1986). These categories reflect the 'framings' used by the respondents in order to interpret the documentaries: interpretations using the 'transparent' framing respond to the veridicality of the television image, evaluating the various filmic representations as if they were events in real life. 'Mediation' frames, on the other hand, resist the rhetorical advances of the film, acknowledging the constructed nature of the diverse elements in it, and as a consequence recognizing that their meanings originate in their existence as representations and not as real life events.

Briefly, my finding is that most respondents across both cultures interpreted the films in similar ways, with a varied employment of 'transparent' and 'mediated' frames which generated readings which were at times critical of the films' arguments and representation. The only group which emerged as markedly different in terms of using a consistently transparent frame for interpreting the documentaries were the Indian non-academics. The picture which emerges most distinctly at the end of my analysis is that while nearly all the viewers from both 'cultures' in categories other than the Indian non-academics generated varying degrees of critical readings of the films from transparent or mediated frames, the Indian non-academics were almost uniformly uncritical, accepting the films' premises.

All interviews contained discussions of the documentary genre's claim to 'truthfully' depict objective reality. One of the significant connections that can be made here is that between the respondents' notion of the authenticity of documentary and their acceptance or (often guarded and heavily qualified) rejection of this claim and their use of specific framings. By way of illustration, here are excerpts from three of the interviews which demonstrate the respondents' stances regarding the nature of documentary.

1 *Interviewer:* What do you think of the claim that documentaries show reality, as opposed to feature films or serials which are fictional?

Indian non-academic: That is correct, because as far as I am concerned, they portray what is exactly happening. So I accept that claim. We have seen it. We are seeing it, and we trust that [our] feelings are correct.

Interviewer: Do you think documentaries portray reality?

Indian non-academic: Yes, those which are permitted to be screened, we have to trust it, and we have to take it into consideration . . . because the government has permitted it to be shown, so we have to trust it, yes.

2 *Interviewer:* Do you think documentaries depict reality?

Indian undergraduate: People have to get what actually goes on. If you put a little bit of artificial element in it, and then try, maybe you are taking away things, you know, not giving them [the audience] the real thing. Sometimes it may not be possible, depending on the type of documentary you want to make . . . Like . . . suppose you want to take a real life situation, like child labour. Sometimes it won't be possible for you to really get across to that actual situation while it's going on and then shoot the film. That is difficult.

3 *Interviewer:* Would you agree with the claim that unlike fictional films, documentaries present a true reflection of reality?

British undergraduate: I would agree with the idea that that's what people say, but that's not necessarily how it is.

Interviewer: Why not?

British undergraduate: Well . . . whatever a documentary is about, it's always going to be biased towards the director's opinion, whereby there's a slant. It'll always be biased. And that's true of films as well.

Excerpt 1 reveals an almost unquestioning acceptance of the documentary genre's claims, especially when approved by forces outside, as in 'the government', whereas Excerpts 2 and 3 demonstrate different degrees of scepticism. These are merely samples from extensive interviews which went on to discuss the particular films which were part of the study. However, these are indicative of an important element in the present context, since it not only suggests a link between the 'horizon of expectation' with regard to the documentary genre and the 'frames' used for the subsequent understanding of the specific films, but also marks this feature as a crucial distinction between the Indian non-academics and the other respondents from both countries.

The *similarities* between the interpretations of the Indian audiences with higher education and those of the British audiences, and equally the *differences* between the interpretations of these Indians and those of their compatriots without higher education, are suggestive. Evidently it undermines, on the one hand, the conflation of culture and geographical space, an approach favoured for a long time by anthropologists and by advocates of nationalist discourses. Even at a preliminary level of analysis the data from this project indicate very strongly the fundamental error in assuming that all Indians share the same cultural resources. On the other hand, it also questions the conflation of culture and ethnicity implicit in the conclusions suggested by Liebes and Katz (1993) in their study which, as we saw traced differences in interpretation along ethnic divides. As our data suggest, the Indian respondents with university education share similar cultural resources (or, in Gadamer's terms, 'historicity' and the 'hermenuetic situation') with the British groups, and what emerges as crucial is not ethnic difference, but difference engendered by higher education.

Both these developments are significant to audience research in an international context, because they contribute to the growing number of critical voices challenging conventional conceptions of culture as unitary and bounded (Clifford and Marcus 1986; Abu-Lughod 1993; Caglar 1997; Clifford 1997a). This has obvious repercussions for the debates concerning cultural imperialism, and the role of the media in the dissemination of western capitalist values and lifestyles. As Amin (1997) argues, the 'multiple and assymetric interdependencies' which characterize the global–local connectivity implies that it is wrong to consider either the global or the local as separate spheres: 'to think of the global as flows of dominance and transformation and the local as fixities of tradition and continuity is to miss the point' (Amin 1997: 129).

To return to the case study, the importance of higher education as a 'sphere' in a person's life-world, with the potential of creating a 'culture' of its own, providing a demonstrably effective 'hermeneutic situation', suggests the presence of a hybrid culture which bridges the gap between indigenous Indian and western cultures. At the same time, the results of the study also underline the inadequacy of conceptions linking culture with geographical and political spaces. Such a conception falls into the trap of distinguishing collectivities along conventional lines, reifying spatial or ethnic criteria as fundamental. Politically as well as intellectually this is not a productive position.

Intrinsic to this are debates concerning the global and the local. In the current climate of economic change, where the balance attempted in India's experiments with 'mixed economy' is being rapidly transformed into a more market-oriented economy, issues of globalization ought to take centre stage.

One of the dichotomies which immediately suggests itself is the notion of the westernized Indian and the non-westernized Indian. As indicated in this study, higher education appears to play an important role in establishing and maintaining this division. Allied to this is the issue of consumerism which seems to have burgeoned in proportion to the recent economic 'reforms' and on which have dovetailed the introduction of and dramatic increase in foreign cable and satellite channels. Given the sheer diversity of the Indian nation-state along the religious, cultural, linguistic as well as social and economic lines, these categories must be taken into account and theorized. In that context, the possibility of a range of intersecting circles of relevance constituting a life-world is heightened. A simple, ethnically based British–Indian dichotomy will be unable to reflect this complexity, merely reproducing ingenuous accounts of pluralistic modes of audience interpretation as that of Liebes and Katz.

Let us for a moment consider one of the strands which make up this complexity – university education, which was an important criterion in the Indian case study. It has been argued (Viswanathan 1987) that in postcolonial contexts such as India, education plays an important role, insidiously continuing the colonial project of domination through the presentation of a certain set of discourses as superior to the indigenous ones. While the colonial period saw the practice of Macaulay's recommendation for the creation, through western education, of 'a class of persons, Indian in blood and colour, but English in taste, in opinions, in morals, and in intellect. To that class we may leave it to . . . enrich those [vernacular] dialects with terms of science borrowed from Western science' (Ashcroft *et al.* 1995: 432), in contemporary India it has helped produce disparities in access to various cultural and economic resources. My case study was more a demonstration of that than an illustration of ethnic differences. The notion of cultural imperialism therefore has to be reconfigured to cleanse it of essentialized implications of 'pure' ethnic cultures, and to take into account the role of institutions such as education and liberal economics in the continuing domination of the west over the rest.

Conclusion

I have attempted to argue in this chapter that there is an urgent need for a theoretical revaluation of the relationship between the socio-cultural contexts of audiences and their interpretations. Without a sufficiently nuanced conceptual framework it becomes easy for instance, to correlate race or ethnic difference with cultural difference, as we saw in the case of Liebes and

Katz (1993), whose attempted explanation of their interesting data is in danger of reifying a colonialist hierarchy of races. Using Gadamer's (1976) philosophical hermeneutics I have sought to demonstrate that our interpretations are ineluctably 'bounded' by our historicity. The significant differences in interpretation between groups of Indian audiences point to the presence of at least two 'cultures' separated by the fault-lines of higher education which appears to have created distinctions far greater than simple ethnic or racial difference. The reasons for this are tied in complex ways with India's colonial past. This is crucial not merely for theoretical developments in audience research, but perhaps more importantly for a reassessment of the nature of cultural imperialism, in which the very real power of the local social and cultural elites (most of whom are educated in western style universities) have to be taken into account.

Notes

1 The use of quantitative methods to analyse essentially qualitative data makes many of the conclusions to their study questionable. For instance, the assumption that frequency of reference to a character or event or emotional reaction indicates the importance accorded to it by the audience, used to justify the counting of such instances as part of the analysis, is methodologically suspect. For further discussion of this problem see Barker and Brooks (1998).

2 Malik's book, *The Meaning of Race*, is a significant contribution to the debates concerning equality and difference. In it he traces the history of racist discourses and makes a convincing argument in favour of a universalist approach to the study of race as a social category, opposing the more fashionable assertion of cultural 'difference'. It is a timely and persuasive corrective to the excesses of the 'politics of difference'. Mohanty's (1989) essay similarly argues against the naivety of liberal pluralism, presenting a philosophically informed case for the examination of cultural differences which takes into account the minimal rationality inherent in cultural practices.

3 I have argued elsewhere (Harindranath 1998) the pertinence of phenomenological sociology to a reappraisal of social context, particularly Schutz's (1972) idea of the individual's life-world as constituting both the 'handed down' knowledge of tradition and culture, as well as the individual's own 'biological situation', forming 'multiple realities'. In combination with philosophical hermeneutics it provides the platform from which to elaborate the social contexts of interpretative activity.

Further reading

Amin, A. (1997) Placing globalization, *Theory, Culture & Society*, 14(2): 123–37.
Corner, J. (1991) Meaning, genre and context: the problematics of 'public

knowledge' in the new audience studies, in J. Curran and M. Gurevitch (eds) *Mass Media and Society*, 1st edn. London: Edward Arnold.

Harindranath, R. (1998) Documentary meanings and interpretative contexts: observations on Indian 'repertoires', in R. Dickinson, R. Harindranath and O. Linne (eds) *Approaches to Audiences: A Reader*. London: Edward Arnold.

Liebes, T. and Katz, E. (1993) *The Export of Meaning: Cross-Cultural Readings of 'Dallas'*. Cambridge: Polity.

Silverstone, R. (1994) *Television and Everyday Life*. London: Routledge.

Tomlinson, J. (1992) *Cultural Imperialism*. London: Pinter.

10

TRANSNATIONAL COMMUNICATIONS AND DIASPORA COMMUNITIES
Marie Gillespie

Introduction

This chapter is based on ongoing research into transnational networks of communications and diaspora communities. It focuses on everyday cultural and discursive practices among British Asian youth living in Southall, a multi-ethnic suburb of London, and a major commercial and cultural centre of the South Asian diaspora. The first section explains how transnational media play a role in sustaining South Asian diaspora formations and consciousness. The second section explains why and how anthropology provides useful tools for studying transnational communications networks among diaspora communities. Finally, in order to illustrate the theoretical and methodological approach, I briefly outline the findings of a case study of the reception of two TV versions of the Mahabharata, a foundational text of Indian society and culture, widely viewed in India and in the diaspora. The case study, which draws upon other similar work, shows how, even though representations of femininity in the epic are intricately interwoven with discourses of patriarchal and religious nationalism, Hindu women in London and Delhi selectively appropriate and contest key narratives for their own purposes, and in doing so subvert patriarchal and nationalist discourses in the construction of their own world-views and identities.

The key argument is that young people who are part of the South Asian diaspora make shared use of the increasingly transnational array of TV programmes and video films available to them, not only to lubricate their daily social interactions, but also to compare and contrast, judge and evaluate the culturally different social worlds that appear on their TV screens (Gillespie

1995). TV talk, though seemingly trivial and inconsequential, is enacted in a variety of private and public arenas, and in some cases constitutes an embryonic public sphere (Gillespie 1998a). It is both a form of self-narration, and a forum in which different vantage points and identities are experimented with and performed. TV talk among Southall youth revolves around issues and concerns which are common to most teenagers today: friends and family, school and locality, growing up and becoming adult, dating, sex and body culture, taste in style, fashion, food and other consumption preferences (Gillespie 1998b). But it is also shaped by the multiethnic and diaspora contexts in which they live, and the culturally diverse media which they consume. Thus subjects of TV talk may include a local racist murder, sex and gender in the latest Bombay blockbuster and in the Australian soap *Neighbours*, the irreverent and subversive humour of the BBC's British Asian comedy sketch series *Goodness Gracious Me*, the lyrics of a Cornershop hit, and the politics of religious nationalism and communalism.

The juxtaposition of representations of very distinct cultural and social practices, and different ways of life, on TV screens in Southall sitting rooms encourages cross-cultural, comparative analyses of media representations. The adoption of such a comparativist and culturally relativist perspective in interpreting different social worlds by youth in diasporas tends to heighten an already well-developed sense of culture consciousness. Those who have the necessary cultural capital can translate with ease across and between distinctive social worlds, languages and cultural spheres and acquire the status of a familial cultural broker. Such everyday analyses of transnational TV are highly contradictory in nature. They often express a cosmopolitan worldview, and articulate shared cultural spaces in which ideas, values, knowledge and institutions undergo processes of convergence, hybridization, synchronization and change (Werbner and Modood 1997). Transnational youth programming, dominated by Americanized teen consumer culture (MTV's 'McCulture'), encourages a self-perception as a world teenager, and mobilizes transnational identifications around consumption practices. Southall youth often voice strong sympathies with environmentalist, feminist and Human Rights movements – generated partly by television coverage of disasters, wars and famines, as well as by various kinds of global totemic media events, such as *Live Aid*, and national charity fund-raising appeals like *Comic Relief*.

National identifications are also important. The ritual enjoyment of *East-Enders* as a 'national soap', or of the evening national news bulletins, tends to affirm, even momentarily, a sense of belonging to a shared British culture. But a heightened and sharpened awareness of racism in the media and in the wider society engenders feelings of disaffection which often results in a hardening of cultural boundaries, the construction of exclusivist identities, or protestations about essentialist definitions of Britishness or Englishness. Religious sectarianism and bigotry, in Southall, in South Asia, in the diaspora and elsewhere, generate fierce criticism of the politics of religious nationalism, and a suspicion of religious absolutism among youth. But an Islamophobic British media may encourage a defensive affirmation of Islam (Islamism). Racism, and the limited sense of belonging to any particular nation or culture, often generate the desire for new kinds of transnational and diaspora identification (Brah 1996).

Diaspora identifications and connections are greatly strengthened by modern communications technologies. The connections may be simply symbolic links between viewers of the same blockbuster Bombay movies, or fans of the same popular music genres or acts; or they may be more concrete links between kin and friends, for example in the form of 'video letters' and home videos of weddings and other rites of passage, especially coming of age celebrations. Such videos serve a range of social, cultural and political functions. They enable families to maintain contact with distant kin; they may be used to introduce eligible marriage partners and their families to each other; they may familiarize Punjabi families in, say, Yuba Valley, California, with the lives of their kin in Southall and vice versa – which amounts to a form of video tourism as well as a cultural exchange. Video (as well as audio) cassettes also serve to construct political and religious communities, in the form of globally circulating propaganda for the Khalistan (Land of the Pure) movement – the campaign for the creation of a separate, sovereign Sikh nation in the Punjab – or documentaries on the life and works of a Sikh sant (holy man), used in religious worship and instruction.

Transnational networks of media and communication are undoubtedly sustaining diaspora formations and enhancing a sense of diaspora consciousness (Cohen 1997). At the same time they are catalysing and accelerating processes of cultural change in a highly differentiated South Asian diaspora, hardening some boundaries while opening up others (Vertovec 1996). Various kinds of transnational ideologies and identifications, some progressive and some regressive, are disseminated in the South Asian diaspora by global communications with unprecedented scope, scale, speed and intensity. It remains to be seen how these varied and contradictory forces will be played out in different locations in the global South Asian diaspora.

Meanwhile Southall youth engage in a process of ongoing negotiation and creative reinvention of their identities. It is these processes of socio-cultural recreation and reinvention that form the focal point of my work. I believe that some of these creative multicultural and anti-racist practices point the way forward for us all, regardless of background, in an increasingly inter-dependent and interconnected world where racism, religious bigotry and ideologies of separation need to be contested and fought.

Electronic capitalism and imagined diaspora communities

In post-colonial Britain, established notions of national culture and national belonging – of what it means to be British and of who belongs – have been challenged and transformed in response to post-war migration and to the increased globalization of economic, political and cultural life. Media and cultural consumption – the production, 'reading' and uses of representations – play a key role in contesting and reconstituting national, religious, gender and ethnic identities. The role of media in the construction of national iden-tities today has been quite well explored in media studies (see, for example, Schlesinger 1987; Morley and Robins 1989). The enormously influential work of Anderson (1983) argues from a historical perspective that 'print-capitalism' was instrumental in forging the 'imagined community' of the nation. The widespread dissemination of newspapers (and the modern novel) led to a heightened awareness of the 'steady, anonymous, simul-taneous experience' of communities of readers (Anderson 1983: 31). The notion of simultaneity was thus crucial to the construction of national con-sciousness in its early modern forms as it is today. The earliest newspapers connected dispersed people to particular discourses of the nation, and the mass ritual and ceremony of reading the newspaper continues to contribute to the construction of ideas of national community. The fact of engaging, in private isolation, in a joint public ritual with significant though absent others, may be as important culturally as any information conveyed.

If the imagined community of the nation became possible because of the advent of newspapers, then this is still more true of the contemporary regu-lation of simultaneous experience through broadcast media schedules (Cardiff and Scannell 1987), perhaps especially as regards the evening broad-cast news on TV and, as we shall see later, soap operas (Morley and Robins 1989). But what kinds of imagined communities may be created as well as eroded by modern TV satellite technology? Satellite TV stations like Zee TV and AsiaNet are already generating complex flows of images and narratives between Indians in India and in the diaspora (there are approximately 20 mil-lion Indians living in the diaspora). We are just beginning to explore the ways in which diaspora communities use transnational communications networks. For example, a new and vibrant independent transnational cinema in which Indians in the diaspora are tackling highly controversial issues of sexual and religious politics. Some of these films would never get past the censors in India, but are being shown at film festivals in India, given media coverage, and generating debate (Triparthi 1997). Yet it is important to bear in mind that ethnic-based transnational audiences are lucrative niche markets, and very much the targets of transnational media corporations. It is important not to exaggerate or romanticize the progressive uses of transnational communications by diaspora communities. It is also premature to announce the end of the nation-state as does Appadurai (1996), but the emergence of an embryonic transnational public sphere of democratic debate is clearly visible, if not inclusive at this stage.

By articulating new kinds of spatial and temporal relationships, communications technologies can transform the politics of representation and the modes of identification available to migrant and diaspora groups. New developments in media are arguably now reducing the importance of geopolitical borders and spatial and temporal boundaries, and so threatening the vitality and significance, even the viability of national cultures, at the same time as they increase the significance of diaspora cultures (Clifford 1997b). As Clifford points out, the language of diaspora appears to be replacing, or at least supplementing, minority discourse. However, the term is under-theorized and overused, and frequently conflates important distinctions between immigrants, guest-workers, ethnic and 'racial' minorities, refugees, expatriates and travellers. This threatens the term's descriptive usefulness (Safran 1991).

We need to recognize patterns of difference and similarity. For example, despite differences in development between different parts of the Hindu diaspora, in nearly every context outside India, Hinduism has emerged as a core feature of ethnic consciousness and community mobilization among Indian immigrants and their descendants (Vertovec 1996: 5). However, a huge diversity of Hindu beliefs and practices have come to pass in different parts of the world which forbids an absolutist or unified definition of Hinduism, and which must alert us to the importance of the comparative study of the structural, contextual and subjective factors which shape patterns of similarity and difference, and different trajectories and strategies of adaptation.

A diaspora perspective, one which situates British Asians in relation to the very complex web of transnational cross-connections in South Asia and in the wider diaspora, is needed to further our understanding of some of the consequences of media and migration in an age of globalization. Many British Asian families have kin not only in India and/or Pakistan but elsewhere in Asia, in the Middle East, in North America, in Africa (many Southall families are 'twice migrants', having formerly lived in East Africa: Bhachu 1985) and also elsewhere in Europe. Bearing this complexity in mind, and the diversity it entails, may help to avoid the pitfalls of ethnic community studies that tend to reify and essentialize ethnic difference.

A diaspora perspective is also important because it acknowledges the ways in which identities have been and continue to be transformed through relocation, cross-cultural exchange and interaction (Hall 1990b). The globalization of media and culture is deeply implicated in this process (Featherstone 1990; Hall 1992a; Appadurai 1996; Hannerz 1997). Ever more sophisticated international communications technologies are used not only by transnational media corporations but also by smaller transnational enterprises serving dispersed ethnic markets, as well as by families, individuals and local communities and groups maintaining and creating specific ties (Gillespie 1997). These processes dissolve distances and suspend time, and in doing so create new and unpredictable forms of connection, identification and cultural affinity, but also of dislocation and disjuncture between people, places and cultures (Giddens 1990, 1991). Thus the new social and cultural conditions of transnationalism require a rethinking of conceptual and methodological tools. An ethnographic approach is in my view essential to tracking complex transnational connections, in order to assess the rapidly changing and augmented economic, political and socio-cultural significance of transnational communities.

Media anthropology and cultural globalization

Media researchers are increasingly looking to anthropology for conceptual and methodological tools to study the ways in which new media markets are transforming national and cultural boundaries (Silverstone 1990; Morley 1991; Silverstone *et al.* 1991; Moores 1993). Anthropology has a long tradition of studying people and places in a cross-cultural and comparative manner. In the past, anthropologists pursued their central interest in human cultural diversity through the study of local cultures, often in remote places with pre-modern social formations. More recently, anthropologists have revised their conventional conception of cultures as immutable, unchanging, bounded wholes untouched by modernity (Clifford and Marcus 1986). They have had to recognize that all cultures are impure, hybrid and constantly changing. Anthropology has also had to reckon with its troubled history of collusion with the violence and deceits of colonialism and imperialism (Asad 1973). It has often been charged with exoticizing, orientalizing, as well as degrading, the people studied, and indeed with 'inventing' 'primitive society' in opposition to a spurious conception of European civilization (Said 1978; Kuper 1992).

This history of complicity with racism cannot be ignored, especially when studying changing cultural and media boundaries. It is an enduring problem for us all, in our daily and in our academic lives, that the labels, categories, systems of classification that we use, and the hierarchies of value that we explicitly or implicitly adopt in our studies, often simplify human and cultural complexity and essentialize cultural difference. The politics and practices of research, and of representation, are very much at the heart of current debates in anthropology. As this agenda is shared by many media studies scholars, anthropology and media studies have much to learn from each other.

Ethnography enables us to track, with rich empirical detail, how global media are used and interpreted by particular people in specific local contexts. Ethnography aims at understanding the world from the point of view of the subjects of research through a long and engaged participation in their everyday lives and practices. It uses a variety of research strategies which, as far as possible, seek to gather data in natural settings. Ethnographic studies contribute to a rich understanding of what people actually do with the media, rather than predictable 'findings' about what the media do to people. Of course this is not meant to imply that media institutions are either benign, or impotent – far from it. Nor do I choose to ignore the many problems that arise from fieldwork experiences and ethnographic practice, not least the difficulties of linking micro-scale and macro-scale analyses of social phenomenon in ethnography (Hammersley 1992). But I do wish to argue the case for the adoption of a more actor-centred approach, for the use of more socially sensitive research tools for studying cultural change today, for the usefulness of multi-sited ethnographies of reception, and for the importance of transnational studies of the media. It remains for you to decide whether the very abbreviated summaries of research presented here live up to the challenge.

Mapping a Hindu nation through sacred TV epics: the Mahabharata in London and Delhi

When two of the most sacred texts of the Hindu religion, the Ramayana and the Mahabharata, were serialized as 'sacred soaps' by the purportedly secular state TV channel Doordarshan, the ratings broke all records in the history of Indian TV. Broadcast consecutively over a four-year period (1988–92), these were the most popular serials ever shown on Indian television and the viewing of them quickly became a ritualized event. All over India, Hindus performed purification rituals, garlanded their TV sets, observed ritual taboos, and participated in what became a national religious ceremony. From 9.30 to 10.15 every Sunday morning for these four years all India stood still. Never before had Indians in such large numbers (80–100 million as compared with a normal daily viewership of 40–60 million) simultaneously communed and consumed a narrative of the nation. Never before had it been possible: television on a mass scale came to India only in the mid-1980s. The television serials were widely perceived not only as sacred epics, but also as domestic/kinship melodramas, and as accurate accounts of ancient Indian history – as 'authentic' sacred narratives 'telling themselves' through the medium of television. Through viewing the serialized episodes in a devotional manner (as in acts of worshipping deities in a temple), viewers found a regular port of entry to a sacred world inhabited by splendid Gods in a Golden Age set in the mists of time in Indian history, prior to the Mughal invasions and to British colonial rule when India was Hindu India. The serials contributed to cementing the belief among vast numbers of Indians that to be truly Indian was to be Hindu. In so doing, they helped to mobilize considerable anti-Muslim sentiment (Singh 1995; Rajagopal 2000) in India and in the Hindu diaspora. This was exploited by the Hindu nationalist political party, the Bharatiya Janata Party (BJP), and several of its sister organisations. This mobilization, which took place on a transnational scale, involved political controversy over a site of worship in Ayodhia (purportedly the birthplace of the God Rama, the hero of the Ramayana), resulting in the deaths of thousands of people, mainly Muslims, in communalist slaughters on and after 6 January 1992. It also heightened tensions between Hindus and Muslims in the South Asian diaspora.

Why and how these serials were open to such exploitation, and how they provoked such a staggering and unanticipated response among viewer-devotees has been the subject of much debate (Lutgendorf 1990; Barucha 1991; Mishra 1991). Their huge popularity in India and the diaspora has been attributed variously to the mesmerizing power of television itself, to the enduring significance of sacred narratives, to the soap operatic ingredients, and/or to the unique manner in which they assisted in the reconstruction of an idealized 'imagined community' of the nation, which generated profound feelings of belonging. But these 'sacred soaps' have been regarded with the utmost disdain by most cultural critics, for whom they spell above all the demise of a long history of rich and diverse linguistic and artistic performance traditions.

There is but a short (and essential) step from discussing performance traditions to exploring the performance of tradition: mobilizations of cultural and religious nationalism which (re-)invent traditions in order to serve particular current political interests (Hobsbawm and Ranger 1983);

performances of national ceremonies (Dayan and Katz 1992); and narrative performances of nationhood (Bhabha 1990a). New media technologies very frequently serve in the reinvention of tradition (Gillespie 1989). The appropriation of the symbolic imagery and the narratives of impending social chaos and disorder in the Mahabharata by the BJP had devastating consequences for some. But in parts of the diaspora, the TV epics were appropriated in more positive ways. In order to understand more fully the discursive and hegemonic power of these TV performances of the Hindu nation in transnational networks of communications though, we need to examine their reception in the various local contexts in which they are used and interpreted, and to avoid monolithic accounts of 'the meaning' of the epic. For, as we shall see, the bringing together of ethnographic studies in various locations can help build up a much more differentiated and nuanced picture of the consequences of these TV epics.

The data for my study were gathered in the homes of Hindu families in Southall and based on my viewing of the TV epics with the family, usually in all-female viewing groups, as well as on extended interviews with women and girls locally. In earlier articles (Gillespie 1989, 1993, 1994), I elaborated how the Ramayana and Mahabharata have long played a central role in Indian popular culture where the narratives are reinscribed and reinvented anew in all art forms and performative genres, not least in every Bombay movie (Mishra 1985). The films and the comic books of the epics are exploited by parents, mothers especially, for didactic purposes in the post-migrant situation. The films especially have provided grandparents and parents with a colourful and lively way of teaching their children about the religious knowledge, beliefs and practices which are integrated into the everyday life-world of all Hindus. They have also been used for language learning and to foster a Hindu world-view more generally, and to catalyse familial debates about issues of cultural continuity and change. I also drew attention to the continuities of devotional viewing in India and the diaspora, the purification rituals, domestic worship and ritual taboos which accompany the viewing of film and TV texts perceived as sacred, and the notion of 'divine vision' (darshan/bhakti) which is seen to connect the devoted believer to the Gods and bestow blessings (Eck 1985).

The TV epics were widely viewed by Hindu families in Southall on local cable TV and/or video. The Mahabharata was also broadcast by BBC2 with subtitles on Saturday afternoons (1990–2). Though the serial in the UK was running well behind India, the sense of 'nearly' simultaneous viewing of a serial form among families in the diaspora and 'back home' was something novel, and much remarked upon by viewers. Time and again families told me that, apart from the pleasures of the serial itself, they enjoyed each episode because, when they were watching it, they felt such a close connection to the relatives back home. What is remarkable here is not only the way the viewers support Anderson's (1983) stress on the significance of imagined temporal identity (simultaneity) in constructing (trans)national community, but also the way in which the TV epics represent national, kinship and religious ties as primary and primordial, equivalent and indeed identical. The mass consumption of mediated performances of sacred texts in India and its diaspora has, in fact, generated the kind of powerful nationalist sentiments which Anderson sought to explain, though this nationalism now takes a religious form. Certainly, we now witness the strengthening of religious forms of nationalism in many contexts, which need to be studied comparatively and transnationally (van der Veer 1995).

The discursive power of the TV epics was greatly assisted by the genre of melodrama. The centrality in the serial, as in all melodrama, of kinship relations and of domestic life and conflicts affirmed connections between discourses of kinship and religion in a nationalized context, and brought to the fore the crucial importance of maintenance of the moral order in the past and in the present (Singh 1995). The TV epics also drew on age-old iconographic conventions. Although the performances of the TV epics take place in the rarefied world of the Hindu gods, these gods have long been domesticated and humanized through the use of popular iconography and performance styles with which Indian viewers are deeply familiar, not least the mythological film genre. The sacred world of the gods is apprehended through narratives of kinship set in a moral order that has to be maintained by Dharma (moral/divine law). The narratives of Hindi melodrama centre around a moral disorder, rather than a narrative enigma which has to be resolved. Viewers are less concerned about what will happen next than how (Thomas 1986). The key narrative question is: how will the moral order be maintained when threatened with chaos? This universalist theme is a screen on to which viewers project their present-day hopes and fears, anxieties and personal conflicts. The BJP was able to use effectively this threat of social and moral disorder to advance their own political purposes. They used the epic to preach that unless India returned to its pristine state as a purified Hindu nation then chaos would reign.

While Ramayana was being widely viewed in Southall, Peter Brook's controversial production of the Mahabharata was screened on British TV. I watched part of it with the mother and daughters of a local Hindu family, the Dhamis, who were to become key informants for my study. Only part of it, because it was met with incomprehension, indeed with revulsion, and switched off after about 20 minutes, whereupon Mrs Dhami and her eldest daughter left the sitting-room to perform a purification ritual upstairs.

Before we examine the ways in which processes of identification are mobilized by the TV epics themselves, it is useful to explain why the Brook version was met with revulsion, not only by this family, but much more widely The Brook version disrupted the identificatory processes typical of the TV epics, and unlike the Indian TV serials, it could not be viewed in a devotional manner. Numerous dichotomies which crystallize the differences between the two versions immediately spring to mind: Indian versus European contexts of production and reception; televised theatre aimed at metropolitan, middle-class elite audiences versus a soap/mythological hybrid genre aimed at mass, largely illiterate Indian audiences at home and abroad; Brook's multicultural casting and interpretation versus a performance and iconographic style which are distinctively Indian; didactic narrative exposition via a 'cosmic' narrator for Hindus, versus 'universalist' mysticism for westerners. Now while all the above go some way to explaining the family's revulsion, they do not tell the whole story and bear the limitations of all binary thinking.

Empirically, deeper and more subtle answers to the question only began to emerge when, several weeks after the screening of the Brook version, Doordarshan's version of the Mahabharata began to be screened on BBC2. There began a long friendship and conversation with the Dhami family, and a long-term engagement with the Mahabharata which we watched together (almost) every week for two years. Over this period we explored many features of different versions of the Mahabharata. Quite spontaneously we performed a contrastive analysis of what the Dhamis referred to as the 'Indian' and 'English' versions. We started a long conversation about the world and the epic texts, about the sacred and the everyday and it became clear that these TV epics served quite a different set of uses.

In the context of Southall where Hindus are a somewhat beleaguered minority in a predominantly Sikh community (celebrations were held on the streets when Indira Gandhi was shot, for example), the TV epics where used in a much more benign assertion of diaspora religious identity. They helped young Hindus articulate a Hindu consciousness and world-view with remarkable sophistication and philosophical depth (see Gillespie 1993, 1994). This sophistication was achieved in part by the contrastive, cross-cultural analyses of the Indian and English versions, and perhaps also by the dialogic nature of the long conversation.

One episode in particular, Draupadi's disrobing (vastraharan), which recounts the public humiliation of one of the key female protagonists of the epic, was discussed at length and in depth over several weeks. It highlights some of the differences between the Indian and English versions which made the latter so distasteful to the Dhami family. It also shows the ways in which the TV epics offer powerful representations not only of what it is to be a woman, but also of what it means to be a Hindu Indian woman in particular. Drawing upon Mankekar's (1993) ethnography of the reception of TV epic among young women in Delhi, it is possible to compare and contrast readings of Draupadi's disrobing by Hindu women and girls living in London and in Delhi. Mankekar's work provides a most useful comparison and contrast to my own work, and made apparent to me the fruitfulness of multi-sited ethnographies.

Draupadi's disrobing

Briefly, the narrative of the Mahabharata centres around the enduring conflict between two rival clans of cousins, the Pandevas and the Kauravas. Draupadi is the polyandrous wife of the five Pandevas brothers. Yudhishtira, the eldest Pandevas (resplendently dressed in white to symbolize his goodness), and Duryodhana (sinister and evil in black), the eldest Kauravas, are the chief protagonists. Duryodhana exploits Yudhishtira's weakness for gambling by tempting him into a game of dice, and so leads him to lose everything that the Pandevas possesses. He even bets and loses his wife Draupadi. The Kauravas then attempt to humiliate her and violate her honour in public by stripping off her sari in the court before the eyes of kings and gods. However, after a powerful display of rage and anger by Draupadi, the God Krishna (who is on the side of the Pandevas) intervenes and magically bestows upon her a sari of infinite length, thus safeguarding her honour. The dramatic intensity of the Doordarshan version is heightened by the use of melodramatic techniques and histrionic traditions typical of some forms of North Indian folk theatre (Lutgendorf 1990). This scene was exhaustively discussed in the Dhami family. The first response was to compare it with the English version. Here one gets a sense of the significance of culturally specific iconographic conventions, such as the semiotics of colour coding, as well as codes of godlike behaviour and dress, when the trauma of Draupadi's violation is discussed:

N: In the English version when they drag her into court, she lets everyone know that she shouldn't be seen in public because she has her period. In the Indian version they just hint at it. It's understood because she is wearing yellow clothes and she's segregated – normally she's all dressed up like a queen.

S: In the Indian version the true strength of her character comes out. She stands up to all the men and she questions all the men in the court . . .

R: And in the English one Bhisma looks at Duryodhana trying to strip her clothes off her but he would never do that.

N: They call her a prostitute and insult her really badly but the hurt of all this doesn't come across in the English one.

R: She swears that she will get her revenge and after that she keeps the wound alive.

S: It's this incident that leads to the war.

R: It's one of the most important moments in the whole Mahabharata – together with the Bhagavat Gita where Krishna tells Arjuna to kill his cousins for the honour of Draupadi and for a better world.

The Brook version did not work for the Dhami women. As the mother said: 'It left a bad taste in my mouth'. One of her daughters added: 'The English version borrowed the story, not the culture'. The dramatic weight and moral significance of this was not properly understood by Brook.

In contrast, the readings of this scene in Doordarshan's version among Hindu women in London and Delhi suggest that it opened up a space for specifically female concerns, and a feminine/ist consciousness to express itself. Draupadi is admired and revered as a symbol of female strength and vulnerability. She is admired because she exposes and challenges the men who attempt to exploit her sexual vulnerability in such a powerful manner. According to Mankekar (1993), watching her disrobing compelled the young women that she worked with to confront and think about their familial and financial, emotional and sexual vulnerabilities. The parallels in the readings of Mankekar's informants and my own are striking. The fact that Draupadi was disrobed by her brother-in-law, in front of all her in-laws signalled a dread. The fact that the ties of kinship could not protect Draupadi from such abuse resonated strongly with a fear that in-laws might fail to protect the best interests of their daughter-in-law in their home. This is a deep-seated anxiety among many young women in India and in the diaspora. Conventionally, the new bride lives with her in-laws where typically she has little power or status, at least until she either provides sons or devises other strategies for overcoming the weakness of her structural position as the property of her husband and his family (Ballard 1982). Despite enormous variations in practices, there is still a dread among many young girls, and this was often expressed to me in Southall and to Mankekar in Delhi, that things may not work out with in-laws.

Draupadi symbolizes that fear and dread. But she also represents a powerful manifestation of female empowerment and rage – an enviable assertiveness that many young women feel is denied to them on the family stage. Yet, some of our informants, both in London and Delhi, point out that her rage, though explosive and absolutely central to the entire narrative in that it leads directly to 'global' war between the two sets of cousins, is ultimately contained within the overarching ideology of family loyalty, respect and honour (izzat), and so is not entirely empowering or subversive. In fact the story of the Mahabharata culminates in a war to end all wars which is fought in the name of Draupadi. The God Krishna actually incites the Pandevas to kill their kin in the name of female honour and chastity – the highest of all moral values. Readings of this scene brought to light, to Mankekar and myself, the many personal battles in the family that women fight for independence, autonomy and individuality. Young women in London and Delhi thus converge in their expression of fears and anxieties and to negotiate identities and gendered subjectivities, and in doing so they rupture the hegemonic nationalist discourse at one moment, only to reinstate it in the next (see Gillespie 1993, 1994).

In another context, as Rajagopal's excellent study of the rise of Hindu nationalism in India highlights, the incitement to war in the world of the Gods can very easily be recontextualized to justify political Hindu violence by young, poor, urban Hindu men disenchanted with the unfulfilled promised of modernity (Rajagopal 2000). The affirmation of India as a Hindu nation (an entirely racist imagining) in the TV epics may be accepted in primordialist manner as a 'true' account of Indian history. Yet, the horrors of the religious violence and slaughter in India among the Hindu youth with whom I worked, have led to a rejection of the kind of racist imagining of the nation, in favour of a more benign cosmological imagining of Hindusim itself. Hinduism is an integral part of the ethnic consciousness and identity of all my Hindu informants (but by no means all Hindus) in the British context, but it coexists alongside a multiculturalist and an anti-racist sensibility, and a cosmopolitan world-view which reacts against rising communal tension inside the town, as well as outside it.

Young people employ various strategies to reconstruct their identities in the post-migrant situation. One of these is to find comfort and solace in a cosmic and religious view of the world which transcends and redefines the problems of everyday life in the real world – problems such as the vulnerability of women, communal tensions, class inequalities, ill health, poverty, alienation at work, consumerist materialism and environmental destruction – all issues which were much discussed by families and young people in Southall in relation to the TV epics. Discourses inherent in the TV epics on the fragility of the social fabric, threats to moral order, or the importance of Dharma (divine law) can equally be applied in Delhi and in London.

Conclusion

The emergence of digital technologies enables diaspora communities to expand and accelerate their communication networks and activities on a global scale with often unpredictable and unforeseen consequences. Old and new media, however, are not universally available and so diaspora communications tend to privilege the affluent, and the flows between different parts of highly differentiated diaspora locations are highly uneven. Huge disparities in education, wealth and social status have profound effects on diaspora politics, formations and consciousness. Nevertheless, the forms of creativity displayed in both cultural production and consumption by members of diaspora groups is often at the cutting edge or avant-garde of media and literary cultures today.

The Indian diaspora also present itself to transnational media companies as a very lucrative market ready to be exploited commercially, and as we have seen, compromised and co-opted by politico-religious movements. But new media, Internet included, may also be used by diaspora communities to foster a concern with human and cultural rights, environmental issues and new forms of cosmopolitan democracy. To understand these contradictory tendencies we need more analyses of how transnational communciations are being used by diaspora communities, and their consequences for nation-states, cultural policies and marginalized groups. This might be achieved through transnational studies of media that effectively combine political economy perspectives with the kind of culturalist approaches to media outlined here. This is as yet an aspiration which awaits realization.

Further reading

Appadurai, A. (1996) *Modernity at Large: The Cultural Dimensions of Globalization*. Minnesota, MN: University of Chicago Press.

Clifford, J. (1997) 'Diasporas', in J. Clifford, *Routes: Travel and Translation in the Late Twentieth Century*. Cambridge, MA: Harvard University Press.

Cohen, R. (1997) *Global Diasporas*. London: Routledge.

Gillespie, M. (1995) *Television, Ethnicity and Cultural Change*. London: Routledge.

Hall, S. (1992) The question of cultural identity, in S. Hall, D. Held and T. McGrew (eds) *Modernity and its Futures*. Cambridge: Polity.

Morley, D. and Robins, K. (1995) *Spaces of Identity: Global Media, Electronic Landscapes and Cultural Boundaries*. London: Routledge.

11

MEDIA AND DIASPORIC CONSCIOUSNESS: AN EXPLORATION AMONG IRANIANS IN LONDON
Annabelle Sreberny

Introduction

As the twentieth century ends with ongoing massive movements of people across state boundaries, the attempt to understand the nature of transnational, diasporic communities takes on not just theoretical significance but also real policy implications, and the study of diasporic media is a logical extension of both.[1]

Diaspora has become a key term in contemporary theorizing about immigration, ethnicity and identity. It works to destabilize some of the assumptions about the national boundedness of the 'ethnic experience', a simplistic focus on processes of assimilation and enculturation and the singularity of ethnic identity, and the obliteration of ethnic history and memory.

Approaches to ethnicity usually focus on the common bonds of language, myth and habit which bind members of an ethnic community together as a subcultural grouping within the territorial confines of a nation-state. Behaviourist approaches analysed the processes of assimilation or acculturation, in which the 'ethnics' became more and more pallid as they blended into the 'melting pot' of the cultural mainstream. In later, more nuanced models, the focus of analysis shifted toward the 'tolerance' or openness of the new host social structure which 'allows' its minority communities to maintain their cultural differences, producing newer tasty metaphors such as the 'tossed salad' of multiculturalism. Yet other work continues to focus on the racism, xenophobia and dynamics of exclusion in western societies; indeed, to critique the self-conscious siege mentality of the new Fortress Europe. What becomes obscured, forgotten, in all these approaches to ethnicity is the cultural memory and attachments to other spaces and places that ethnic communities often hold dear.

The causes of the continually shifting 'ethnoscape' (Appadurai 1990) of our globalized epoch are diverse. People may be escapees from military conflict, political refugees, economic migrants or 'guest-workers'. The massive contemporary movements include Afghanis, Iranians, Turks, Kurds, Russians, Albanian Kosovans, Romani, Vietnamese, Chinese, Algerians and Hutus, to name but a few obvious groupings. Settlement may not always be permanent, while even 'temporary' settlement can last for decades. The configurations produced are varied and complex. For example, Iran now has a semi-permanent population of well over 1 million Afghani refugees, whereas Iran has itself exported over 1 million refugees and migrants to many different countries. The visible contemporary movement of peoples prompts a focus on transnational communities which are caught, or live, between at least two and often more places, their original homes of dispersal and their new homes of arrival, neither fully at home in nor totally detached from either and often creating a significant third space of globalized diasporic connections.

These new transnational communities require a rethinking of some older conceptualizations of diaspora. For example, Cohen (1997) tries to elaborate a nine point model:

> Normally [sic], diasporas exhibit several of the following features: 1) dispersal from an original homeland, often traumatically; 2) alternatively, the expansion from a homeland in search of work, in pursuit of trade or to further colonial ambitions; 3) a collective memory and myth about the homeland; 4) an idealization of the supposed ancestral home; 5) a return movement; 6) a strong ethnic group consciousness sustained over a long time; 7) a troubled relationship with host societies; 8) a sense of solidarity with co-ethnic members in other countries; and 9) the possibility of a distinctive creative, enriching life in tolerant host countries.
>
> (Cohen 1997: 180)

But such a model suggests a sense of tradition already invented, a group consciousness already strong and rootedness as the driving force in the diasporic experience. Instead these are precisely the elements that need to be made theoretically problematic and explored empirically.

The play between fit and non-fit, belonging and longing has been explored through a variety of constructs: for example, in both Simmel's 'stranger' (see Wolff 1950) and Turner's 'liminality' (1969), where existence is lived on the edge, partial, 'ambiguous, neither here nor there, betwixt and between all fixed points of classification' (Turner, quoted in Naficy 1993: 8, 10). Naficy suggests that such a state of flux is always a potential 'becoming', an 'exilic "slipzone" of fusion and admixture' (Naficy 1993: 7), labelling the diasporic actors he is analysing as 'exilic liminars' even as he deconstructs this singularity by analysing a number of fault-lines that appear and disappear among Iranians living in California.

Gilroy (1993) shifted the analytic focus of diasporic experience from a somewhat limited and static focus on 'roots' to a more inclusive, dynamic analysis of 'routes'. He builds on du Bois's (1986) notion of 'double consciousness' which gives a sense of 'both/and', of having two identities; in du Bois's work of being both American and Black, with 'two souls, two thoughts, two unreconciled strivings, two warring ideals' (du Bois in Gilroy 1993: 126). While this is a significant conceptual move in that the traces of the past are carried into the present, this approach remains too bipolar to adequately capture the complexity and richness of some contemporary diasporic consciousness: we seem to need even more than simply 'here' and 'there'. Brah (1996) presses the anti-essentialist argument further, suggesting that 'the concept of diaspora offers a critique of discourses of fixed origins while taking account of a homing desire, as distinct from a desire for a homeland' (Brah 1996: 16). She proffers the idea of 'diaspora space' which 'foregrounds the entanglement of genealogies of dispersion with those of "staying put" . . . it is a cartography of the politics of intersectionality' (Brah 1996: 16). It is precisely the contradictions of and between location and dislocation, the 'border crossings' and the 'diasporic identities' that need to be explored in their complexity: 'diaspora space is the intersectionality of dispora, border and dis/location as a point of confluence of economic, political, cultural and psychic processes, of peoples, cultures, capital, commodities' (Brah 1996: 208).

A further shift seems to be needed, to examine the movements across space and time that lead to novel hybrid, complex 'third spaces' of cultural practice and identification. Global diasporic consciousness may be a particular vivid example of this imaginary third space of identification. So, the play around the term 'diaspora' offers approaches that can be historically and spatially more dynamic, that explore the sense of both fit and non-fit, belonging and longing that seems to exemplify the diasporic experience, as well as the multiple identifications and third-or-more spaces in which diaspora is conducted. Such a construction supports the conceptual move from identity viewed as 'either/or' to a sense of identifications as 'and/and' (Melucci 1996) and seems preferable to the claim of identity as 'hybridity', a new mixing which seems to simply highlight some putative pristine original states.

A focus on ethnicity has tended to imply a group looking inward to its new national host context. A focus on exile has meant an often nostalgic gaze 'back' to the old, political, home. A focus on diaspora seems to invite a looking around, not only in and back but also a scoping all-around gaze, multi-directional.

Such emergent diasporic consciousness, like ethnic identity, appears increasingly to be supported by the diffusion of new technologies and new kinds of cultural production. Research is beginning to map the existence and range of diasporic media channels (Dayan 1998; Karim 1998). Yet while such work on the production side of diasporic media is a useful start, the use of various media forms as part of the lived experience of diaspora, indeed the means through which contemporary diasporic consciousness may be defined and sustained, remains relatively unexplored.[2]

In this chapter, diasporic experience is the focus, and I examine how the contemporary media forms of diasporic communities both bind trans-national communities, maintain minority ethnic cultural identities and lineages of affect to old homes as well as creating ties to new homes. The metaphor of media as 'binding' is a useful one, and the chapter seeks to show the multiplicity of ties that are produced and maintained. But it is also vital to examine media use and habits within a broader map of cultural activities endorsed by diasporic communities. Too easy theoretical moves claim many peoples and their media as 'diasporic' while what is needed is rich empirically grounded material about how diaspora is experienced, lived in the everyday, and what kinds of roles the media play within the complex set of psychological, sociological and cultural dynamics that comprise diasporic reality.

Inventing the script of diaspora: a brief note on Iranian immigration

There have been earlier periods when exile was adopted as a political strategy by Iranians, for example, from the mid-nineteenth century as a protest against autocratic Qajar rule, and during the 1970s against repressive Pahlavi rule (see Sreberny-Mohammadi and Mohammadi 1991).[3] In both these periods, the exile population were predominantly male intellectuals, members of an educated middle class, their numbers were small and the timeframe was temporary. The movement out of Iran during and after the Islamic Revolution is really the first major out-movement of people that Iran has experienced; guestimates have totalled this at around 2 million, while Bozorgmehr (1998) suggests that 1990 census figures from ten major western countries total only about 640,000 Iranians.[4] Whatever the precise figures, a transnational diaspora has been created with major population clusters in New York, Washington, DC and Los Angeles its heartland; in London, Paris, Berlin, the Spanish Riviera, a limbo community in Turkey; in Perth, Australia; Japan; Costa Rica; and elsewhere.

Since the late 1970s there have been different waves of migration to Britain. Some wealthy families had bought property in London before the revolution, and many Iranian students studied in Britain during the Pahlavi period, so Royalist sympathizers fled the early stages of the revolution to real estate investments they had made long before. After the declaration of the Islamic Republic and its new forms of repression, socialist and liberal elements left, followed by young men who did not wish to be drafted to fight in the war with Iraq; followed by young women and families, when the gender restrictions became too confining. For most of the participants in the project, this was the first time they have lived for any length of time outside Iran. They are essentially writing the script of what it means to be the Iranian diaspora.

For many, their time in the UK was intended to be a necessary sojourn from their real life back home in Iran, which would be resumed when conditions allowed for their return. Yet that frame of mind has been tempered by the length of time actually now resident in Britain, the lack of dramatic change in Iranian politics and the various realities that start to impinge on the collective psyche. These people, as the first migrant generation who have directly experienced the leaving and arriving of diasporic movement, are inventing a life-script for themselves which is frequently challenged by all sorts of disturbances: familial, economic, linguistic, cultural and political.

Elusive 'community': the 'Iranians living in London' (ILIL)

There is an easy temptation in English to refer to people as 'the such-and-such community'. To ask 'Where is the Iranian community in London?' is to assume that one exists. Rather, we discovered that such a community is elusive for a number of different reasons. To ask 'Where are Iranians living in London?' is a very different search. What follows is about the ILIL.

The statistical invisibility of 'others'

There was no prior research work on the ILIL and very limited statistical data. It is very hard to disentangle Iranians from the general 1991 Census data. While a specific code was given to those born in Iran (685), the data have never been analysed down to this level of specificity. So Iranians are included in a generic 'Middle East' category, and thus remain statistically elusive.

This fits a general trend whereby people of Middle East background (like many others) tend to become invisible within the prevailing categories of ethnicity in use in Britain. For example, Modood *et al.*'s (1997) analysis of ethnic minorities in Britain utilized six ethnic categories: White, Caribbean, Indian/African Asian, Pakistani, Bangladeshi and Chinese (Modood *et al.* 1997: 11). Since the last five are fairly specific categories, Middle Easterners would presumably be counted as 'White', producing a rather gross category which actually contains a far greater range of ethnic difference than do the others. Also, as Lewis (1994: 13) among others has noted, UK Census data do not include religious affiliation, so assessments about the total numbers of Muslims in Britain vary significantly, from under 1 million to over 2 million.

Iranians are often clustered under a generalized 'other' category in descriptions of British ethnic groups. The 1991 Census data use a 'Chinese'/'other' category beyond the dominant ethnic minority markers; this is then subdivided into 'Other-Asian' and bizarrely 'Other-Other' (CRER/CRE 1993). With no definition provided of the boundaries of Asia, which are always blurred on the western edge, it is not clear into which of these 'other' categories Iranians would be fitted. Figures from the 1991 Census indicated that Iranian nationals resident in the UK, essentially individuals born in Iran, totalled 32,262, approximately half of whom (16,856) lived in inner and outer London. More recent Labour Force Surveys give slightly higher figures, and Home Office figures suggest an estimated 16,000–20,000 temporary visas have been given each year of the 1990s to Iranians, all of which suggests that official figures might be quite conservative approximations of the numbers of Iranians in Britain. Furthermore, as Census data are based on place of birth so Iranian children born in the UK, whether of two or one Iranian parents, do not show as Iranian. Also, those whose immigration status is unclear, who may have overstayed their visa period or indeed gained illegal entry, are unlikely to have been included on Census forms. Thus official figures are probably an underestimation of the real number of people with some kind of Iranian heritage or affiliation who are living in Britain.

As mentioned, just over half the 1991 Census total of Iranians resident in Britain were based in outer and inner London, mainly but still sparsely clustered into the north-west boroughs of Brent, Barnet and Ealing in outer London, and in Hammersmith and Fulham, Kensington and Chelsea and Westminster in inner London. This project was conducted in London only.

Iranians as an elusive research subject

The project triangulated a number of research methods, wary that the method could construct a research object that did not otherwise exist in a coherent form. We mapped the visible development of Iranian economic and socio-cultural activities across London: the grocery shops, video stores, restaurants and bakeries, estate agents and hairdressers that have sprung up in particular areas of London, around Kensington, Olympia, Temple Fortune and Ealing Broadway. Iranians also come together as a 'community in action' around numerous cultural events, such as traditional and contemporary musical performances, poetry readings, religious and cultural celebrations like Noruz (New Year), even the all-Persian disco nights at the Hammersmith Palais. Ongoing activities include the English-language classes, the burgeoning local community, advice and legal centres, and libraries. We developed a bilingual questionnaire which was left for self-completion in many of the above locales, and advertised the project on Iranian cable television. We conducted a number of interviews with well-known figures on the London scene, and organized many focus groups across a number of cultural organizations. Our attention to media channels as significant voices of and about Iranians – whether originating from inside the Islamic Republic, from London itself, or from other parts of the Iranian diaspora – was always contextualized within other forms of cultural expression and social interaction, which themselves had strong 'diasporic' elements.

Community and locale: the elusiveness of place

A great deal of effort was spent in trying to track down and map the emerging institutional infrastructure of the Iranian diaspora: community organizations and centres, language schools and libraries, grocery shops, video rental stores and restaurants. This was compiled with the help of listings in community newspapers, and through interviews with key figures in the community who provided assessments and analyses of the nature of the Iranian community and its locations, as well as a degree of serendipity and chance. This work revealed the geographic spread and internal cultural and ethnic diversity of Iranians in London. It also revealed considerable flux in the community, some activities ending and new activities developing during the course of the project. A detailed picture has been built up of the various 'spaces' across London which serve as markers of ethnicity and often become the focal points for local community formation. In addition, a year-long calendar of cultural, political and social events was developed which shows how Iranian ethnicity is expressed through various kinds of 'performances' that bring together people from across London, but do not constitute any long-term or clear sense of community. Indeed, one pronounced feeling is the sense that Iranians in London do not constitute a single 'community' or only in the gross sense of being different from other groupings based on national background, such as Turks or Pakistanis. Rather, Iranians are forming many local groupings dependent upon the particular area of London in which they live, or according to some pre-existing but newly elaborated ethnic, linguistic or politico-cultural line of difference. That is, simply, there are many real and potential Iranian communities in London, not just a single one.

The wide dispersion of Iranians across the capital gives them a physically amorphous existence, physical dispersion being one factor among many militating against the development of a strong sense of Iranian community. This is radically different to the experience of some other minorities in other cities, where, for example, Pakstanis in certain wards of inner-city Bradford number 50–70 per cent of the population, or the heavy concentration of people of Bangladeshi background in Tower Hamlets. Such different patterns of dispersal or concentration may go a long way to explaining the different patterns of community infrastructure and intra-community dynamics that exist among minority ethnic communities in Britain.

Media environment

The media environment available to Iranians in London is one of the richest in the diaspora outside Los Angeles, comprising a variety of print and broadcast channels with differing orientations and claims on the audience, both reinforcing and complicating the dynamics of looking in, looking back and looking around.

The press environment includes a number of daily newspapers: *Nimrooz*, which is privately owned and produced in London; *Kayhan*, which has its editorial office in Paris although it is published in London; and *Etela'at*, which maintains editorial offices in both London and New York, whose masthead proclaims it as 'The Only International Persian Daily Newspaper' and which includes a page of news in English. *Kayhan Havai'i* is a weekly newspaper, published from Tehran, and increasingly a number of Persian newspapers from Iran are available on the Net. All these newspapers carry a great deal of news and commentary about events inside the Islamic Republic. *Etela'at* in particular appears to address the globally dispersed Iranian diaspora, with the advertising on a single page offering the services of immigration lawyers in California and Ontario, travel agents in Frankfurt and North Carolina, foreign exchange dealers and tea packers in London; indeed, it may only be by appealing to the global diaspora of over 1 million Iranians that a sufficient readership is invoked to produce adequate advertising revenue.

There was strong feeling among respondents, supported by the findings on actual use, that the Persian print media were heavily politicized and read mainly by middle-aged men who tended to manifest a strong political nostalgia for Iran, the 'looking back' syndrome:

> All the Persian press is for a male readership and for the 40-plus age group and not for the younger generation . . . I think the Persian press outside the country is for only ten per cent of the Iranian population. The rest are not interested in politics. And since there are different political tendencies and divisions even within this ten per cent, so the circulation of this political press is very low and they cannot be all-embracing.
>
> (Male journalist)

> Many changes occur within our host country of residence; we are largely ignorant of them and are not interested in them. They do not have any reflection within our media. If we deal with any issues beyond our country and community, they are very general issues. Our press and media activity is not marked by local features. The Persian magazines published in London could have as well been published in other corners of Europe.
>
> (Male academic/psychologist)

A wide range of political journals (*Ruzegar-e No* from Paris), literary reviews (*Cheshm Andaz*) and satirical magazines (*Asghar-Agha* from London) are produced by exile groups, and middle-aged male newspaper readers supplement their daily feed of news and information with heavy consumption of these. Other kinds of titles, including film and women's magazines (*Banu* from London, *Nemeye Digar* from New York), are also produced from different locations. These print forms circulate through and help to maintain the global diaspora, whereby Iranians in the US, Europe and Australia are bound together through the circulation of cultural products as well as performers. The more overtly political activities are enjoyed more by middle-aged men, while women and young people also participate in this globalized culture through attendance at popular events such as sell-out musical concerts. Locally within London, a free weekly newspaper, *Niazmandihah*, is available which carries advertising about Iranian events, shops and services, the closest thing to a community newspaper for the ILIL.

Persian radio in London has had a chequered history. First privately owned, the licence was later given to the oppositional Mojaheddin-Khalgh who developed far more politically inflected programming, but then it was once again returned to private hands; such dramatic shifts in focus and audience appeal has made it difficult to sustain a regular listenership, although *Radio Spectrum* has now been broadcasting for a number of years and seeks a range of content, some of which does focus on issues inside Iran but also includes more locally inflected issues as well as popular phone-in formats. Limited hours of Persian television, *Rangarang*, are also available on selected cable stations in the London area; while it tries to cover local events and produces some of its own programming, it also carries material from Los Angeles, the heartland of Iranian diasporic culture (Naficy 1993). Television is popular across generations, but especially the young, and is well used by women, who tended to see local broadcast media as the best vehicles for constructing a sense of an Iranian community in London. Of all media, radio was the one most frequently singled out as offering real potential as a community-building vehicle but which had never really taken such a purpose seriously:

> In my opinion, radio and television are the only media which are capable of playing this role in the community and linking the community together and filling the gap. The other media are very political and right from the beginning establish their readership and audience in order to maintain their continuity . . . but my assumption is that radio and television are potentially capable of creating a sense of community.
>
> (Female language teacher)

More and more material is circulating directly from Tehran, including award-winning films, and by 1999 a 24-hour television channel supported by the Islamic Republic was available via cable.

One of the central problems that cultural producers face is the lack of a critical mass of consumers to support the activity financially. Some commented that cultural spending was not yet well established as a habit among Iranians, who prefer more conspicuous consumption:

> We Iranians spend money on some items but not on newspapers and theatre tickets. My friends can spend lots of money on clothes and dinner out, and even pay for me, but when it comes to a newspaper, they do not want to spend money. They do not have the habit.
>
> (Male cultural entrepreneur)

That helps to explain the diasporic reach of many print titles, intent not so much on generating a global politics, but rather benefiting from advertising and subscription revenues across many locales.

Thus diasporic space is constructed through a great variety of cultural activities and media channels, still mainly 'looking back' as well as 'looking around'. It was women in the main who complained about the lack of realism of Iranian media and cultural activities, which still did not take seriously the rootedness in the new place – London – of their 'Iranian' lives. It was women who most vigorously asked for local media that offered legal advice, talked about how to negotiate the British social security and health systems, that staged discussions precisely about the dilemmas of life in diaspora and the complex pulls of longing and belonging that all experienced.

Institutionalization of a minority community

The range and variety of diasporic media indicate not only the political and social concerns of the Iranian diaspora but also its institutionalization in different countries, its ongoing nostalgic obsession with Iran as well as the development of a discernible transnational community with many key nodes, including London. But it is important that the development and purposes of diasporic media be connected to other forms of diasporic community organization, and that the symbiotic nature of these different kinds of community structures be noted and explored. For example, much mediated content focuses on well-known persona – whether political, musical or literary – who traverse the diaspora giving performances and helping to put a particular place or organization on the diasporic map. The development of community organizations is one measure of the degree of longevity and sense of ongoing residency in a new host culture, operating as spatial locations that can become the nexus of different kinds of community activities. During the period of this study there were at least eight semi-permanent locations across London which provided a community focus for Iranians; some claimed to represent, even if only nominally, the entire Iranian Community Centre while others clearly identify the part of London in which they operate, as in Harrow Iranian Community Centre. Most of these centres offered drop-in facilities, legal advice and social security information, organized activities such as Noruz festivities, lectures and musical events; many also organized regular Persian language classes.

Thus simply locationally, even within the single city of London, it appears that there is no singular Iranian community but a number of more locally based communities which represent different waves of immigration, different political loyalties and class backgrounds. Outside Iran, religious and ethnic differences have also come to the fore and are evidenced through Armenian churches, Sefardi synagogues, minority language (for example Armenian and Kurdish) classes and an eclectic cultural calendar of festivities, celebrations and religiously significant dates. Yet time and again in interviews, while this ethno-religious diversity was recognized – and clearly constitutes yet further community divisions – it was felt to be less divisive than the political fault-lines that run across Iranians. Again, such empirical work shows the elusiveness of a singular Iranian community and evidence of many overlapping and not mutually exclusive subcommunities.

Looking backwards, forwards and around

The discourse of the ILIL reflects a strong awareness of moving through a psychological transition, one which was frequently referred to as a movement from exile to diaspora. Many respondents played with the language of dispersion.

> A political refugee (*panahandeh*) in the host country always lives in the past with the hope that one day he [*sic*] will finally return to his homeland. On the other hand, an émigré (*mohajer*) is cut off from his past in his country and is thinking about his future in this country.
>
> (Male poet)

> a political refugee is a mid-way passenger in the host country, in a globalized coffee-house, while an émigré is here to build a new home and nest for himself . . . a political refugee worries about all the problems in his own country in the faraway place, but an émigré is inevitably facing his own problems here . . . the political refugee, as much as possible, does not open his suitcase and even when he sits on a bench, sits on the edge as if he is waiting for the good news to arrive and to go back home. But an émigré opens his suitcase and lies down on the bench and wants to live here.
>
> (Male poet)

> over time political refugees become emigrants . . . a political refugee tries not to be absorbed in this society, while for an émigré the biggest problems and struggles are those related to his desire to be assimilated within the society which he has chosen for his future life.
>
> (Male writer)

A growing realism about their situation was also apparent among respondents, with a sense that Iranians were shifting psychologically from thinking of themselves as exiles focused on return to immigrants trying to build a new life in Britain. Many respondents talked evocatively about the continuing difficulty of making such a shift: their dreams were still located in an Iranian landscape even after many years of living abroad; that they could not bear to tell themselves that they had truly 'left' Iran; that nostalgia ran through the community, many of whom lived mentally with suitcases packed at the ready. From this, a sense of generational divide was emerging, the older generation wanting to retain a sense of Iranianness and to instil it in their children. The latter were already products of British education and immersed in British culture, being avid consumers of British media, at the same time as they also acknowledged racism and a sense of imperfect fit into the cultural mainstream.

Identity

Living in a diasporic space provokes urgent questions about what constitutes personal and cultural identity. Iranian concern about identity tended to centre a great deal on language, with worries about the younger generation not speaking Persian and the generational conflicts that developed around getting children to attend language schools. This concern is supported by our finding that 28 per cent of our respondents, even in all-Iranian households, speak English at home. Additionally, ethnic minorities within the Iranian diaspora tend to speak their own language at home (Azari, Armenian, Assyrian or Kurdish). Younger respondents suggested an emergent 'Pinglish' was in active use, with the adoption of Persian terms within an English sentence structure. For many Iranians in this study, their identity was very closely bound up with language:

> In my opinion, Iranian culture and this Iranism (*Irangari*) is very much related to our Persian (*Farsi*) language because the essential core of the Iranian culture is the Persian language . . . If we want to keep the Iranians together as a group of unified people who know themselves and those around them, we have to value those who know their language and speak it.
>
> (Female teacher)

Language bound them to Iran but also to other Iranians, especially family and friends who did not necessarily live close by, but perhaps remained in Iran or lived elsewhere in the global diaspora. One interviewee suggested that because family is so important, persuading Iranian children to learn

Persian in order to be able to talk to those they love, particularly to be able to communicate with grandparents, was a sound strategy:

> Children should love to learn Persian because they love those who speak Persian.
>
> (Female teacher)

A very different position was espoused by a writer, who considered the concern about Persian language to be a nostalgia that covered fear of loss of one's own identity:

> even if all the 4 million Iranians around the world forget Persian, no harm will come to Persian. It is not Persian that is in danger, but it is your own identity which is in danger.
>
> (Male poet)

Family use of English was sometimes described as a necessary strategy to help children integrate into British schools, but often betrayed an anger with Iranian politics that was displaced onto Persian. As yet little attempt has been made to develop Persian-language media content that acknowledges the mixed heritage of Persian youth and explores this in the language of their cultural heritage; in that sense, the London-based media may be missing an opportunity to keep Persian alive as a cultural vehicle for the next generation.

'Living in limbo': between Iran and the UK

The sense of living imaginatively both 'here' and 'there' was vividly described by many respondents. Some referred to the Iran of their dreamscapes, others to their continuing desire to return:

> Even now, after such a long time, the geographical context of my dreams and nightmares is usually Sarab [a neighbourhood of Mashad] and very rarely is it London, despite the many years that I have lived here.
>
> (Male writer)

> I cannot consider myself an immigrant, or perhaps I just cannot face it. I think that I have intentionally chosen to live here temporarily . . . but I am not prepared to accept that I have 'left' Iran.
>
> (Female teacher)

Still we have not accepted the fact of migration and to look upon our life as migrants. Many of us still have our luggage in the corner of the house waiting to return to Iran.

(Male businessman)

Again, diasporic media may play to all poles of affect: they can help Iranians relocate within the British cultural space, the inward turn; or they can exacerbate feelings of dislocation, the temporariness of the Iranian existence in England and intense involvement with affairs inside the Islamic Republic, the backward look; or they can bind Iranians to the emerging transnational Iranian community, the truly diasporic vision. Indeed, avid consumption of Persian diasporic media can lead to looking in all directions at once, maintaining a deterritorialized Iranian cultural identity as well as engagement with the fatherland, although by far the weakest invitation is toward realistic engagement with the new 'home'.

Issues of generation and gender

An internal discourse about the different generations and thus different experiences of migration was frequently evoked:

The first generation is living in their memories and most of them are not facing the realities of the life in migration. On the other hand, the new generation is emerging who are very familiar with the conditions of life in the host society. Thus the generation gap is huge in migration. So it is very difficult to speak about a totality called the Iranian community.

(Male entrepreneur)

It seems very silly that the first generation of emigrants and political refugees insist on bringing up their children, the second generation, exactly like themselves. They have to realize that these children are not anymore Iran's children, they are the children of wherever they have been born. They are Iran's gift to the world.

(Male writer)

In some comments, the theoretical shift from identity as either–or to more encompassing ideas of multiple identities of and–and were echoed and elaborated from experience:

Our children have two different motherlands – one that is their ancestral/historical motherland – the one in which their parents want them to believe – and another real one which is here because they have been born here and they are the children of here.

(Male poet)

Among the most popular of cultural events are traditional Iranian music concerts and participation at Iranian festivals such as Noruz which do draw generations and genders together. These were also the events which provided some semblance of a broader inclusive Iranian community that came together periodically but otherwise had little continuity or strong sense of itself.

Religion

While there is evidence for growing concern about identity among Iranians, this does not focus centrally upon religion. The majority of respondents (63 per cent) said they were Muslim, with very small percentages each of Christians, Zoroastrians, Jews and Bahaii, while one-quarter of respondents refused any religious identifier. In terms of practice, 62 per cent of our respondents said they were not religious and in relation to participation in Iranian collective activities, participation in religious gatherings was the lowest. It could be argued that a community running from an Islamic theocracy is not likely to manifest very strong religious tendencies; it may also be that Iranians now value a context which supports the private practice of religion and consequently take it for granted. Circumstantial evidence suggests a heightened interest in Iranian mysticism and attendance at Sufi gatherings, so further work that explores religious meaning, identity and practice within the Iranian diaspora would be a useful elaboration of our early findings. Religious content finds little space across media forms, and joking comments were made about the dominance of boring mullahs on television inside the Islamic Republic.

For a relatively small population, Iranians seem able to maintain a fairly wide range of cultural activities and media, of which concert-going – to both popular and traditional music – was the most popular activity. Yet the most frequently given answer to the question 'If you were to show a stranger something of Iranian culture, where would you take them' was 'To my house', suggesting both the incompleteness and inadequacy of public places to represent Iran as well as the intensity of Iranian identity maintenance that happens inside private space.

Conclusion

This chapter has tried to argue through some of the complexities in understanding the contemporary phenomenon of diaspora, including the manifold ways in which diasporic media can function. I challenge the easy slippage into the notion of a single 'diasporic community' by highlighting not only the generational and gender divisions that run among Iranians living in London, but also other major fault-lines structured political factionalism, different waves of migration and internal linguistic and ethnic differentiation: all have their own media, own gatherings, community structures and disputes.

Indeed what the space of diaspora does for Iranians is allow for an interrogation of ethnicity and identity in a way that rarely developed 'at home' in Iran. In many ways, it is the national signifier 'Iranian' that binds the ILIL together because religion and language are so strongly striated within them. This means that, unlike Cohen (1997) and other authors, we cannot assume coherence, a single 'community' with a united purpose. Only richly textured empirical analysis, using different methods to generate material, can give us nuanced understanding of the complexity of the diasporic process.

Living in diaspora is to be able to access a global Iranian 'collective consciousness' in a way that is impossible actually living inside the Islamic Republic because of the gatekeeping controls on media and cultural product currently in effect inside Iran. But to be a diasporic Iranian is a perversion of Gandhi's famous slogan: it is to have no simple 'home' but to be surrounded by the multiple voices of one's fellow countrymen and women.[5] Openness and access come at great cost, the mediated irony of contemporary diaspora.

Notes

1 An earlier version of this chapter was presented to the Joint Session of the Political Economy section and the Working Group on Race, Ethnicity and the Media, International Association for Media and Communication Research Conference, Glasgow, 30 July–2 August 1998.

2 A major exception to this is the fascinating research project on Floating Lives: The Media of Asian Diasporas, led by Stuart Cunningham and John Sinclair in Australia.

3 The Economic and Social Research Council (ESRC) project Multiculturalism, Moslems and the Media, funded under the ESRC programme on Media Economics and Media Culture, made some of these issues the central focus of research. The project was designed as a parallel comparative analysis of the dynamics of the Pakistan population in Bradford and Iranians in London, examining their construction of political and cultural identities in specific urban locales yet within the particular historical contexts of their diasporic experiences, and the role of

cultural and media practices in the maintenance and redefinition of identity. This chapter focuses solely on the Iranian material.
4 The ten countries are the USA, Canada, West Germany, Sweden, Great Britain, France, Norway, Australia, Israel and Japan.
5 'I want the windows of my home to be open to the cultures of the world, but I don't want to be blown off my feet by any one of them' (Mahatma Gandhi).

Further reading

Appadurai, A. (1990) Disjuncture and difference in the global cultural economy, in M. Featherstone (ed.) *Global Culture*. London: Sage.

Brah, A. (1996) *Cartographies of Diaspora: Contesting Identities*. London: Routledge.

Dayan, D. (1998) Particularistic media and diasporic communications, in T. Liebes and J. Curran (eds) *Media, Ritual and Identity*. London: Routledge.

Gilroy, P. (1993) *The Black Atlantic: Modernity and Double Consciousness*. London: Verso.

Naficy, H. (1993) *The Making of Exile Culture: Iranian Television in Los Angeles*. Minneapolis, MN: University of Minnesota Press.

Sreberny-Mohammadi, A. and Mohammadi, A. (1991) Iranian exiles as opposition, in A. Fathi (ed.) *Iranian Refugees and Exiles since Khomeni*. Costa Mesa, CA: Mazda.

Part IV

AFTERWORD: ON THE RIGHT TO COMMUNICATE

12 | MEDIA AND THE PUBLIC SPHERE IN MULTI-ETHNIC SOCIETIES
Charles Husband

Introduction

In the late twentieth century there is no need to argue that the mass media are an important facet of our social world. Entertainment media are not allowed to be innocent forms of relaxation; but, whether soap opera or Disney cartoon, their ideological content and potential for shaping beliefs, values and identities is open to scrutiny. News is equally a target of heated analysis as its ability to frame the events in our world and reflect partisan interests is studied and contested. We have several decades now of cumulative, and increasingly sophisticated, research examining the media's 'representation' of the world to us. Many of the authors in this book have made significant contributions to this process. Nor has this analysis been narrowly focused upon imagery and language but it has also placed the content of media within a broader framework which has sought to make explicit the process of media production and the economic logic of media industries. This political economy of the media and related accounts of the professional networks and interests that shape the media we routinely encounter is essential to an adequate understanding of 'race', racism and the media. And since the early 1990s the available literature which addresses this theme has become increasingly visible across the world (see, for example, Riggins 1992; Jakubowicz et al. 1994; Husband 1996; Gandy 1998).

The intention of this chapter is to step back from an immediate concern with exploring how the media construct images of majority and minority ethnic identity, and how these may impact upon the audience. Rather the aim here will be to ask some questions about what functions we expect the media to fulfil in multi-ethnic societies. In stepping back from an immediate concern with media effects we may perhaps be able to explore some of our taken-for-granted assumptions about what we expect of the media in a multi-ethnic society. I will use the idea of citizenship and of the public sphere to open up our understanding of the ways we may choose to lay down a framework of expectations for how the media should operate in a multi-ethnic society. This shift from a reactive, what *do* the media do, to a pro-active, what *should* the media do, can generate a surprisingly awkward sense of personal exposure. Instead of examining data and 'facts' about what the media have done, in which our own values and preference can be quietly implicit in our confident analysis, here we must deliberately make explicit our political stance as individuals in a particular society.

Our critical evaluation of the role of the media in a multi-ethnic society cannot, from this perspective, be allowed to operate without an explicit statement of *our* definition of multiculturalism. Multiculturalism is not just a descriptive account of ethnic diversity, it is always also a political philosophy of how these diverse ethnic identities are supposed to coexist (Goldberg 1994). Our own identity as a member of dominant or minority ethnic communities is necessarily relevant. It is relevant to how we feel about our society's negotiation of ethnic diversity. It is relevant to how we approach our understanding of what that diversity is; for the history of a society carries within it deeply embedded notions of who are the 'real' members of the society. We will therefore necessarily examine the construction of *national* identities and their relation to the legal status of *citizen*. We will explore how a society provides for a political recognition of diversity. And we will explore how a notion of *the right to communicate* may shape our expectation of the proper role of the mass media in a multi-ethnic society.

The public sphere

Before proceeding any further, and in anticipation of our later discussion of the multi-ethnic public sphere, it is appropriate that we should briefly signal the relevance of the concept of the public sphere to the argument being developed. In mass communication literature and in conferences since the late 1980s the idea of the public sphere has recurred so frequently as to almost have enjoyed vogue status. Within the development of democratic theory there is a long vein of discussion addressing the question of how and through what means shall the ruled communicate their views and wishes to the ruler. The conception of the public sphere as a communicative and institutional space wherein the principles of democracy can be practised and the rights of citizenship be nurtured and expressed, has been modified as democracy within nation-states has itself evolved (cf. Habermas 1989; Dahlgren 1991). With the increasing social complexity and mobility that characterizes late-twentieth-century societies the mass media have been perceived as having an increasingly central role in facilitating dialogue among citizens. Curran (1991) has provided a particularly robust account of the critical importance of the media in relation to the public sphere. He argues:

> According to classical theory, the public sphere (or in more traditional terminology, 'public forum') is the space between Government and society in which private individuals exercise formal and informal control over the state: formal control through the election of governments and informal control through the pressure of public opinion. The media are central to this process. They distribute the information necessary for citizens to make an informed choice at election time; they facilitate the formation of public opinion by providing an independent forum of debate; and they enable the people to shape the conduct of government by articulating their views. The media are thus the principal institutions of the public sphere or, in the rhetoric of nineteenth century liberalism, 'the fourth estate of the realm'.
>
> (Curran 1991: 2)

Perhaps it is the contemporary concerns about the operation of democracy itself in developed nation-states (Galbraith 1992; Hutton 1995) that have given particular weight to the concerns about the potential of the media to invigorate democracy. The additional complementary anxieties relating to the ownership and control of the media, the assault upon public service broadcasting and the argued homogenization of media content serves to amplify these concerns by suggesting that the media themselves are increasingly incapable of representing a diversity of voices. Thus it is from an explicit assertion of the essential role of the mass media in facilitating civility between citizens, and democracy within the nation-state, that I shall seek to outline a model of the multi-ethnic public sphere later in this chapter.

Differentiated citizenship

In the contemporary world the nation-state is taken for granted as a form of political organization. The state provides a system of institutions which provide the legal and organizational infrastructure for regulating a territorial space, the country. The political taken-for-grantedness of liberal social democracy as a way of constructing an administrative system with an authority to regulate people's lives in very many societies frequently serves to hide the fact of its relatively recent history. And the painful struggle of the newly constructed states that have emerged from the Soviet Union, as they seek to adapt to this model, serve to remind us that social democracy is not a natural or inevitable form of social organization.

The notion of a people united by a common identity, a nation, can express itself through many political forms; in recent history, for example, it found itself congenially associated with German and Italian fascism. However, the essence of what Anderson (1983) famously called 'the imagined community' is the idea of a fundamental connectedness between members of 'the nation'. The political potency of this form of collective identity is revealed in the construction and institutional practices of the nation-state when the territory regulated by the state is seen as the uniquely privileged domain of members of the nation. This view of the world is usually constructed and sustained by a supportive 'invention of tradition' (Hobsbawm and Ranger 1983) in which a selective amnesia toward the past allows for a consistent and positive account of the 'national history' to be disseminated.

From the point of view of the argument here this picture becomes additionally problematic when the legal status of citizenship is introduced into the relationship between the individual and the nation-state. To quote Brubaker (1989: 3) 'Citizenship today means membership of a nation-state'. The implications of this are expanded by Bottomore (1992: 18) who argues that citizenship is a status 'bestowed on those who are full members of a community' and that 'all who possess the status are equal with respect to rights and duties with which the status is endowed'. If only it were that simple; for in a world in which we have seen very considerable cross-border migration, and indeed international migration flows (Castles and Miller 1993), the exclusion of residents of a country from citizenship status, and the denial of access to the exercise of their rights to citizens who are defined as ethnic-minorities is an evident and contentious problem. If, as in Germany, the conception of the nation is tied to an essentially exclusive notion of the 'volk' then how may migrants and minority ethnic residents be accepted as full members? The very different ways in which countries have responded to their changing ethnic diversity (see, for example, Heckmann and Bosswick 1995) and the continuing power of national identities in constructing boundaries to social solidarity both contribute to making citizenship status a major issue in multi-ethnic societies (Balakrishnan 1996; Dijkink 1996).

Bottomore (1992) has helpfully distinguished between 'formal' and 'substantive' citizenship. The former he defines as membership in a nation-state and the latter as 'an array of civil, political and especially social rights, involving also some kind of participation in the business of government'. Clearly where there is racism and xenophobia in a country, formal citizenship may not guarantee substantive citizenship rights. The history of the emergence of distinct ethnic minority populations within a nation-state is routinely defined in relation to the majority ethnic population's expectations and self-image. Where, as in Britain, Germany and France, there is a history of overseas empire then the particularities of that history tends to inform their response to ethnic diversity. Ethnic and racial stereotypes are readily available to inform their perception of ethnic minorities. Or in countries like Norway or Ireland, with their own history of being oppressed, they may find it easy to believe that they have no propensity for racism or xenophobia. The reality would seem to be that all majority populations have exploited their national identity in order to (a) police access to formal citizenship and (b) qualify ethnic minority citizens' access to substantive citizenship rights. It is in this context that we may explore the value of the concept of differentiated citizenship.

In an important 1989 article Young provided an insightful critique of 'the ideal of universal citizenship'. She showed how a routine assumption of universal equality in fact often marginalized the experience and interests of minorities; and this led her to advocate an alternative, differentiated citizenship. More recently Kymlicka (1995) has developed this model in an explicit exploration of *Multicultural Citizenship*. At the heart of his argument is the assertion that recognizing the rights of ethnic groups, as groups, is not inconsistent with those general liberal democratic principles that are familiar in western European democracies. In developing his analysis he distinguishes between multinational states and polyethnic states. In multinational states, the cultural diversity has resulted from the incorporation of previously self-governing, territorially concentrated cultures into a large state. This has characteristically been the consequence of federation or conquest; it would include countries like Switzerland or Spain, and indigenous peoples such as native Americans in North America, the Sami in the Nordic states and Australian Aborigines. In polyethnic states, the cultural diversity arises from individual and family migration and is typical of much nineteenth- and twentieth-century migration of both persons seeking a better life and refugees fleeing oppression.

For Kymlicka (1995) the different historical circumstances underlying these forms of ethnic diversity have considerable political implications for the construction of the different facets of differentiated citizenship. Thus, he argues for differentiating between the rights to be allowed *national minorities* in multinational societies and those to *ethnic groups* in polyethnic states. He persuasively argues that the distinct historical experience of national minorities allows for their pursuing self-government rights which would not be available to minority ethnic groups. These self-government rights typically are attached to jurisdiction over a particular territory which is designated as being historically linked to the national minority.

Kymlicka in fact proposes three forms of group-differentiated rights, which as we shall see below have quite significant implications for communication policy and the operation of the mass media in multi-ethnic societies. Self-government rights he defines as the delegation of powers to national minorities, while polyethnic rights he defines in terms of financial support and legal protection for certain practices associated with particular ethnic or religious groups. Finally there are special representation rights which he defines in relation to guaranteed seats for ethnic or national groups within the central institutions of the larger state (Kymlicka 1995: 6–7, 26–33).

Clearly for a nation-state to allow a national minority to have jurisdiction over its own 'nation', while they are simultaneously citizens of the broader state, requires a moral and legal recognition of their distinctive experience, and their unique location within the state. This particular expression of differentiated citizenship is central to the current work in producing the international legal instrument – the UN Draft Declaration on the Rights of Indigenous Peoples. Indeed in Australia, New Zealand, North America and Europe there are already clear instances of the application of elements of self-government rights to indigenous peoples (Gayim and Myntti 1997). Where such rights have been allowed, it has facilitated policies which have contributed to the retention of traditional law, the resilience of community languages and it has provided a basis for a cultural resistance to the dominance of majority values and practices. In part this has been through media policies which have guaranteed media run by and for indigenous peoples (Browne 1996) and in some instances has provided for the community regulation of the flow of majority media into indigenous communities (Dowmunt 1993). This certainly constitutes a radical departure from the economic liberalism that characterizes so much of media policy, for it represents a collective decision determining individual media choice. As such this is very different to the individualism located in such notions as 'consumer sovereignty'. The Australian experience of the BRACS (Broadcasting to Remote Aboriginal Communities System) provides one example of such self-government shaping the media environment of an indigenous people (Batty 1993).

Polyethnic rights provide the basis for the state seeking to support initiatives which may protect specific religious and cultural practices which may not be sustained through simple market forces. Indeed polyethnic rights may include legislation which seeks to prevent the cultural and identity concerns of minority ethnic groups being marginalized or suppressed by the deliberate, or unthinking, discrimination of the majority ethnic population within the country (New Community 1994). Special state support for media policies and funding to address the media interests of minority ethnic groups are one particular expression of polyethnic rights. However, as with the special provision for national minorities, the state's facilitation of ethnically specific media is no guarantee of their viability or success. Where the minority ethnic group is small or widely dispersed then they may have difficulty in constituting a commercially viable audience. Finance recurs as a major issue in the development and longevity of minority ethnic media (see Bovenkerk-Teerink 1994; Hussein 1994; Ngui 1994).

For this reason alone it is apparent why special group representation rights are the important third element in group differentiated rights: they serve to place the particular interests of national minorities and minority ethnic groups within the power-broking institutions of society. If this representation is to be meaningful then these representatives must have a realistically powerful presence when participating in the struggle over the allocation of resources and the definition of priorities. Clearly special group representation within the state institutions may itself be a critical precursor to the recognition and definition of self-government and polyethnic rights. Significant minority representation within the senior management of public service broadcasting systems and broadcasting authorities would be necessary expressions of this right in multi-ethnic societies.

The essential linkage between the concept of differentiated citizenship and the explicit formulation of a model for multicultural coexistence lies in the fundamental recognition of the individual as social. Following Young (1989), there is a recognition that citizenship rights founded in universal respect for the individual may not adequately accommodate the competing rights and expectations of minority ethnic groups. Group differentiated rights therefore start from an acceptance of social solidarity within ethnic and national minority identities as intrinsic to individual identities. However, they then allow for the political expression of groupness through policies targeting group rather than universalist individual rights. Consequently a multicultural policy based upon the assimilation of minorities to the majority culture is not compatible with group differentiated rights. Assimilationist policies may claim to guarantee the universal formal rights of the citizen but they in effect demand that migrants and national minorities surrender their social and cultural substantive rights.

Differentiated citizenship is compatible with a multicultural policy which recognizes cultural diversity and permits cultural pluralism: that is the coexistence of differing cultural traditions and values within the country. However, as has often been seen in Europe, cultural pluralism has in effect been tolerated in the private domain of the home, while the public domain of work and the state has remained the exclusive terrain of the majority population (Wrench and Solomos 1993). The language of host and migrant, of culture lag or cultural deficit, and of 'the national interest' have all in different ways provided an acceptable coded language through which cultural pluralism has been effectively constrained (Centre for Contemporary Cultural Studies 1983; Smith 1994).

The privatization of cultural pluralism to domestic space is most explicitly challenged by promotion of structural pluralism: a deliberate promotion of ethnic diversity in institutional and structural terms. European examples of resistance to the construction of mosques, or the British resistance to the creation of Muslim schools, reveal how different is the acceptability of institutional autonomy, as opposed to private diversity (Husband 1994c). In media terms this is the difference between accepting that what people do in the privacy of their own homes is their own business, and acceptance of the proliferation of media which are linguistically and politically targeting and expressing the interests of specific ethnic communities. Very often the official state policies that affirm tolerance of minority ethnic cultures have built within them an implicit fear of diversity itself. And this fear then justifies a widely held consensus that there is a natural threshold of tolerance beyond which 'reasonable' people cannot be expected to go (Blommaert and Verschueren 1998).

The autonomy of ethnic groupings to pursue their own interests within the broad political framework of the state is a key characteristic of structural pluralism. It reflects in real terms the analytic insight into ethnic identity provided by Wallman (1986) when she distinguished between ethnicity as 'consciousness of kind' – a social psychological sense of identity – and ethnicity as 'structure' – the infrastructure of institutions and organizations that enable the living of one's ethnicity. There is a sense in which ethnicity is social psychological, a sense of who I am. But in the absence of a place where I can speak my language, buy my foodstuffs and my music, and express my faith with others; then how shall I express my identity in action. Nor does this celebration of my ethnic or national minority identity make me necessarily a less trustworthy and responsible citizen. Patriotism toward a country does not depend upon a shared 'national' identity. Switzerland alone is an adequate demonstration of this fact. Consequently the model of multiculturalism that allows for this connectedness between the fabric of society and a personal sense of ethnic identity is one which incorporates and promotes the necessary structural pluralism consistent with a true acceptance of the diversity present in the country. Differentiated citizenship, and the associated group differentiated rights provide the necessary political framework for this to be possible. But, as we shall see below, not necessarily without difficulty.

The right to communicate

The political framework offered by differentiated citizenship provides a sound platform upon which to begin to sketch a model of a multi-ethnic public sphere. However, there is a further tool that I would wish to bring on board first, and this derives directly from hotly contested communication theory. The right to communicate has a long and fraught history (Hujanen 1988, 1989) and as an inclusive conception of communication seeks to draw together those established rights including freedom of speech, of the press, of information and assembly. There is an inherent virtue in this, in that as an overarching right it asserts the necessary interdependence of each on the other. Whether it be concerns about globalization and the homogenizing of culture (Featherstone 1990) or the critical place of information in shaping and limiting political freedoms (Herman and McChesney 1997) or the many variations on a concern with 'cultural imperialism' (Tomlinson 1992; Sinclair *et al.* 1996) there is ample evidence of widespread concerns about potential limitations upon our communicative freedoms. Consequently the right to communicate may legitimately be seen to be another essential framing variable in the construction of a model of the multi-ethnic public sphere.

In order to effectively use this tool it is appropriate to first develop an understanding of it, and I would argue that the right to communicate is best placed within the human rights discourse as a 'third generation human right'. As Mbaye (1986) has argued:

> civil and political rights are based on the principle of liberty, whereas economic, social and cultural rights derive from the principle of equality. In the case of the former rights, an abstention is required of the state: in effect the state must avoid preventing the exercise by individuals of the rights and liberties that are recognised as theirs . . . Conversely, for the enjoyment of the second category of rights the state must make provision for their achievement.
>
> Such rights could be categorised by saying that civil and political rights are 'rights of', while economic, social and cultural rights are 'rights to'. These first and second generation rights are now completed by third generation rights, the achievement of which can no longer be

obtained merely by abstention or provision on the part of the state, but requires solidarity between people and states. These rights of solidarity are basically the right of peace, the right to the environment and the right to development. There are however, other such rights.

(Mbaye 1986: 28–9)

Thus if we conceive of the right to communicate as a third generation right then we may reasonably expect that the state will abstain from arbitrarily interfering with individuals' communicative freedoms, and will in a complementary manner through its policies and actions ensure a material infrastructure of resources and institutions which will facilitate the exercise of these freedoms. And of course, given the argument above we would expect in a multi-ethnic society that these second generation obligations would be promoted through the application of a group differentiated rights philosophy.

There is, however, a fly in this potentially potent ointment. Only a little reflection will make us aware that a great deal of the contemporary debates around freedom of speech or the challenge to hate speech is all too frequently carried out within a myopic and egotistical first generation rights discourse. To caricature it, this often takes the form of a simplistic but robust assertion that 'I will not have my rights of utterance constrained'. Translated into a broader communication policy these sentiments reduce a right to communicate to a unidirectional interpretation of first and second generation rights as a licence to encode and decode, transmit and receive, on your own terms. This radical individualism is inconsistent with a society's ability to sustain a respect for diversity, sustained through differentiated citizenship. This self-centred, egotistical and hence ethnocentric, approach to communication is not open to learning, is not concerned with dialogue and reciprocal exchange; rather it commodifies communicative acts as personal exploitation of a resource – communication.

Such a perspective on communication is entirely inappropriate to the promotion of civility and inter-ethnic dialogue in a multi-ethnic society. Faced with these circumstances I have proposed (Husband 1996, 1998) the necessary modification of the right to communicate by the attachment of a qualifying complementary right – *the right to be understood*. This entirely utopian, but necessary, concept draws not upon the individualistic tradition of European human rights thinking which is implicit in the Universal Declaration of Human Rights (see International Commission on Jurists (ICJ) 1986: 25) but rather draws upon the African Charter on Human and People's Rights (ICJ 1986) which is informed by the value of solidarity with others, as outlined by Mbaye (1986) above. It outlines the duties of the individual toward the community and affirms the essential social and collective nature of rights. As such its centre of gravity is compatible with the legal framework of differentiated citizenship outlined above. As I have argued elsewhere:

> The Right to be Understood would place upon all a duty to seek comprehension of the other. The right to be understood qualifies the right to communicate by rejecting and condemning egocentric and ethnocentric routines of engaging with the communicative acts of others.
>
> (Husband 1998: 139)

In building a conceptual framework for the construction of a multi-ethnic public sphere the first and second generation principles of the right to communicate clearly define the necessary functions of the state in guaranteeing an equitable communications environment. The third generation demands of the right to be understood lays a burden of responsibility upon the citizens operating within that environment. It asserts that all must accept the burden of trying to understand, and as such is consistent with the communicative openness and curiosity implicit in models of intercultural communication.

The multi-ethnic public sphere

Given the arguments above it is now clear that a multi-ethnic public sphere must reflect the diversity present in society in such a way as to facilitate the autonomous expression of ethnic identity of both minority and majority ethnic groups, and of national minorities. Additionally it must provide for the exchange of information and cultural products *across* these communities of identity. A wide diversity of media serving audiences defined exclusively in terms of distinct ethnic identities may be consistent with group differentiated rights, but it would be a Babel of parallel and exclusive public spheres that would have no sympathy with a right to be understood.

Thus the defining elements of a model of a viable multi-ethnic public sphere are threefold. First, the state must fulfil its first generation human rights obligations by creating the space for the expression of individual, and collective, communicative freedoms. Second, through the adoption of the philosophy of differentiated citizenship, and the application of the attendant group differentiated rights, the state should fulfil its second generation human rights functions in enabling the emergence and continued vitality, of a diverse media structure reflective of the ethnic diversity present in the society. Finally, consistent with third generation human rights thinking, the state should promote 'the right to be understood' as a principle which should inform the exercise of the communicative rights promoted by the two prior actions. This is certainly a utopian model. But if we are to assess the adequacy of the mass media in sustaining a rich and engaged democratic exchange within contemporary societies it is necessary to establish explicit benchmarks.

If we begin to explore how such a media infrastructure may be developed it is immediately apparent that contemporary changes in mass media technologies and structures are already highly favourable to the promotion of diversity within the media environment. Since the late 1980s the very considerable proliferation of direct broadcasting by satellite (DBS) and the continuing expansion of cable systems have significantly increased the number of channels available. If we add to this the impact of video cassette technology and the emergence of digital video discs then the opportunity for consumer choice in the audio visual media has expanded enormously. Niche marketing in the music industry and digital compression in radio has further extended this repertoire. In addition to which, although personal computer ownership has not achieved the penetration nationally or internationally that some partisan commentators might suggest, it is clear that the entry of information technology into the domestic sphere has opened up new opportunities for the richness of CD-ROM multimedia and Internet services to enter the home. In essence in developed western societies we live in a media rich world. However, this statement must be carefully qualified by an explicit recognition of the high levels of poverty operating within these societies. This is so much so that we may reasonably talk of a quarter of some national populations and a much higher proportion of some minority ethnic communities having only a marginal access to the world just described above. Consequently it is this disparity of access to the media which must also be addressed in constructing media policies for a multi-ethnic society.

However, it is the case that in the contemporary world of the mass media we are witnessing increased consumer choice paralleled by increasing audience fragmentation. While there is a discernible global restructuring of the mass media, there is also a proliferation of media which are targeting quite distinct audiences. Thus the current media environment is already compatible with the diversity of media implicit in the above model of a multi-ethnic public sphere. Diversity of choice and niche marketing are already intrinsic to the contemporary mass media.

While this contemporary context is propitious for the development of the multi-ethnic public sphere there are, however, sound reasons for caution. The demography of minority ethnic communities and minority national populations may not be such as to render them commercially viable audiences for particular media. Where these populations are small in number, or widely dispersed, they may not constitute a viable economic base for a medium dedicated to servicing their needs. Clearly the size of the African American or Hispanic populations in the United States makes them potentially attractive audiences. But small communities of Tamil or Sudanese refugees or the numerically small and dispersed populations of Sami in the Nordic states present an economic challenge to would-be media providers.

In many instances a commercial basis for minority ethnic media is not sustainable. In this context we may look to the state to fulfil its second generation obligations within a differentiated groups rights approach, namely to provide a state subsidy to ensure the presence of an appropriate media infrastructure. Although to some this will sound like a radical manifestation of 'the nanny state' there are in fact many instances of just such policies around the world (for example in Australia, Canada, Great Britain, Norway and New Zealand). Not surprisingly perhaps, the literature on such state subsidy indicates that frequently the state's operation of polyethnic rights principles is often marked by tokenism and niggardly funding (Husband 1996). Additional difficulties are also apparent in the managerial struggle over just who is in control of such initiatives when they are established. The experiences of indigenous broadcasting in Australia and New Zealand amply suggest the difficulties which may arise over the representativeness of the 'ethnic' management structure and the tensions between the ethnic and the commercial imperatives built into the enterprise (Batty 1993; Pattel-Gray 1998).

State subsidy of minority ethnic media is a logical expression of polyethnic differentiated group rights and is intrinsic to the creation of a realistically diverse multi-ethnic public sphere. Given that the majority ethnic communities are frequently xenophobic or racist, and that often the state policy on managing diversity is negotiated through an inherently continuing assimilationist ethos, whatever the formal rhetoric, then not surprisingly such initiatives may well generate majority resentment. That telling concept, 'Victimization of the majority', evokes exactly that sort of righteous resentment which majority nationalism can invoke in a majority confronted by initiatives aimed at minority interests. However, if a multi-ethnic society is to enjoy long-term peace and cohesion it is exactly such myopic ignorance which must be confronted through a vibrant public sphere. There is nothing in the democratic process that guarantees that the public sphere is an arena of sweetness and light. On the contrary, in multi-ethnic societies marked by inequalities and quite different cultural agendas, the short-term impact of the public sphere proposed here must necessarily generate a disquietingly 'robust' exchange between the participants. The necessary fundamental recognition that a society is irretrievably multi-ethnic must render majority self-interest, and the attendant complacent hypocrisy in denying equitable citizenship status to all, a condition whose days are numbered. The period of transition may, however, be uncomfortable to many.

Nor can we assume that the facilitation of a diverse media environment will necessarily be uniquely positive in its utilization by minority ethnic communities. Taylor (1992) has spoken about the transition from a politics of recognition, where individuals responded to each others as equals with reciprocal respect, to a politics of difference, where groups in defining their distinctiveness refuse to be homogenized to a universal similarity. This has close affinities to Young's (1989) critique of universalism in human rights discourse. In effect the politics of difference insists that in recognizing my difference, if you wish to treat me equally then you may have to treat me differently. This of course is entirely compatible with the adoption of differentiated citizenship and the application of differentiated group rights. The difficulty may arise when an ethnic group's definition of itself incorporates prejudicial views of outgroups or restricts the individual freedoms of members of its own ingroup. For such a group their use of dedicated ethnic media may constitute a propaganda machine for their own intolerance. Possession of minority ethnic status is no guarantee of political virtue, and Kymlicka (1995) rightly addresses the question of how shall we tolerate intolerant minorities. The answer is in essence, as we would intolerant majorities: we would not.

The picture painted so far of the multi-ethnic public sphere is one characterized by a great diversity of media operating on commercial, and on a semi or fully subsidized basis. Here the focus is upon guaranteeing the opportunity for access and participation in the media, on an equitable basis, to all ethnic communities in society. This is about giving voice. It is about reducing or removing the economic, professional or political constraints upon employing the media as a core route to participation in the public sphere. And in and of itself this is good. But on its own it would be an inadequate media base for a multi-ethnic public sphere. There is an audience driven logic to much of the media located in this sector which is likely to give them relatively narrow demographic profiles: they will serve quite distinct audiences. How then does this relate to a right to be understood? Where is the exchange across boundaries?

In order to develop a balanced media system that can ensure not only the unbridled voice of particular interest groups, but also channels where interest groups engage across ethnic boundaries then there must but complementary media. One obvious candidate for this role is public service broadcasting (PSB). Although widely believed to be on the defensive, the tradition of public service broadcasting contains values compatible with the ethos of the right to be understood. It is not solely market driven, can be unembarrassed in its advocacy of a collective public good, and has an ability to target a wide range of audiences on its own terms. Given the lamentable lack of social diversity present in the staffing and management of many PSB institutions then it is likely that both special representation rights and aspects of polyethnic rights must necessarily be invoked in order to construct media institutions with the ability and legitimacy to address ethnically diverse audiences. Indeed given the increasing audience choice and market segmentation it is also reasonable to hypothesize that for the major commercial national media a judicious embracing of a PSB ethos in serving 'the mainstream' may increasingly sit comfortably with their own market placement. The 'mainstream' in these terms then becomes the heterogeneous citizenry in pursuit of high quality media that may not be readily accessible across the range of 'niche' media.

Conclusion

Thus the argument in this chapter has been to make explicit the necessary elements for the construction of a multi-ethnic public sphere. Drawing upon a conceptual framework of political philosophy the fallibility of much multicultural policy has been exposed and the necessity of pursuing a policy of differentiated citizenship has been argued. This provides a legal-political framework in which the distinctive histories and current experiences of differing ethnic groups can be formally recognized by the state. Once this is in place then the pursuit of communication rights can be advanced through group differentiated policies. However, the Eurocentrism in much human rights discourse is recognized and challenged by the invoking of a complementary right to be understood. This conceptual framework in interaction provides the means within which an appropriate multi-ethnic public sphere may be developed.

This is undoubtedly a utopian project, but not a futile one. It establishes the benchmark criteria for a multi-ethnic media environment. This is defined by the complementarity of media giving voice to specific ethnic community interests and media facilitating an inter-ethnic multi-interest exchange. Finally, as a utopian project it is not naively optimistic. In challenging the vested interests and xenophobia of the majorities, and the partisan intolerance within segments of the marginalized minority communities this model anticipates an equalitarian structural pluralism achieved through some distressing exchanges in the public sphere.

Further reading

Curran, J. (1991) Rethinking the media as public sphere, in P. Dahlgren and C. Sparkes (eds) *Communication and Citizenship*. London: Routledge.

Goldberg, D.T. (ed.) (1994) *Multiculturalism: A Critical Reader*. Oxford: Blackwell.

Husband, C. (ed.) (1994) *A Richer Vision: The Development of Ethnic Minority Media in Western Democracies*. London: John Libbey.

Kymlicka, W. (1995) *Multicultural Citizenship*. Oxford: Oxford University Press.

Young, I.M. (1989) Polity and group difference: a critique of the ideal of universal citizenship, *Ethics*, 99(2): 250–74.

DISCUSSION OF KEY TERMS AND CONCEPTS

Diaspora/diasporic consciousness

Literally 'to disperse' or 'scatter', the term *diaspora* refers to the movement of populations and groups – whether forced or voluntary. *Diasporic consciousness* thus refers to the distinctive forms of consciousness associated with communities and groups that have experienced social and cultural dislocation and the complex forces of attachment and belonging, isolation and difference that are experienced in everyday life and which, to use W.E.B. Du Bois's term, can result in a form of 'double consciousness' (see Gilroy 1993; Gillespie, this volume; Sreberny, this volume)

Ethnic minorities in the UK and the US

The presence of ethnic minorities in the US and the UK has been forged by historical and contemporary flows of people and the operations of power. Disparate *native, immigrant, migrant and refugee groups and communities* – some indigenous, some long settled, others newly arrived, yet others transitory and/or transnational and transcultural – today characterize these two societies. Ethnic minorities and *diasporic communities* are richly differentiated by *different histories* (and *her-stories*), the *politics of exile* and encounters with their 'host' societies and with each other. They are also characterized by different demographics, languages, religions, traditions, customs and internal processes of cultural negotiation, adaptation and change. Ethnic minority populations in both the UK and the US have experienced, and many continue to experience, structural inequalities, processes of disadvantage and racist discrimination in many areas of social activity and endeavour, and significant numbers also continue to confront harassment, personal violence and attack. These lived realities have been informed by the actions and policies of state, and generated struggles for civil rights and political participation (see Omi and Winant 1995; Solomos and Back 1996).

Ethnic minorities in the UK

Many minority ethnic populations in the UK, like those in the US have been historically shaped by processes of slavery and conquest (Fryer 1984). Unlike the US, however, the majority of the UK's racialized ethnic minority communities have arrived and settled relatively recently, though inter-state relations, flows of people from and to former British colonies, and sedimented white ethnocentric attitudes all betray the continuing influence of former British imperialism and colonialism. At the 1991 Census count Britain's population of just under 55 million people included 1.5 per cent 'Indians', 0.9 per cent 'Pakistanis', 0.9 per cent 'Black Caribbeans', 0.4 per cent 'Black Africans', 0.3 per cent 'Bangladeshi', 0.3 per cent 'Chinese' and 0.4 per cent 'other Asians'. Britain's ethnic minority population today comprises approximately 5.5 per cent of the population (UK Office of Population Census and Surveys, 1991 Census). These official designations, as with those for the US below, however, are at best crude descriptors of both ethnicity and identity and can be criticized, at worst, for harbouring essentialist ideas of 'race' (for more on language and terms see Ross, this volume).

Ethnic minorities in the US

The historical emergence of the US is inextricably bound up with arrival of diverse European settlers and the enforced and voluntary incorporation of others. 'The American obsession with the melting pot has its origins in conquest, slavery and the exploitation of foreign labour: from the Indians uprooted and banished to reservations; the Mexicans conquered and subjugated by expansionism; the Africans abducted and forced into perpetual servitude; and the Asians coaxed and cajoled into exploitative indentureships' (Small 1994: 9). Across the nineteenth and twentieth centuries influxes of people from different countries, and for a variety of economic and political reasons, have contributed to today's US 'All Races' (*sic*) population of 272,402 million including 12.8 per cent 'Black', 0.9 per cent 'American Indian, Eskimo and Aleut', 4.0 per cent 'Asian and Pacific Islanders' and 11.4 per cent 'Hispanic origin (of any race)' (US Census Bureau, Population Estimates Program, 1999). Currently 'people of colour' comprise approximately 20 per cent of the population and form an overwhelming majority in many urban centres.

Hybrid-culture/hybridity

Cultures are always in flux and they contain the elements and traces of historical encounters with other peoples, cultures and forms of political struggle. Nowhere is this more pronounced than in *post-colonial societies*. Post-colonial societies are theorized today as 'the totality of practices, in all their rich variety, which characterise the societies of the post-colonial world from the moment of colonisation to the present day' (Ashcroft *et al.* 1995: xv). The encounters between indigenous peoples and local cultural practices and western forms of rule, power and culture are thought to variously have produced cultural forms of assimilation, co-option, synthesis, resistance and subversion often expressed in and through *hybrid-cultures* – cultural forms that are also increasingly produced in the *globalizing* present. Salman Rushdie, when describing his 'symptomatic' and controversial book, positively evaluates the cultural fusions that can result: 'The Satanic Verses celebrates hybrid-ity, impurity, intermingling, the transformations that come out of new and unex-pected combinations of human beings, cultures, ideas, politics, movies, songs . . . It is the great possibility that mass migration gives the world, and I have tried to embrace it' (Rushdie 1991: 394). (See also Bhabha 1990a; Ashcroft *et al.* 1995; Harindranath, this volume; Gray, this volume, on globalizing trends in television and the representations of 'blackness'.)

Institutionalized racism

Generally the term *institutionalized racism* is now used to refer to how discrimina-tory processes and outcomes are not always the product of individual bigotry and racist prejudices, but may in fact be the product of institutionalized *norms, culture* and *unthinking or unwitting practices* that unintentionally and/or insensitively reproduce wider structures of disadvantage and processes of discrimination. Advanced in the 1960s as a corrective to simplistic ideas that confined 'racism' to individual prejudice and overt acts of racist behaviour, the concept has subsequently been used in generalizing and/or contradictory ways and can thus be criticized in the context of *anti-racist politics* for losing analytical bite, letting 'responsible' indi-viduals within organizations off the hook, and polarizing issues of racism into a sim-plistic opposition of white and black interests, thereby reproducing the *essentialism* inherent to ideas of 'race'. Carefully deployed and analytically specified, however, the concept of institutionalized racism continues to have relevance for the analysis of media institutions, professional and routine practices, and the production of detri-mental and discriminatory 'representational' outcomes. (For discussion of unin-tended professional outcomes and corporate and organizational practices leading to processes of ethnic minority under-representation and misrepresentation, see Wilson, this volume; Cottle, this volume.)

Multiculturalism

Multicultural societies are societies – now the vast majority – that are composed of a *plurality of cultures* and communities, each sustaining different (though often overlapping) beliefs, traditions, practices and ways of life. Societies can respond to the fact of *multicultures* in a number of different ways. *Monoculturalism* asserts the superiority of the dominant culture, denies respect or value to the cultures of others and therefore seeks to *assimilate* communities and cultures into its world-view and way of life. *Multiculturalism* generally seeks to recognize, positively evaluate and celebrate cultural diversity and *integrate* minority cultures and communities without undermining their claims to distinctiveness. Contemporary multiculturalism has often been criticized in the context of *anti-racist politics* for failing to address struc-tural and systemic inequalities, its superficial and seemingly static understanding of cultural diversity, and its tendency to *exoticize* the cultures of others. In recent years it nonetheless represents a significant advance in normative thinking and has informed such policies as *affirmative action* in the US and *multicultural education* in the UK. Multiculturalism can in fact assume a diversity of forms (Parekh 1997) and today, unsurprisingly therefore, is one of the most hotly contested terms (and normative doctrines) in the field of 'race', racism and ethnicity (Goldberg 1994; Husband, this volume).

Problematics of 'race', racism and ethnicity

The notion of 'problematics' in this context refers to the wider theoretical and political frameworks that conceptualize and prioritize different research 'problems' or questions and which structure our thinking and debates about the social and discursive realities of 'race', racism and ethnicity. Developing on the ideas of others, three general 'problematics', described below, today contend for wider theoretical recognition and help to structure the field (see Hall 1988, 1999; Miles 1993; Solomos and Back 1996, 1999; Miles and Torres 1999).

Problematic 1: the 'race relations' problematic

The 'race relations' problematic is deeply embedded within common-sense views in both the UK and the US and continues to inform academic discussion and study to this day (Mason 1999). Early sociological approaches to the study of *'race'* had sought to theorize *'race relations'* in terms of *inter-group processes* of adjustment, assimilation and in relation to conflicts over status claims and resources (Park *et al.* 1923; Rex and Moore 1967). This way of conceptualizing 'race relations' has subsequently been criticized for failing to adequately theorize the systemic processes and persistent structures of inequality, the exclusions of power and the prevalent culture and experience of racisms that condition such 'inter-group' encounters. Moreover, the very terms deployed, 'race relations', appear to presume *'race'* not only as a self-evident category but also as the key explanatory factor thought to explain *racial conflict situations*. This appears, then, to endorse erroneous common-sense ideas of 'race' as biologically real (Miles 1982; Miles and Torres 1999) even though most sociologists would today argue that 'race' can be taken as 'real' only in terms of its *material consequences* and *discursive effects* (Mason 1995; Omi and Winant 1995).

Problematic 2: the 'racism/racialization' problematic

Based on the critique of the 'race relations' problematic, Robert Miles, among others, has consistently argued that what we should actually be studying is how material inequalities and signifying processes combine to 'racialize' groups as 'races' and thereby help sustain, for example, the structures and processes of class inequality and the exploitation of migrant workers. *Racialization* 'refers to a process of categorisation, a representational process of defining an Other (usually, but not exclusively) somatically' (Miles 1989: 75; cf. Small 1999). In the context of the US Michael Omi and Howard Winant have proposed a view of *racial formations*, which is defined as 'the sociohistorical process by which racial categories are created, inhabited, transformed and destroyed' (Omi and Winant 1994: 55), and they analyse the role played by 'race' in political projects and in relation to hegemonic structures of power. In the UK influential analyses of the so-called *'new racism'* have been theorized not as 'the result of autonomous racial conflicts' or as 'the outcome of abstract laws of capitalist development' (Solomos *et al.* 1982: 27) but in relation to an 'organic' crisis of capitalism in which 'race' becomes discursively mobilized and articulated, in relation to the state's attempts to 'police the crisis' and maintain hegemonic dominance (Hall *et al.* 1978; Hall 1980a). Today however, the term 'new racism' is often used to refer to public statements and cultural forms of representation which racially essentialize others but which do not necessarily involve a conjunctural analysis of state and politics (see, for example, van Dijk, this volume).

Together these positions and debates help to define the 'racism/racialization' problematic in opposition to common-sense views of 'race relations' and the focus shifts to the historical and contemporary processes by which social groups become 'racialized' or *'raced'* and how ideologies and discourses of 'race' are both constituted by, and constitutive of, racist exclusions and practices – whether in relation to the state, institutions or everyday practices (see Fiske, this volume). *Multiracial feminists* have here played a leading role in opening up the discursive complexities of *sexuality*, *gender* and class and how these are variously refracted within and through discourses and representations of 'race'. Together, these theoretical concerns and coordinates point to the relevance of attending to (and challenging) media representations of 'race' (see Dines and Humez 1995; McLintock 1995; Berry and Manning-Miller 1996), as well as media institutional under-representation and processes of *institutionalized racism* (Cohen and Gardner 1982; Wadsworth 1986).

Problematic 3: the 'new ethnicities' problematic

Recently a third, 'new ethnicities' (Hall 1988) problematic has emerged which seeks to engage with the cultural complexities of ethnic identities, processes of identity formation and change and with the *'new cultural politics of difference'* (West 1993). These writers theorize the discursive complexities and 'positionalities' involved in *ethnic identity* – approached not as essentially fixed or *primordial* – but as culturally fluid, internally contested and politically engaged (Brah 1996; Hall 1999; Yuval-Davis 1999). The earlier and strategic political mobilization of *'the essential black subject'* (Hall 1988) here gives way to an acknowledgement of important ethnic minority differences and the multiple *'subject positions'* found within and between these.

These changes are often contextualized in relation to the contradictory processes and flows of *globalization* and how these can lead both to the defensive reassertion of *'ethnic absolutisms'* organized around *tradition* as well as to 'new ethnicities' organized around processes of cultural *translation* comprising cultural crossover and syncretism, and *post-colonial hybridity* (Gilroy 1987; Bhabha 1990a; Robins 1991; Hall 1992a, 1992b) – processes, furthermore, that are increasingly media dependent (Morley and Robins 1995) and actively negotiated within local settings and cultural milieux (Back 1996). Many of today's diasporic communities, with their simultaneous identifications with place(s), within myths and memories, and between different cultures and homes, thus problematize essentializing ideas of cultural *'roots'*, and point rather to the influence of the disparate *'routes'* travelled and how these inform biographies, the complex layering of ethnic identities and outlooks, and the formation of collective projects (Gilroy 1993; Clifford 1997a; Hall 1999).

This emergent problematic thus encourages us to take seriously – for the first time perhaps – issues of ethnic minority differences and the complexities of media use, appropriation and sense-making within processes of identity formation, contestation and change. How *diasporic communities* and those positioned at the margins of society creatively utilize media technologies and integrate mainstream media within their daily lives and local cultural practices are theoretically prefigured in this problematic. Interestingly, the focus on processes of identity formation and change at the margins, is thought to also help illuminate processes of *hegemonic 'ethnicity'* and the construction of *'whiteness'* at the centre (Hall 1988; Julian and Mercer 1988).

White backlash culture

Across the 1990s in both the United States and the United Kingdom a white backlash against anti-racist, anti-homophobic and anti-sexist initiatives and policies took place. The advances won in normative thinking around multiculturalism and anti-racism, and embodied in anti-racist strategies and multicultural policies, was increasingly subject to ridicule and attack. This *white backlash* continues to variously find expression within and across today's media (see Gabriel 1998, this volume).

REFERENCES

Abu-Lughod, L. (1993) Writing against culture, in R. Fox (ed.) *Recapturing Anthropology*. Santa Fe, NM: School of American Research Press.

Ainley, B. (1998) *Black Journalists, White Media*. Stoke-on-Trent: Trentham.

Albert-Honore, S. (1996) Empowering voices: KUCB and Black Liberation Radio, in V.T. Berry and C.L. Manning-Miller (eds) *Mediated Messages and African-American Culture*. London: Sage.

Allan, S. (1999) *News Culture*. Buckingham: Open University Press.

Allen, T. and Seaton, J. (eds) (1999) *The Media of Conflict: War Reporting and Representations of Ethnic Violence*. London: Zed Books.

American Society of Newspaper Editors (ASNE) (1998) News release on Annual Newsroom Employment Survey. Reston, VA: ASNE.

Ames, J.D. (1938) Editorial treatment of lynchings, *Public Opinion Quarterly*, 2(1): 77–84.

Amin, A. (1997) Placing globalization, *Theory, Culture & Society*, 14(2): 123–37.

Ananthakrishnan, S.I. (1994) The development of local radio and ethnic minority initiatives in Norway, in C. Husband (ed.) *A Richer Vision*. London: John Libbey.

Anderson, B. (1983) *Imagined Communities: Reflections on the Origin and Spread of Nationalism*. London: Verso.

Anwar, M. and Shang, A. (1982) *Television in a Multi-Racial Society: A Research Report*. London: Commission for Racial Equality.

Appadurai, A. (1990) Disjuncture and difference in the global cultural economy, in M. Featherstone (ed.) *Global Culture*. London: Sage.

Appadurai, A. (1996) *Modernity at Large: The Cultural Dimensions of Globalization*. Minnesota, MN: University of Chicago Press.

Asad, T. (ed.) (1973) *Anthropology and the Colonial Encounter*. New York: Humanities Press.

Ashcroft, B., Griffiths, G. and Tiffin, H. (eds) (1995) *The Postcolonial Studies Reader*. London: Routledge.

Auletta, K. (1997) American Keiretsu, *The New Yorker*, 20 and 27 October: 225–8.

Back, L. (1996) *New Ethnicities and Urban Culture: Racisms and Multiculture in Young Lives*. London: UCL Press.

Bagdikian, B. (1987) *The Media Monopoly*, 2nd edn. Boston, MA: Beacon.

Balakrishnan, G. (1996) *Mapping the Nation*. London: Verso.

Ballard, R. (1982) South Asian families in Britain, in R. Rappoport (ed.) *Families in Britain*. London: Routledge & Kegan Paul.

Banon Hernandez, A.M. (1996) *Racismo, discurso periodistico y didactica de la lengua* (Racism, media discourse and language pedagogy). Almeria: Universidad de Almeria.

Barker, C. (1997) Television and the reflexive product of the self: soaps, teenage talk and hybrid identities, *British Journal of Sociology*, 48(4): 611–28.

Barker, C. (1998) 'Cindy's a shit': Moral identities and moral responsibility in the 'soap talk' of British Asian Girls, *Sociology*, 32(1): 65–81.

Barker, M. (1981) *The New Racism*. London: Junction.

Barker, M. and Brooks, K. (1998) *Knowing Audiences: 'Judge Dredd', Its Friends, Fans and Foes*. Luton: University of Luton Press.

Barry, A. (1988) Black mythologies: representation of Black people on British television, in J. Twitchin (ed.) *The Black and White Media Show Book*. Stoke-on-Trent: Trentham.

Barucha, R. (1991) A view from India, in D. Williams (ed.) *Peter Brook and the Mahabharata: Critical Perspectives*. London: Routledge.

Batty, P. (1993) Singing the electric: Aboriginal television in Australia, in T. Dowmunt (ed.) *Channels of Resistance: Global Television and Local Empowerment*. London: British Film Institute.

BBC (1995) *People and Programmes*. London: BBC.

Beattie, L., Khan, F. and Philo, G. (1999a) Race, advertising and the public face of television, in G. Philo (ed.) *Message Received*. London: Longman.

Beattie, L., Miller, D., Miller, E. and Philo, G. (1999b) The media and Africa: images of disaster and rebellion, in G. Philo (ed.) *Message Received*. London: Longman.

Bell, A. and Garrett, P. (eds) (1998) *Approaches to Media Discourse*. Oxford: Blackwell.

Bell, D. (1994) Representing Aboriginal women: who speaks for whom?, in O. Mendelsohn and U. Baxi (eds) *The Rights of Subordinated Peoples*. Delhi: Oxford University Press.

Bell, D. (1996) White women can't speak, *Feminism and Psychology*, 6(2): 197–203.

Benjamin, I. (1995) *The Black Press in Britain*. Stoke-on-Trent: Trentham.

Ben-Tovim, G., Gabriel, J., Law, I. and Stredder, K. (1986) *The Local Politics of Race*. London: Macmillan.

Bernal, M. (1987) *Black Athena: The Afroasiatic Roots of Classical Civilisation*. London: Free Association Books.

Berry, V.T. and Manning-Miller, C.L. (eds) (1996) *Mediated Messages and African-American Culture*. London: Sage.

Bhabha, H. (ed.) (1990a) *Nation and Narration*. London: Routledge.

Bhabha, H. (1990b) DissemiNation: time, narrative and the margins of the modern nation, in H. Bhabha (ed.) *Nation and Narration*. London: Routledge.

Bhachu, P. (1985) *Twice Migrants*. London: Tavistock.

Bhavnani, K-K. and Phoenix, A. (eds) (1994) *Shifting Identities Shifting Racisms*. London: Sage.

Blommaert, J. and Verschueren, J. (1998) *Debating Diversity*. London: Routledge.

Bobo, J. (1995) The Color Purple: Black women as cultural readers, in G. Dines and J.M. Humez (eds) *Gender, Race and Class in Media*. London: Sage.

Bodroghkozy, A. (1995) Is this what you mean by color TV? Race, gender and contested meanings in NBC's *Julia*, in G. Dines and J.M. Humez (eds) *Gender, Race and Class in Media*. London: Sage.

Bottomore, T. (1992) Citizenship and social class, fifty years on, in T.H. Marshall and T. Bottomore *Citizenship and Social Class*. London: Pluto.

Bourdieu, P. (1984) *Distinction: A Social Critique of the Judgement of Taste*. London: Routledge & Kegan Paul.

Bourne, S. (1998) *Black in the British Frame*. London: Cassell.

Bovenkerk-Teerink, W. (1994) Ethnic minorities and the media: the case of the Netherlands, in C. Husband (ed.) *A Richer Vision*. Paris: Unesco.

Bowers, D. (1967) A report on activity by publishers in directing newsroom decisions, *Journalism Quarterly*, 44(1): 49–50.

Bozorgmehr, M. (1998) From Iranian studies to studies of Iranians in the United States, *Iranian Studies*, 31(1): 5–26.

Brah, A. (1996) *Cartographies of Diaspora: Contesting Identities*. London: Routledge.

Braham, P. (1982) How the media report race, in M. Gurevitch, T. Bennett, J. Curran and J. Woollacott (eds) *Culture, Society and the Media*. London: Methuen.

Brasch, W.M. (1981) *Black English and the Mass Media*. Amherst, MA: University of Massachusetts Press.

Breed, W. (1955) Social control in the newsroom: a functional analysis, *Social Forces*, 33(4): 326–35, reprinted in W. Schramm (ed.) (1960) *Mass Communications*, 2nd edn. Champaign, IL: University of Illinois Press.

Broadcasting Standards Council (BSC) (1992) *The Portrayal of Ethnic Minorities on Television*, research working paper no. 7. London: BSC.

Browne, D.R. (1996) *Electronic Media and Indigenous Peoples*. Ames, IA: Iowa State University Press.

Browne, D.R. (1999) The snail's shell: electronic media and emigrant communities, *Communications*, 24(1): 61–84.

Brubaker, W.R. (1989) *Migration and the Politics of Citizenship in Europe and North America*. Lenham: University Press of America.

Burgess, J.A. (1985) News from nowhere: the press, the riots and the myth of the inner city, in J.A. Burgess and R.A. Gold (eds) *Geography, the Media and Popular Culture*. London: Croom Helm.

Burrough, B. and Masters, K. (1997) Cable guys, *Vanity Fair*, January: 76–9: 126–31.

Butler, J. (1993) Endangered/endangering: schematic racism and white paranoia, in R. Gooding-Williams (ed.) *Reading Rodney King: Reading Urban Uprising*. London: Routledge.

Butterworth, E. (1967) The 1962 smallpox outbreak and the British press, *Race*, 7(4): 347–64.

Caglar, A. (1997) Hyphenated identities and the limits of 'culture', in T. Modood and P. Werbner (eds) *The Politics of Multiculturalism in the New Europe*. London: Zed Books.

Campbell, C.P. (1995) *Race, Myth and the News*. London: Sage.

Cannon, L.W., Higginbotham, E. and Leung, M.L.A. (1991) Race and class bias in qualitative research on women, in J. Lober and S.A. Farrell (eds) *The Social Construction of Gender*. New York: Sage.

Carby, H. (1982) White women listen! Black feminism and the boundaries of sisterhood, in Centre for Contemporary Cultural Studies (eds) *The Empire Strikes Back*. London: Hutchinson.

Cardiff, D. and Scannell, P. (1987) Broadcasting and national unity, in J. Curran, A. Smith and P. Wingate (eds) *Impacts and Influences*. London: Methuen.

Carey, J. (1989) *Communication as Culture*. London: Unwin Hyman.

Carter, B. (1995) Broadcast networks come back strong, *New York Times*, Business Day, 2 August: C1, C6.

Carter, B. (1998) A wiley upstart that did a lot of things right, *New York Times*, Arts and Leisure Section, 4 January: 34–5.

Cashmore, E. (1997) *The Black Culture Industry*. London: Routledge.

Castles, S. and Miller, M.J. (1993) *The Age of Migration*. London: Macmillan.

Cayton, H. (1942) Fighting for white folks?, *The Nation*, 26 September: 267.

Centre for Contemporary Cultural Studies (eds) (1983) *The Empire Strikes Back*. London: Hutchinson.

Centre for Research in Ethnic Relations (CRER)/Commission for Racial Equality (CRE) (1991) Census factsheet no.1: settlement patterns of ethnic minorities in Britain. National Ethnic Minority Data Archive. Warwick: CRER/CRE.

Clifford, J. (1997a) *Routes: Travel and Translation in the Late Twentieth Century*. Cambridge, MA: Harvard University Press.

Clifford, J. (1997b) Diasporas, in J. Clifford, *Routes: Travel and Translation in the Late Twentieth Century*. Cambridge, MA: Harvard University Press.

Clifford, J. and Marcus, G.E. (eds) (1986) *Writing Culture: The Poetics and Politics of Ethnography*. Berkeley, CA: University of California Press.

Cohen, C. and Gardner, P. (eds) (1982) *It Ain't Half Racist Mum*. London: Comedia.

Cohen, R. (1997) *Global Diasporas*. London: Routledge.

Coleman, M. *et al.* (1986) Blacks in the newsroom of *The Washington Post*, a report to the editors of *The Washington Post*, Naples, FL, 6 February: 4.

Corea, A. (1995) Racism and the American way of media, in J. Downing, A. Mohammadi and A. Sreberny-Mohammadi (eds) *Questioning the Media*, 2nd edn. London: Sage.

Corner, J. (1991) Meaning, genre and context: the problematics of 'public knowledge' in the new audience studies, in J. Curran and M. Gurevitch (eds) *Mass Media and Society*, 1st edn. London: Edward Arnold.

Corner, J. (1995) *Television Form and Public Address*. London: Edward Arnold.

Corner, J. and Richardson, K. (1986) Documentary meanings and the discourse of interpretation, in J. Corner (ed.) *Documentary and the Mass Media*. London: Edward Arnold.

Cottle, S. (1991) Reporting the Rushdie affair: a case study in the orchestration of public opinion, *Race and Class*, 32(4): 45–64.

Cottle, S. (1992) 'Race', racialization and the media: a review and update of research, *Sage Race Relations Abstracts*, 17(2): 3–57.

Cottle, S. (1993a) *TV News, Urban Conflict and the Inner City*. Leicester: Leicester University Press.

Cottle, S. (1993b) 'Race' and regional television news: multi-culturalism and the production of popular TV, *New Community*, 19(4): 581–92.

Cottle, S. (1994) Stigmatizing Handsworth: notes on reporting spoiled space, *Critical Studies in Mass Communication*, 11(3): 231–56.

Cottle, S. (1997) *Television and Ethnic Minorities: Producers' Perspectives*. Aldershot: Avebury.

Cottle, S. (1998) Making ethnic minority programmes inside the BBC: professional pragmatics and cultural containment, *Media, Culture and Society*, 20(2): 295–317.

Cottle, S. (1999) From BBC newsroom to BBC news centre: On changing technology and journalist practices, *Convergence: The Journal of Research into New Media Technologies*, 5(3): 22–43.

Cottle, S. (2000a) Rethinking news access, *Journalism Studies*, 1(3).

Cottle, S. (2000b) Elite discourse as mediated ritual: *The Guardian* reporting of the racist murder of Stephen Lawrence 1993–1999.

Critcher, C., Parker, M. and Sondhi, R. (1977) *Race in the Provincial Press*. Paris: Unesco.

Croteau, D. and Hoynes, W. (1997) *Media/Society: Industries, Images, and Audiences*. Thousand Oaks, CA: Pine Forge Press.

Curran, J. (1991) Rethinking the media as public sphere, in P. Dahlgren and C. Sparkes (eds) *Communication and Citizenship*. London: Routledge.

Curtis, L. (1984) *Nothing But the Same Old Story*. London: Information on Ireland.

Dahlgren, P. (1991) Introduction, in P. Dahlgren and C. Sparkes (eds) *Communication and Citizenship*. London: Routledge.

Daniels, T. (1990) Beyond negative or positive images, in J. Willis and T. Wollen (eds) *The Neglected Audience*. London: British Film Institute.

Daniels, T. (1994) Programmes for Black audiences, in S. Hood (ed.) *Behind the Screens: The Structure of British Television in the Nineties*. London: Lawrence and Wishart.

Daniels, T. and Gerson, J. (eds) (1989) *The Colour Black: Black Images in British Television.* London: British Film Institute.

Dates, J.L. and Barlow, W. (eds) (1994) *Split Image: African Americans in the Mass Media,* 2nd edn. Washington, DC: Howard University Press.

Davis, M. (1990) *City of Quartz: Excavating the Future in Los Angeles.* London: Verso.

Davis, S.G. (1997) *Spectacular Nature: Corporate Culture and the Sea World Experience.* Berkeley, CA: University of California Press.

Dayan, D. (1998) Particularistic media and diasporic communications, in T. Liebes and J. Curran (eds) *Media, Ritual and Identity.* London: Routledge.

Dayan, D. and Katz, E. (1992) *Media Events: The Live Broadcasting of History.* Cambridge, MA: Harvard University Press.

Deepe Keever, B.A., Martindale, C. and Weston, M.A. (eds) (1997) *U.S. Coverage of Racial Minorities: A Sourcebook, 1934–1996.* Westport, CN: Greenwood.

Dennis, E.E. and Pease, E.C. (eds) (1997) *The Media in Black and White.* New Brunswick, NJ: Transaction.

Dickinson, R., Harindranath, R. and Linné, O. (eds) (1998) *Approaches to Audiences: A Reader.* London: Edward Arnold.

Dijkink, G. (1996) *National Identity and Geopolitical Visions.* London: Routledge.

Dines, G. and Humez, J.M. (eds) (1995) *Gender, Race and Class in Media.* London: Sage.

Dovidio, J.F. and Gaertner, S.L. (eds) (1986) *Prejudice, Discrimination, and Racism.* Orlando, FL: Academic Press.

Dowmunt, T. (ed.) (1993) *Channels of Resistance: Global Television and Local Empowerment.* London: British Film Institute.

Downing, J. (1985) 'Coillons . . . Shryned in an Hoggs Toord': British news media discourse on race, in T. van Dijk (ed.) *Discourse and Communication.* Berlin: Walter de Gruyter.

Downing, J. (1988) 'The Cosby Show' and American racial discourse, in G. Smitherman-Donaldson and T. van Dijk (eds) *Discourse and Discrimination.* Detroit, MI: Wayne State University Press.

Downing, J. (1994) Communication training programmes for members of ethnic minorities groups in the United States of America: an overview, in C. Husband (ed.) *A Richer Vision.* London: John Libbey.

D'Souza, D. (1992) *Illiberal Education: The Politics of Race and Sex on Campus.* New York: Vintage.

D'Souza, D. (1995) *The End of Racism: Principles for a Multiracial Society.* New York: Free Press.

Du Bois, W.E.B. (1986) *Dubois Writings.* New York: Library of America.

Dyer, R. (1977) Victim: Hermeneutic project, *Film Forum,* 1: 2.

Dyer, R. (1988) White, *Screen,* 28(4): 44–64.

Dyer, R. (1997) *White.* London: Routledge.

Dyson, M.E. (1993) *Reflecting Black: African American Cultural Criticism*. Minneapolis, MN: University of Minnesota Press.

Eck, D. (1985) *Darshan: Seeing the Divine Image in India*. Chambersburg, PA: Anima.

Edelstein, A.S. (1997) *Total Propaganda: From Mass Culture to Popular Culture*. London: Lawrence Erlbaum.

Edwards, R. (1996) White woman researcher–black women subjects, *Feminism and Psychology*, 6(2): 169–75.

Ehrenreich, B. (1990) The usual suspects, *Mother Jones*, September/October: 7.

Elliott, P. (1972) *The Making of a Television Series*. London: Constable.

Entman, R.E. (1990) Modern racism and the images of Blacks in local television news, *Critical Studies in Mass Communication*, 7(4): 332–45.

Essed, P. (1991) *Understanding Everyday Racism: An Interdisciplinary Theory*. Newbury Park, CA: Sage.

Essed, P. (1994) Contradictory positions, ambivalent perceptions: a case study of a black woman entrepreneur, in A. Bhavnani and A. Phoenix (eds) *Shifting Identities Shifting Racisms*. London: Sage.

Ettema, J.S. (1990) Press rites and race relations: a study of mass mediated ritual, *Critical Studies in Mass Communication*, 7(4): 309–31.

Fanon, F. (1986) *Black Skin, White Masks*. London: Pluto.

Featherstone, M. (ed.) (1990) *Global Culture: Nationalism, Globalisation, Modernity*. London: Sage.

Ferguson, M. and Golding, P. (eds) (1997) *Cultural Studies in Question*. London: Sage.

Fife, M. (1987) Promoting racial diversity in US broadcasting: federal policies versus social realities, *Media, Culture and Society*, 9(1): 481–505.

Fiske, J. (1993) *Power Plays, Power Works*. London: Verso.

Fiske, J. (1994a) *Media Matters: Everyday Culture and Political Change*. Minneapolis, MN: University of Minnesota Press.

Fiske, J. (1994b) Radical shopping in Los Angeles: race, media and the public sphere of consumption, *Media, Culture and Society*, 16(3): 469–86.

Fiske, J. (1996) *Media Matters: Race and Gender in U.S. Politics*, revised edn. Minneapolis, MN: University of Minnesota Press.

Fisler, P.L. and Lowenstein, R.L. (eds) (1968) *Race and the News Media*. New York: Praeger.

Foucault, M. (1972) *The Archaeology of Knowledge*, trans. A.M. Sheridan Smith. London: Tavistock.

Foucault, M. (1979) *Discipline and Punish: The Birth of the Prison*, trans A. Sheridan. Harmondsworth: Penguin.

Foucault, M. (1981) *The History of Sexuality: An Introduction*, trans. R. Hurley. Harmondsworth: Penguin.

Fowler, R. (1991) *Language in the News: Discourse and Ideology in the British Press*. London: Routledge.

Fowler, R., Hodge, B., Kress, G. and Trew, T. (1979) *Language and Control*. London: Routledge & Kegan Paul.

Fox, D.T. (1993) Honouring the treaty: indigenous television in Aotearoa, in T. Dowmunt (ed.) *Channels of Resistance: Global Television and Local Empowerment*. London: British Film Institute.

Frachon, C. and Vargaftig, M. (eds) (1995) *European Television*. London: John Libbey.

Frankenberg, R. (1993) *The Social Construction of Whiteness: White Women, Race Matters*. London: Routledge.

Fryer, P. (1984) *Staying Power*. London: Pluto.

Gabriel, J. (1994) *Racism, Culture, Markets*. London: Routledge.

Gabriel, J. (1996) What do you mean when Minority means you?, *Screen*, 37(2): 129–51.

Gabriel, J. (1998) *Whitewash: Racialized Politics and the Media*. London: Routledge.

Gabriel, J., Law, I., Stredder, K. and Bernal, M. (1987) *Black Athena: The Afroasiatic Roots of Classical Civilization*. London: Free Association.

Gadamer, H-G. (1975) *Truth and Method*. New York: Continuum.

Gadamer, H-G. (1976) *Philosophical Hermeneutics*. Berkeley, CA: University of California Press.

Galbraith, J.K. (1992) *The Culture of Contentment*. London: Sinclair-Stevenson.

Galtung, J. and Ruge, M. (1981) Structuring and selecting news, in S. Cohen and J. Young (eds) *The Manufacture of News*. London: Constable.

Gandy, O. (1998) *Communication and Race: A Structural Perspective*. London: Edward Arnold.

Gans, H. (1979) *Deciding What's News*. New York: Vintage.

Garvey, D. (1971) Social control in the television newsroom. Unpublished PhD thesis, Stanford University, CA.

Gayim, E. and Myntti, K. (1997) *Indigenous and Tribal Peoples Rights: 1993 and After*. Rovaniemi: Northern Institute for Environmental and Minority Law, University of Lapland.

Geertz, C. (1973) *The Interpretation of Cultures*. New York: Basic Books.

Giddens, A. (1990) *The Consequences of Modernity*. Cambridge: Polity.

Giddens, A. (1991) *Modernity and Self-Identity*. Cambridge: Polity.

Gillborn, D. (1995) *Racism and Antiracism in Real Schools*. Buckingham: Open University Press.

Gillespie, M. (1989) Technology and tradition: audio-visual culture among South Asian families in west London, *Cultural Studies*, 3(2): 226–39.

Gillespie, M. (1993) From Sanskrit to sacred soap: a case-study in the reception of two contemporary TV versions of 'The Mahabharata', in D. Buckingham (ed.) *Reading Audiences*, Manchester: Manchester University Press.

Gillespie, M. (1994) Sacred serials, devotional viewing and domestic worship, in R. Allen (ed.) *To Be Continued: Soap Operas around the World*. New York: Routledge.

Gillespie, M. (1995) *Television, Ethnicity and Cultural Change*. London: Routledge.

Gillespie, M. (1997) Multicultural broadcasting in Britain, in K. Robbins (ed.)

Programming for People: From Cultural Rights to Cultural Responsibilities, United Nations World Television Forum Report. Rome: European Broadcasting Union/RAI.

Gillespie, M. (1998a) Media, minority youth and the public sphere, in *Zeitschrift für Erziehungs-wissenschaft* vol. 1. Berlin: Verlag Leske + Budrich, Opladen.

Gillespie, M. (1998b) Being cool and classy: style hierarchies in a London Punjabi peer culture, *International Journal of Punjab Studies*, 5(2): 160–78.

Gilroy, P. (1987) *There Ain't No Black in the Union Jack*. London: Hutchinson.

Gilroy, P. (1992) The end of anti-racism, in J. Donald and A. Rattansi (eds) *'Race', Culture and Difference*. London: Sage.

Gilroy, P. (1993) *The Black Atlantic: Modernity and Double Consciousness*. London: Verso.

Givanni, J. (ed.) (1995) *Remote Control*. London: British Film Institute.

Glasser, T.L. and Craft, S. (1998) Public journalism and the search for democratic ideals, in T. Liebes and J. Curran (eds) *Media, Ritual and Identity*. London: Routledge.

Goldberg, D.T. (1990) The social formation of racist discourse, in D.T. Goldberg (ed.) *Anatomy of Racism*. Minneapolis, MN: University of Minnesota Press.

Goldberg, D.T. (1993) *Racist Culture: Philosophy and the Politics of Meaning*. Oxford: Blackwell.

Goldberg, D.T. (ed.) (1994) *Multiculturalism: A Critical Reader*. Oxford: Blackwell.

Golding, P. and Murdock, G. (1996) Culture, communications and political economy, in J. Curran and M. Gurevitch (eds) *Mass Media and Society*, 2nd edn. London: Edward Arnold.

Gooding-Williams, R. (ed.) (1993) *Reading Rodney King: Reading Urban Uprising*. London: Routledge.

Gordon, P. and Rosenberg, D. (1989) *Daily Racism: The Press and Black People in Britain*. London: Runnymede Trust.

Gray, H. (1986) Television and the new black man: black images in prime-time situation comedy, *Media, Culture and Society*, 8: 223–42.

Gray, H. (1989) Television, black Americans and the American dream, *Critical Studies in Mass Communication*, 6: 376–86.

Gray, H. (1995) *Watching Race: Television and the Struggle for 'Blackness'*. Minneapolis, MN: University of Minnesota Press.

Greenslade, L., Madden, M. and Pearson, M. (1997) From visible to invisible: the problem of the health of Irish people in Britain, in L. Marks and M. Worboys (eds) *Migrants, Minorities and Health: Historical and Contemporary Studies*. London: Routledge.

Griffin, C. (1996) 'See whose face it wears': difference, otherness and power, *Feminism and Psychology*, 6(2): 185–91.

Habermas, J. (1989) *The Structural Transformation of the Public Sphere*. Cambridge: Polity.

Hall, S. (1978) Racism and reaction, in Commission for Racial Equality (eds) *Five Views of Multi-Racial Britain*. London: Commission for Racial Equality.

Hall, S. (1980a) Race, articulation and societies structured in dominance, in Unesco (eds) *Sociological Theories: Race and Colonialism*. Paris: Unesco.

Hall, S. (1980b) Recent developments in theories of language and ideology: a critical note, in S. Hall, D. Hobson, A. Lowe and P. Willis (eds) *Culture, Media, Language*. London: Hutchinson.

Hall, S. (1980c) Encoding/decoding in S. Hall, D. Hobson, A. Lowe and P. Willis (eds) *Culture, Media, Language*. London: Hutchinson.

Hall, S. (1981) The determination of news photographs, in S. Cohen and J. Young (eds) *The Manufacture of News*. London: Constable.

Hall, S. (1988) New ethnicities, in K. Mercer (ed.) *Black Film, British Cinema*, ICA documents 7. London: British Film Institute.

Hall, S. (1990a) The whites of their eyes: racist ideologies and the media, in M. Alvarado and J.O. Thompson (eds) *The Media Reader*. London: British Film Institute.

Hall, S. (1990b) Cultural identity and diaspora, in J. Rutherford (ed.) *Identity: Community, Culture, Difference*. London: Lawrence and Wishart.

Hall, S. (1991) The local and the global: globalization and the media, in A.D. King (ed.) *Culture, Globalization and the World System: Contemporary Conditions and the Representation of Identity*. London: Macmillan.

Hall, S. (1992a) The question of cultural identity, in S. Hall, D. Held and T. McGrew (eds) *Modernity and its Futures*. Cambridge: Polity.

Hall, S. (1992b) What is this 'Black' in black popular culture?, in G. Dent (ed.) *Black Popular Culture*. Seattle, WA: Bay Press.

Hall, S. (1992c) The west and the rest: discourse and power, in S. Hall and B. Gieben (eds) *Formations of Modernity*. Cambridge: Polity.

Hall, S. (1995) Black and white in television, in J. Givanni (ed.) *Remote Control*. London: British Film Institute.

Hall, S. (1997) The Spectacle of the 'Other', in S. Hall (ed.) *Representation: Cultural Representations and Signifying Practices*. London: Sage.

Hall, S. (1999) Interview with Stuart Hall: culture and power, in R. Torres, L.F. Miron and J.X. India (eds) *Race, Identity and Citizenship: A Reader*. Oxford: Blackwell.

Hall, S., Chritcher, C., Jefferson, T., Clarke, J. and Roberts, B. (1978) *Policing the Crisis: Mugging, the State, and Law and Order*. London: Macmillan.

Halloran, J. (1974) Mass media and race: a research approach, in Unesco (eds) *Race as News*. Paris: Unesco.

Halloran, J. (1977) Introduction, in Unesco (eds) *Race, Ethnicity and the Media*. Paris: Unesco.

Halloran, J.D., Bhatt, A. and Gray. P. (1995) *Ethnic Minorities and Television: A Study of Use, Reactions and Preferences*. Leicester: Centre for Mass Communication Research, University of Leicester.

Hammersley, M. (1992) *What's Wrong with Ethnography?* London: Routledge.

Hannerz, U. (1997) *Transnational Connections*. London: Routledge.

Hansen, A. and Murdock, G. (1985) Constructing the crowd: populist discourse and press presentation, in V. Mosco and M. Wasco (eds) *Popular Culture and Media Events: The Critical Communication Review*, vol. III. Norwood, NJ: Ablex.

Harindranath, R. (1996) Cross-cultural interpretation of television: a phenomeno-logical hermeneutic inquiry. Unpublished PhD thesis, University of Leicester.

Harindranath, R. (1998) Documentary meanings and interpretative contexts: obser-vations on Indian 'repertoires', in R. Dickinson, R. Harindranath and O. Linne (eds) *Approaches to Audiences: A Reader*. London: Edward Arnold.

Hartmann, P. and Husband, C. (1974) *Racism and the Mass Media*. London: Davis Poynter.

Hartmann, P., Husband, C. and Clark, J. (1974) Race as news: a study in the hand-ling of race in the British press from 1963 to 1970, in Unesco (eds) *Race as News*. Paris: Unesco.

Harvey, D. (1989) *The Condition of Postmodernity*. Oxford: Blackwell.

Heckmann, F. and Bosswick, W. (1995) *Migration Policies: A Comparative Perspec-tive*. Stuttgart: Ferdinand Enke Verlag.

Herman, E. and McChesney, R. (1997) *The Global Media: The New Missionaries of Corporate Capitalism*. London: Cassell.

Hickman, M. and Walter, B. (1995) Deconstructing whiteness: Irish women in Britain, *Feminist Review*, 50 (Summer): 5–19.

Hillyard, P. (1993) *Suspect Community: People's Experience of the Prevention of Terrorism Act in Britain*. London: Pluto.

Hobsbawm, E. and Ranger, T. (eds) (1983) *The Invention of Tradition*. Cambridge: Cambridge University Press.

Holland, P. (1981) The New Cross fire and the popular press, *Multi-Racial Edu-cation*, 9(3): 61–80.

Hollingsworth, M. (1990) *The Press and Political Dissent*. London: Pluto.

hooks, b. (1981) *Ain't I a Woman? Black Women and Feminism*. Boston, MA: South End Press.

hooks, b. (1989) *Talking Back: Thinking Feminist, Thinking Black*. Boston, MA: South End Press.

hooks, b. (1992) *Black Looks, Race and Representation*. Boston, MA: South End Press.

hooks, b. (1994) *Outlaw Culture: Resisting Representations*. London: Routledge.

hooks, b. (1996) *Reel to Real: Race, Sex and Class at the Movies*. London: Rout-ledge.

Hujanen, T. (1988) *The Role of Information in the Realization of the Human Rights of Migrant Workers: Conclusions and Recommendations*. Tampere, Finland: Department of Journalism and Mass Communication, University of Tampere.

Hujanen, T. (1989) *Information, Communication and the Human Rights of Migrants*. Lausanne: Bureau Lausannois pour les Immigrés.

Hunt, D. (1997) *Screening the Los Angeles 'Riots': Race, Seeing and Resistance*. Cambridge: Cambridge University Press.

Hunt, D. (1999) *O.J. Simpson Facts and Fictions: News Rituals in the Construction of Reality*. Cambridge: Cambridge University Press.

Husband, C. (ed.) (1994a) *A Richer Vision: The Development of Ethnic Minority Media in Western Democracies*. London: John Libbey.

Husband, C. (1994b) *'Race' and Nation: The British Experience*. Perth, WA: Paradigm.

Husband, C. (1994c) The political context of Muslim communities' participation in British society, in B. Lewis and D. Schnapper (eds) *Muslims in Europe*. Paris: Acte Sud.

Husband, C. (1996) The right to be understood: conceiving the multi-ethnic public sphere, *Innovation*, 9: 205–15.

Husband, C. (1998) Differentiated citizenship and the multi-ethnic public sphere, *Journal of International Communication* 5(1 and 2): 122–33.

Husband, C. and Chouhan, J.M. (1985) Local radio in the communication environment of ethnic minorities in Britain, in T. van Dijk (ed.) *Discourse and Communication*. Berlin: Walter de Gruyter.

Hussein, A. (1994) Market forces and the marginalization of Black film and video production in the United Kingdom, in C. Husband (ed.) *A Richer Vision*. London: John Libbey.

Hutton, W. (1995) *The State We're In*. London: Jonathan Cape.

Ignatiev, N. (1995) *How the Irish Became White*. London: Routledge.

Ignatiev, N. and Garvey, J. (eds) (1996) *Race Traitor*. New York: Routledge.

Institute for Journalism Education (IJE) (1985) *The Quiet Crisis: Minority Journalists and Newsroom Opportunity*. Berkeley, CA: IJE.

International Commission on Jurists (IJC) (1986) *Human and Peoples' Rights in Africa and the African Charter*. Geneva: ICJ.

Ismond, P. (1997a) From Asia vision to Asia net, in S. Cottle (ed.) *Television and Ethnic Minorities*. Aldershot: Avebury.

Ismond, P. (1997b) Identity TV, in S. Cottle (ed.) *Television and Ethnic Minorities*. Aldershot: Avebury.

Jacobs, R.N. (1996) Civil society and crisis: culture, discourse, and the Rodney King beating, *American Journal of Sociology*, 101(5): 1238–72.

Jager, S. and Link, J. (1993) *Die Vierte Gewalt: Rassismus und die Medien* (The fourth power: racism and the media). Duisburg: DISS.

Jahoda, G. (1999) *Imagined Savages: Ancient Roots of Modern Prejudice in Western Culture*. London: Routledge.

Jakubowicz, A. (1995) Media in multicultural nations: some comparisons, in J. Downing, A. Mohammadi and A. Sreberny-Mohammadi (eds) *Questioning the Media*, 2nd edn. London: Sage.

Jakubowicz, A., Goodall, H., Martin, J. *et al.* (1994) *Racism, Ethnicity and the Media*. St Leonards, NSW: Allen & Unwin.

Jensen, K.B. (1986) *Making Sense of the News*. Arhus: University of Arhus Press.

Jhally, S. and Lewis, J. (1992) *Enlightened Racism: The Cosby Show, Audiences and the Myth of the American Dream*. Boulder, CO: Westview.

Joshua, H., Wallace, T. and Booth, H. (1983) *To Ride the Storm: The 1980 Bristol 'Riots' and the State*. London: Heinemann.

Julian, I. and Mercer, K. (1988) Introduction: De Margin and De Centre, *Screen*, 29(4): 2–10.

Karim K. (1998) From ethnic media to global media: transnational networks among diasporic communities. Paper presented to the Joint Session of the Political Economy section and the Working Group on Race and Ethnicity, International Association for Media and Communication Research Conference, Glasgow, 30 July–2 August.

Keighron, P. and Walker, C. (1994) Working in television: five interviews, in S. Hood (ed.) *Behind the Screens: The Structure of British Television in the Nineties*. London: Lawrence and Wishart.

Kelley, R. (1996) Kickin' reality, kickin' ballistics: gangsta rap and postindustrial Los Angeles, in W.E. Perkins (ed.) *Droppin' Science: Critical Essays on Rap Music and Hip Hop Culture*, Philadelphia, PA: Temple University Press.

Kellner, D. (1990) Advertising and consumer culture, in J. Downing, A. Mohammadi and A. Sreberny-Mohammadi (eds) *Questioning the Media*. Newbury Park, CA: Sage.

Kerner, O. (1968) *Report of the National Advisory Committee on Civil Disorders*. New York: Bantham Books.

Knopf, T.A. (1973) Sniping: a new pattern of violence?, in S. Cohen and J. Young (eds) *The Manufacture of News*, 1st edn. London: Constable.

Koon, S. (1992) *Presumed Guilty: The Tragedy of the Rodney King Affair*. Washington, DC: Regnery Gateway.

Kumar, K. (1977) Holding the middle ground, in J. Curran, M. Gurevitch and J. Woollacott (eds) *Mass Communication and Society*. London: Edward Arnold.

Kuper, A. (1992) *The Invention of Primitive Society*. London: Routledge.

Kushnick, L. (1970) Black Power and the media, *Race Today*, 2: 439–42.

Kymlicka, W. (1995) *Multicultural Citizenship*. Oxford: Oxford University Press.

Larbalestier, J. (1990) The politics of representation: Australian Aboriginal women and feminism, *Anthropological Forum*, 6(2): 143–57.

Lash, S. and Urry, J. (1987) *The End of Organized Capitalism*. Cambridge: Polity.

Law, I. (1997) *Privilege and Silence: 'Race' in the British News during the General Election Campaign, 1997*. Leeds: Race and Public Policy Unit, University of Leeds.

Lewis, J. (1982) The story of a riot: the television coverage of civil unrest in 1981, *Screen Education*, 40: 15–33.

Lewis, J. (1991) *The Ideological Octopus*. London: Routledge.

Lewis, P. (1994) *Islamic Britain*. London: I.B. Tauris.

Liebes, T. (1988) Cultural differences in the retelling of television fiction, *Critical Studies in Mass Communication*, 5(4): 277–92.

Liebes, T. and Katz, E. (1986) Patterns of involvement in television fiction: a comparative analysis, *European Journal of Communication*, 1: 2.

Liebes, T. and Katz, E. (1993) *The Export of Meaning: Cross-Cultural Readings of 'Dallas'.* Cambridge: Polity.

Lipsitz, G. (1994) *Dangerous Cross Roads.* London: Verso.

Livingstone, S. (1990) *Making Sense of Television: The Psychology of Audience Interpretation.* Oxford: Pergamon.

Lorde, A. (1981) The master's tools will never dismantle the master's house, in C. Moraga and G. Anzaldua (eds) *This Bridge Called My Back: Writings by Radical Women of Color.* Watertown, MA: Persephone Press.

Lule, J. (1997) The rape of Mike Tyson: race, the press and symbolic types, in D. Berkowitz (ed.) *Social Meanings of News.* London: Sage.

Lutgendorf, P. (1990) Ramayan: the video, *The Drama Review: A Journal of Performance Studies*, 34(2): 127–77.

Luttrell, W. (1992) Working-class women's ways of knowing: effects of gender, race and class, in J. Wrigley (ed.) *Education and Gender Equality.* London: Falmer.

Lynch, F. (1989) *Invisible Victims: White Males and the Crisis of Affirmative Action.* Westport, CT: Greenwood.

Malik, K. (1996a) *The Meaning of Race.* London: Macmillan.

Malik, K. (1996b) Universalism and difference: race and the postmodernists, *Race and Class*, 37(3): 1–17.

McConahay, J.B. (1982) Is it the buses or the Blacks? Self-interest versus racial attitudes as correlates of anti-busing attitudes in Louisville, *Journal of Politics*, 44: 692–720.

MacDonald, J.F. (1992) *Blacks and White TV.* Chicago: Nelson Hall.

McGarry, R.G. (1994) *The Subtle Slant: A Cross-Linguistic Discourse Analysis Model for Evaluating Inter-Ethnic Conflict in the Press.* Boone, NC: Parkway.

McLaughlin, G. (1999) Refugees, migrants and the fall of the Berlin Wall, in G. Philo (ed.) *Message Received.* London: Longman.

McLintock, A. (1995) *Imperial Leather: Race, Gender and Sexuality in the Colonial Context.* London: Routledge.

Mankekar, P. (1993) Television tales and a woman's rage: a nationalist recasting of Draupadi's disrobing, *Public Culture*, 5(3): 469–92.

Martindale, C. (1985) Covering causes of social upheaval. Paper presented to the Association for Education in Journalism and Mass Communication Annual Meeting, Memphis, TN, August.

Martindale, C. (1986) *The White Press and Black America.* Westport, CT: Greenwood.

Mason, D. (1995) *Race and Ethnicity in Modern Britain.* Oxford: Oxford University Press.

Mason, D. (1999) The continuing significance of race? Teaching ethnic and racial studies in sociology, in M. Bulmer and J. Solomos (eds) *Ethnic and Racial Studies Today.* London: Routledge.

Massey, D. (1984) *Spatial Divisions of Labour: Social Structures and the Geography of Production.* London: Macmillan.

Masters, K. (1997) Hollywood vertigo, *Vanity Fair*, February: 66–72.

Mazingo, S. (1988) Minorities and social control in the newsroom: thirty years after breed, in G. Smitherman-Donaldson and T. van Dijk (eds) *Discourse and Discrimination*. Detroit, MI: Wayne State University Press.

Mbaye, K. (1988) Introduction to the African Charter on human and peoples' rights, in International Commission on Jurists (eds) *Human and Peoples' Rights in Africa and the African Charter*. Geneva: ICJ.

Melucci, A. (1996) *The Playful Self*. Cambridge: Polity.

Mercer, K. (ed.) (1988) *Black Film, Black Cinema*, ICA documents 7. London: British Film Institute.

Mercer, K. (1989) General introduction, in T. Daniels and J. Gerson (eds) *The Colour Black: Black Images in British Television*. London: British Film Institute.

Mercer, K. (1994) *Welcome to the Jungle*. London: Routledge.

Merton, R. (1949) *Social Theory and Social Structure*. Glencoe, IL: Free Press.

Miles, R. (1982) *Racism and Migrant Labour*. London: Routledge & Kegan Paul.

Miles, R. (1984) The riots of 1958: notes on the ideological construction of 'race relations' as a political issue in Britain, *Immigrants and Minorities*, 3(3): 252–75.

Miles, R. (1989) *Racism*. London: Routledge.

Miles, R. (1993) *Racism After 'Race Relations'*. London: Routledge.

Miles, R. and Torres, R.D. (1999) Does 'race' matter? Transatlantic perspectives on racism after 'race relations', in R.Torres, L.F. Miron and J.X. India (eds) *Race, Identity and Citizenship: A Reader*. Oxford: Blackwell.

Mishra, V. (1985) Toward a theoretical critique of Bombay cinema, *Screen*, 26(3–4): 133–49.

Mishra, V. (1991) The great Indian epic and Peter Brook, in D.Williams (ed.) *Peter Brook and The Mahabharata: Critical Perspectives*. London: Routledge.

Modood, T., Berthoud, R., Lakey, J., Nazroo, J., Smith, P., Virdee, S. and Beishon, S. (1997) *Ethnic Minorities in Britain*. London: Policy Studies Institute.

Mohammadi, A. (ed.) (1997) *International Communication and Globalization*. London: Sage.

Mohanty, S.P. (1989) Us and them: on the philosophical bases for political criticism, *New Formations*, 8: 55–80.

Montagu, A. (1997) *Man's Most Dangerous Myth: The Fallacy of Race*. London: Altamira.

Moores, S. (1993) *Interpreting Audiences: The Ethnography of Media Consumption*. London: Sage.

Morar, N. (1995) *Multicultural Programmes Department*, department publication. Birmingham: BBC.

Morley, D. (1980) *The 'Nationwide' Audience*. London: British Film Institute.

Morley, D. (1991) Television and ethnography, *Screen*, 3(1): 1–15.

Morley, D. and Robins, K. (1989) Spaces of identity, *Screen*, 20(4): 3–15.

Morley, D. and Robins, K. (1995) *Spaces of Identity: Global Media, Electronic Landscapes and Cultural Boundaries*. London: Routledge.

Mullan, B. (1996) *Not a Pretty Picture: Ethnic Minority Views of Television*. Aldershot: Avebury.

Murdock, G. (1982) Large corporations and the control of the communication industries, in M. Gurevitch, T. Bennett, J. Curran and J. Woollacott (eds) *Culture, Society and the Media*. London: Methuen.

Murdock, G. (1984) Reporting the riots: images and impacts, in J. Benyon (ed.) *Scarman and After*. Oxford: Pergamon.

Murray, N. (1986) Anti-racists and other demons: the press and ideology in Thatcher's Britain, *Race and Class*, 27: 1–20.

Naficy, H. (1993) *The Making of Exile Culture: Iranian Television in Los Angeles*. Minneapolis, MN: University of Minnesota Press.

National Association of Black Journalists (NABJ) (1992) *An NABJ Print Task Force Report: The L.A. Unrest and Beyond*. Reston, VA: NABJ.

New York Times Magazine (1998) Now what? The dawn of the post network, Post Broadcast, Post Mass Television Age, *New York Times Magazine*, 20 September.

Ngui, M. (1994) Behind the rhetoric: employment practices in ethnic minority media in Australia, in C. Husband (ed.) *A Richer Vision*. London: John Libbey.

Nightingale, V. (1996) *Studying Audiences: The Shock of the Real*. London: Routledge.

Omi, M. (1989) In living color: race and American culture, in I. Angus and S. Jhally (eds) *Cultural Politics in Contemporary America*. London: Routledge.

Omi, M. and Winant, H. (1995) *Racial Formations in the United States*, 2nd edn. London: Routledge.

Paletz, D.L. and Dunn, R. (1969) Press coverage of civil disorders, *Public Opinion Quarterly*, 33: 328–45.

Parekh, B. (1997) National culture and multiculturalism, in K. Thompson (ed.) *Media and Cultural Regulation*. London: Sage.

Park, R.E., Burgess, E. and Mackenzie, R. (1923) *The City*. Chicago: University of Chicago Press.

Pattel-Gray, A. (1998) *Indigenous Communications in Aotearoa New Zealand, Australia and the Pacific*. London: World Association for Christian Communication.

Peak, S. and Fisher, P. (eds) (1996) *The Media Guide*. London: Fourth Estate.

Pease, T. and Smith, J.F. (1991) *The Newsroom Barometer: Job Satisfaction and the Impact of Racial Diversity at U.S. Daily Newspapers*. Athens, OH: Ohio University Press.

Petley, J. and Romano, G. (1993) After the deluge: public service television in western Europe, in T. Dowmunt (ed.) *Channels of Resistance: Global Television and Local Empowerment*. London: British Film Institute.

Pettigrew, T.F. and Meertens, R.W. (1995) Subtle and blatant prejudice in western Europe, *European Journal of Social Psychology*, 25(1): 57–75.

Philo, G. and Beattie, L. (1999) Race, migration and media, in G. Philo (ed.) *Message Received*. London: Longman.

Pieterse, J. (1995) *White on Black: Images of Africa and Blacks in Western Popular Culture*. New Haven, CT: Yale University Press.

Pilger, J. (1986) *Heroes*. London: Pan.

Pilger, J. (1998) *Hidden Agendas*. London: Vintage.

Pines, J. (1988) Black independent film in Britain: historical overview, in J. Twitchin (ed.) *The Black and White Media Show Book*. Stoke-on-Trent: Trentham.

Pines, J. (ed.) (1992) *Black and White in Colour: Black People in British Television since 1936*. London: British Film Institute.

Polman, D. (1995) British using video to help stop crime: use of surveillance cameras widespread, *Wisconsin State Journal*, 21 February: 7A.

Rajagopal, A. (2000) *Politics after Television: Religious Nationalism and the Retailing of Hindutva 1987–1993*. Cambridge: Cambridge University Press.

Ramaprasad, J. (1996) How four newspapers covered the 1992 Los Angeles 'Riots', in V.T. Berry and C.L. Manning-Miller (eds) *Mediated Messages and African-American Culture*. London: Sage.

Reeves, B. and Nass, C. (1996) *The Media Equation*. Cambridge: Cambridge University Press.

Reeves, J.L. and Campbell, R. (1994) *Cracked Coverage: Television News, the Anti-Cocaine Crusade, and the Reagan Legacy*. Durham, NC: Duke University Press.

Rex, J. and Moore, R. (1967) *Race, Community and Conflict*. London: Oxford University Press.

Riggins, S.H. (1992) *Ethnic Minority Media: An International Perspective*. London: Sage.

Roach, C. (1990) The movement for a new world information and communication order: a second wave?, *Media, Culture and Society*, 12(3): 283–307.

Roach, C. (1993) The MacBride Round Table as a non-governmental organization? Paper delivered to the Fifth MacBride Round Table, Dublin City University, Dublin, June.

Robins, K. (1991) Tradition and translation: national culture in global context, in J. Corner and S. Harvey (eds) *Enterprise and Heritage: Crosscurrents of National Culture*. London: Routledge.

Rodney, W. (1988) *How Europe Undeveloped Africa*. London: Bogle L'Ouverture.

Roediger, D. (1991) *The Wages of Whiteness: Race and the Making of the American Working Class*. London: Verso.

Roscoe, J. (1999) *Documentary in New Zealand: An Immigrant Nation*. Palmerston North: Dunmore Press.

Ross, K. (1992) *Television in Black And White: Ethnic Stereotypes and Popular Television*, research paper in ethnic relations no. 19. Coventry: Centre for Research in Ethnic Relations, University of Warwick.

Ross, K. (1996) *Black and White Media: Black Images in Popular Film and Television*. Cambridge: Polity.

Rushdie, S. (1991) *Imaginary Homelands*. London: Granta/Penguin.

Russell, D.E.H. (1996) Between a rock and a hard place: the politics of white feminists conducting research on black women in South Africa, *Feminism and Psychology*, 6(2): 176–80.

Safran, W. (1991) Diasporas in modern society: myths of homeland and return, *Diaspora*, 1: 83–99.

Said, E.W. (1978) *Orientalism: Western Conceptions of the Orient.* London: Routledge & Kegan Paul.

Said, E.W. (1986) An ideology of difference, in H. Gates (ed.) *'Race', Writing and Difference.* Chicago: University of Chicago Press.

Salam, S. (1995) A mirror crack'd from side to side: black and independent producers and the television industry, in C. Frachon and M.Vargaftig (eds) *European Television.* London: John Libbey.

Scarman, Lord (1986) *The Brixton Disorders, 10–12 April 1981.* Harmondsworth: Penguin.

Schlesinger, P. (1987) On national identity: some conceptions and misconceptions criticised, *Social Science Information,* 26(2): 219–64.

Schutz, A. (1972) *The Phenomenology of the Social World.* London: Heinemann.

Seymour-Ure, C. (1974) Enoch Powell's 'Earthquake', in C. Seymour-Ure, *The Political Impact of the Mass Media.* London: Constable.

Shohat, E. and Stam, R. (1994) *Unthinking Eurocentrism: Multiculturalism and the Media.* London: Routledge.

Sibley, D. (1995) *Geographies of Exclusion.* London: Routledge.

Silverstone, R. (1990) TV and everyday life: towards an anthropology of the TV audience, in M. Ferguson (ed.) *Public Communication.* London: Sage.

Silverstone, R. (1994) *Television and Everyday Life.* London: Routledge.

Silverstone, R. *et al.* (1991) Listening to a long conversation: an ethnographic approach to the study of information and communication technologies in the home, *Cultural Studies,* 5(2): 204–27.

Sinclair, J., Jacka, E. and Cunningham, S. (1996) *New Patterns in Global Television.* Oxford: Oxford University Press.

Singer, B. (1970) Mass media and communication processes in the Detroit riot of 1967, *Public Opinion Quarterly,* 34(2): 236–45.

Singh, S. (1995) The epic on tube: plumbing the depths of history. A paradigm for viewing the TV serialization of the Mahabharata, *Quarterly Review of Film and Video,* 16(1): 77–99.

Small, S. (1994) *Racialised Barriers: The Black Experience in the United States and England in the 1980s.* London: Routledge.

Small, S. (1999) The contours of racialization: structures, representations and resistance in the United States, in R. Torres, L.F. Miron and J.X. India (eds) *Race, Identity and Citizenship: A Reader.* Oxford: Blackwell.

Smith, A.M. (1994) *New Right Discourse on Race and Sexuality.* Cambridge: Cambridge University Press.

Smitherman-Donaldson, G. and van Dijk, T.A. (eds) (1987) *Discourse and Discrimination.* Detroit, MI: Wayne State University Press.

Snead, J. (1994) 'Black independent film': Britain and America, in J. Snead, *White Screens, Black Images.* London: Routledge.

Solomos, J. (1986) Political language and violent protest: ideological and policy responses to the 1981 and 1985 riots, *Youth and Policy,* 18: 12–24.

Solomos, J. (1989) *Race and Racism in Contemporary Britain.* London: Macmillan.

Solomos, J. and Back, L. (1996) *Racism and Society*. London: Macmillan.

Solomos, J. and Back, L. (1999) Marxism, racism and ethnicity, in R. Torres, L.F. Miron and J.X. India (eds) *Race, Identity and Citizenship: A Reader*. Oxford: Blackwell.

Solomos, J., Findley, B., Jones, S. and Gilroy, P. (1982) The organic crisis of British capitalism and race: the experience of the seventies, in Centre for Contemporary Cultural Studies (eds) *The Empire Strikes Back*. London: Hutchinson.

Sreberny, A. (1999) *The Iranian Diaspora in London: A Research Report*. Leicester: Centre for Mass Communication Research, University of Leicester.

Sreberny-Mohammadi, A. and Mohammadi, A. (1991) Iranian exiles as opposition, in A. Fathi (ed.) *Iranian Refugees and Exiles since Khomeini*. Costa Mesa, CA: Mazda.

Sreberny-Mohammadi, A. and Mohammadi, A. (1994) *Small Media, Big Revolution: Communication, Culture and the Iranian Revolution*. Minneapolis, MN: University of Minnesota Press.

Sreberny-Mohammadi, A., Winseck, D., McKenna, J. and Boyd-Barrett, O. (eds) (1998) *Media in Global Context*. London: Edward Arnold.

Sterngold, J. (1998a) A racial divide widens on network TV, *New York Times*, National Desk, 29 December: 1.

Sterngold, J. (1998b) How cable captured the mini series and the high ground, *New York Times Magazine*, 20 September: 86–7.

Stone, J. and Lasus, H. (1998) Immigration and ethnic relations in Britain and America, in T. Blackstone, B. Parekh and P. Sanders (eds) *Race Relations in Britain*. London: Routledge.

Sumner, C. (1982) 'Political hooliganism' and 'rampaging mobs': the national press coverage of the Toxteth riots, in C. Sumner (ed.) *Crime, Justice and the Mass Media*. Cambridge: Cambridge University Press.

Sundquist, E. (1996) *The Dubois Reader*. Oxford: Oxford University Press.

Swanson, C. (1949) Midcity daily: the news staff and its relation to control, *Journalism Quarterly*, 26: 20–8.

Tait, A.A. and Barber, J.T. (1996) Black entertainment television: breaking new ground and accepting new responsibilities?, in V.T. Berry and C.L. Manning-Miller (eds) *Mediated Messages and African-American Culture*. London: Sage.

Tatla, D.S. and Singh, G. (1989) The Punjabi press, *New Community*, 15(2): 171–84.

Taylor, C. (1992) *Multiculturalism and 'The Politics of Recognition'*. Princeton, NJ: Princeton University Press.

The Economist (1997a) Boot up the television set, *The Economist*, Business Section, 28 June–14 July: 73–5.

The Economist (1997b) Hollywood's fading charms, *The Economist*, 22 March: 81–9.

The Economist (1997c) Once more with feeling, *The Economist*, 12 April–18 April: 64–5.

Thomas, R. (1986) Indian cinema: pleasures and popularity, *Screen*, 26(3–4): 116–32.

Thussu, D.K. (ed.) (1998) *Electronic Empires: Global Media and Local Resistance*. London: Edward Arnold.

Tomlinson, J. (1992) *Cultural Imperialism*. London: Pinter.

Triparti, S. (1997) The march of Vishnu, *Index on Censorship*, 26(6): 84–9.

Troyna, B. (1981) *Public Awareness and the Media: A Study of Reporting on Race*. London: Commission for Racial Equality.

Tuchman, G. (1972) Objectivity as a strategic ritual: an examination of newsmen's notions of objectivity, *American Journal of Sociology*, 77: 660–79.

Tuchman, G. (1978) *Making News: A Study in the Construction of Reality*. New York: Free Press.

Tumber, H. (1982) *Television and the Riots*. Broadcasting Research Unit. London: British Film Institute.

Turner, V. (1969) *The Ritual Process*. Routledge & Kegan Paul.

Twitchin, J. (1988) Stereotypical thinking in TV news and current affairs, in J. Twitchin (ed.) *The Black and White Media Show Book*. Stoke-on-Trent: Trentham.

United States Government (1996) *Telecommunications Act of 1996*. Washington, DC: US Government Printing Office.

Van der Veer, P. (1995) *Religious Nationalism: Hindus and Muslims in India*. Berkeley, CA: University of California Press.

Van Dijk, T. (1987) *Communicating Racism: Ethnic Prejudice in Thought and Talk*. Newbury Park, CA: Sage.

Van Dijk, T.A. (1988a) *News Analysis: Case Studies of International and National News in the Press*. Hillsdale, NJ: Lawrence Erlbaum.

Van Dijk, T.A. (1988b) *News as Discourse*. Hillsdale, NJ: Lawrence Erlbaum.

Van Dijk, T.A. (1991) *Racism and the Press*. London: Routledge.

Van Dijk, T.A. (1993) *Elite Discourse and Racism*. Newbury Park, CA: Sage.

Van Dijk, T.A. (1996) Discourse, power and access, in C.R. Caldas-Coulthard and M. Coulthard (eds) *Texts and Practices: Readings in Critical Discourse Analysis*. London: Routledge.

Van Dijk, T.A. (1997a) *Racismo y Análisis Crítico de Los Medios* (Racism and the critical analysis of the media). Barcelona: Paidos.

Van Dijk, T.A. (ed.) (1997b) *Discourse Studies: A Multidisciplinary Introduction*. London: Sage.

Van Dijk, T.A. (1998). *Ideology: A Multidisciplinary Study*. London: Sage.

Vertovec, S. (1996) Comparative issues in, and multiple meanings of, the South Asian religious diaspora. Paper given to Conference on Comparative Study of South Asian Diaspora Religious Experience in Britain, Canada and USA, School of Oriental and African Studies, London, 4–6 November.

Viswanathan, G. (1987) The beginning of English Literary Study in British India. *Oxford Literary Review*, 9 (1 & 2).

Wadsworth, M. (1986) Racism in broadcasting, in J. Curran (ed.) *Bending Reality: The State of the Media*. London: Pluto.

Wallman, S. (1986) Ethnicity and the boundary process in context, in J. Rex and D. Mason (eds) *Theories of Race and Ethnic Relations*. Cambridge: Cambridge University Press.

Walton, H. (1986) *White Researchers and Racism*, working paper no. 10. Manchester: University of Manchester.

Ware, V. (1992) *Beyond the Pale: White Women, Racism and Identity*. London: Verso.

Waters, E. (1977) About recapturing a fading mission, *Editor and Publisher*, 12: 20.

Watkins, C.S. (1998) *Representing Hip-Hop Culture and the Production of Black Cinema*. Chicago: University of Chicago Press.

Weaver, D. and Wilhoit, G.C. (1992) *The American Journalist in the 1990s*. Arlington, VA: Freedom Forum.

Webster, J.G. and Phalen, P.F. (1997) *The Mass Audience: Rediscovering the Dominant Model*. London: Lawrence Erlbaum.

Werbner, P. and Modood, T. (1997) *Debating Cultural Hybridity: Multicultural Identities and the Politics of Anti-Racism*. London: Zed Books.

West, C. (1993) The new cultural politics of difference, in S. During (ed.) *The Cultural Studies Reader*. London: Routledge.

Williams, P. (1991) *The Alchemy of Race and Rights*. Cambridge, MA: Harvard University Press.

Wilson, C. (1991) *Black Journalists in Paradox: Historical Perspectives and Current Dilemmas*. Westport, CT: Greenwood.

Wilson, C. and Gutierrez, F. (1995) *Race, Multiculturalism, and the Media: From Mass to Class Communication*, 2nd edn. Thousand Oaks, CA: Sage.

Wodak, R., Nowak, P., Pelikan, J., Gruber, H., de Cillia, R. and Mitten, R. (1990) 'Wir sind alle unschuldige Tater': *Diskurshistorische Studien zum Nachkriegsantisemitismus* ('We are all innocent perpetrators': discourse historic studies in post war antisemitism). Frankfurt/Main: Suhrkamp.

Wolff, K. (trans./ed.) (1950) *The Sociology of George Simmel*. London: Collier-Macmillan.

Wrench, J. and Solomos, J. (1993) *Racism and Migration in Europe*. Oxford: Berg.

Young, I.M. (1989) Polity and group difference: a critique of the ideal of universal citizenship, *Ethics*, 99(2): 250–74.

Young, I.M. (1997) *Intersecting Voices*. Princeton, NJ: Princeton University Press.

Yuval-Davis, N. (1999) Ethnicity, gender relations and multiculturalism, in R. Torres, L.F. Miron and J.X. India (eds) *Race, Identity and Citizenship: A Reader*. Oxford: Blackwell.

Ziegler, D. and White, A. (1990) Women and minorities on network television news: an examination of correspondents and newsmakers, *Journal of Broadcasting and Electronic Media*, 34: 215–23.

Zook, K.B. (1994) How I became the prince of a town called Bel Air: nationalist desire in Black television. Doctoral dissertation, University of California, Santa Cruz.

INDEX